# THE
# WESTERN IMPACT ON
# WORLD MUSIC

# THE
# WESTERN IMPACT ON WORLD MUSIC

## Change, Adaptation, and Survival

## Bruno Nettl

**SCHIRMER BOOKS**
*A Division of Macmillan, Inc.*
NEW YORK

Collier Macmillan Publishers
LONDON

Schirmer Books
A Division of Macmillan, Inc.
866 Third Avenue, New York, N. Y. 10022

Collier Macmillan Canada, Inc.

Library of Congress Catalog Card Number: 84–13953

Printed in the United States of America

printing number
1   2   3   4   5   6   7   8   9   10

**Library of Congress Cataloging in Publication Data**

Nettl, Bruno, 1930–
    The Western impact on world music.

    Includes index.
    Bibliography: p.
    1. Ethnomusicology.   2. Music and society.
3. Music—History and criticism.   I. Title.
ML3798.N48   1985          780'.07          84–13953
ISBN 0-02-870860-1

*For Gloria*

# Contents

# REGULARITIES

# Preface

This is an essay on the effects of Western musical culture on the musical traditions of the non-Western world, especially during the last hundred years. Through synthesis and with many illustrations, it tries to show both the unity and the diversity of these effects, also examining the ways in which they have been studied by ethnomusicologists.

Although it begins and ends with theoretical considerations, emphasis is less on theory and interpretation than on illustration. It was in Madras, in 1981, while drafting some of the materials presented here, that I was particularly struck by the many different ways in which Western musical culture impinged on traditional music and musical life, the many sounds, events, persons, concepts, instruments, institutions that were involved. I determined to try to bring this kind of experience closer to readers by devoting a major part of my effort to a group of vignettes whose function it is, as it were, to bombard them with samples of the complexity of musical change.

The vignettes in the Illustrations section are therefore purposely presented in only partially systematic order. The first four ("Powwow," "Harmony," "Two Cities," and "Compatibles"), a microcosm of the total sampling showing Western music affecting different parts of the music system, are followed by some dealing with instruments ("Violins," "Pianos," "Emblems," "Orchestras") from which we move gradually to modes of transmission ("Victrolas," "Notes," "Music School") and then to the overlapping group of urban institutions ("Migrants," "Streets," "Concerts") and characteristically urban styles ("Pop," "Juju," "National Music"). From a group on religious music ("Old-Time Religion," "Indigenizers," "New-Time Religion") we move to a group of vignettes on some of the kinds of individuals involved in the musical interaction ("Innovators," "Americans," "A Champion," "Visitors," "Ethnomusicologists"). A look at the related "Opinions" is followed by vignettes on preservation and conservation ("Treasures," "Macuma," "Conferences") and finally by three whose thrust is the issue of boundaries among musics ("*Māhour,*" "Duck Dance," "Concertos").

My interest in musical change as part of intercultural contact goes back three decades, has provided a focus for field work among the Blackfoot people of Montana, in Iran, and in South India, and has led to graduate seminars and an NEH-sponsored Seminar for College Teachers at the University of Illinois in Urbana. It should also have led to a comprehensive book, but the subject is so vast that even this small attempt to synthesize depends largely upon illustrations drawn from cultures in which I have had personal experience. During the last few years, I have had the good fortune of having several graduate students in my seminars whose projects or theses intersected with the subject at hand. Six of them kindly wrote vignettes on their research, and these have been integrated into the text but appear under the authors' names. I am grateful to them—Carol Babiracki, William Belzner, Victoria Lindsay-Levine, Christopher Waterman, Steven Whiting, and Paul Wolbers—for permitting me to use these materials.

In keeping with the informal style of writing, I have avoided footnotes but placed a list of references after each of the forty short subdivisions; these indicate materials on which the preceding pages are based and direct the reader further. A (hopefully) thorough but hardly comprehensive bibliography appears at the end of the book.

If this essay has a message, it must surely be that the coming of Western music, rather than bringing about the homogenization of world music, has actually helped to make the twentieth century a period of great musical diversity. Even so, this admittedly optimistic view of the musical scene certainly does not imply approval of the colonization, conquest, and exploitation of Third World peoples by Europeans and North Americans of which our subject here is an indirect result. Morality does not guarantee great art, and immoral acts have often been shown to result in interesting music. In retrospect, the musical diversity of the modern world may be one of the more acceptable results of the introduction of Western culture to the rest of the world.

In part, this project results from several months' residence in Madras in the period 1981–82, and I wish to acknowledge grants from the National Endowment for the Humanities and the American Institute of Indian Studies that made it possible. I am also grateful to the University of Illinois Research Board for providing grants that made it possible to appoint two research assistants, Victoria Lindsay-Levine in the fall of 1982, and Steven Whiting in the spring of 1984, who contributed in significant ways to the project, compiling portions of the bibliography, doing a lot of badly needed editorial work, providing helpful criticism, and coming up with good ideas. If my memory serves me correctly, it was William Kay Archer who first, some twenty years ago, drew my attention to the interest of the specific subject of this essay. I am of course grateful to him, and also to Gerard Behague, Charles Capwell, Jean Christensen, Jack Ashworth, Helen Myers, David Stigberg, William Belzner, Philip Bohlman, Carol Babiracki, and Christopher Waterman, as well as to the twelve professors who participated in the NEH summer seminar in 1979—and many others—for stimulating discussion and criticism. And of course to the musicians of Browning, Tehran, and Madras, who lived the subject of this book and made it come to life for me.

BN
March 1, 1984

## Abbreviations in the References

EM       Ethnomusicology: Journal of the Society for Ethnomusicology
JIFMC   Journal of the International Folk Music Council
YIFMC  Yearbook of the International Folk Music Council
YTM    Yearbook for Traditional Music

# THE
# WESTERN IMPACT ON
# WORLD MUSIC

# APPROACHES

# 1
# The Fourth Age

During the last hundred years, the most significant phenomenon in the global history of music has been the intensive imposition of Western music and musical thought upon the rest of the world. And surely an important aspect of this event is the formidable number of responses that the world's cultures have made in order to maintain, preserve, modify, or virtually abandon their musical traditions. While the coming of Western music is often seen as the death-knell of musical variety in the world, examination of its many effects shows the world's musics in the twentieth century, in part as a result of the pressure generated by Western musical culture, in a state of unprecedented diversity.

That the last hundred years have seen a change of special magnitude is suggested in Walter Wiora's book, *The Four Ages of Music,* one of the few serious attempts to propose a scheme for understanding the entire history of music. Only in the first and fourth of these (overlapping) ages does Wiora see a unified musical world. In the first, he speculatively suggests, the world was homogeneous, music beginning everywhere more or less in the same way, all cultures roughly sharing an early history of music. In the second and third periods, the cultures of the world diverged, each building a music appropriate to its values, social structure, aesthetic, and technology. But in the fourth age, that of "global industrial culture" since the industrial revolution, the world's musics have again converged, united by the intensive diffusion of elements derived from European society—its technology, economic and political organization, and much more—and along with these, the coming of Western music not only as a system of sound but also as a set of concepts and attendant technology and behavior. The world's cultures come together, as well, in their need to confront Western culture musically. The twentieth century must be seen as a period of the most intensive interchange of musical ideas.

In most places, the introduction of Western music goes back a few hundred years, but its imposition became vastly more intensive in the twentieth century. Virtually all of the world's people have been exposed to masses, hymns, marches, rock and roll, waltzes, and jazz; to violins, pianos, guitars; to chords, notated music books, records, radio; to orchestras, bands, choruses; even to opera and oratorio, Monteverdi and Schoenberg. In different ways, at various rates of speed, and with varying enthusiasm, they have accepted this music, and one may hear it, performed with great or moderate expertise, and feel that everywhere, it has to some extent been accepted by the people as their own. The performances of jazz in West Africa, Palestrina masses in Oceania, Schubert in China, electronic music in Japan are important aspects

3

of cultural interaction in music. But the use of gamelan techniques, African percussion sounds, and raga principles by composers of Europe and the Americas must be regarded in the first instance as aspects of the history of Western music. The facet of interaction between Western and non-Western music of concern to us here, however, is the way in which the world's musical traditions have responded to the invasion. If indeed Wiora's fourth age characterizes a world united by effects that have come from Western culture and music, it is the variety of responses and of ways in which the world's musics have managed to maintain themselves in the face of the onslaught that requires us to interpret this age as far more than a mere expansion of the history of Western music.

To describe all that has happened in world music of this century, culture by culture, would easily require a set of volumes. This one volume only suggests a few regularities and provides a group of illustrations, but these ought also to be preceded by a consideration of some of the ways in which the events have been or could be studied. There are three more or less parallel events that comprise a kind of backdrop for this essay: (1) the exposure of the non-Western world to Western music; (2) the recognition, by Western musical scholars, of the existence of non-Western musics as independent units worthy of attention; and (3) the eventual acceptance of musical repertories, styles, and institutions resulting explicitly from the interaction of non-Western and Western as materials for study. The reader may be surprised to find the facts of musical interaction and change and the history of scholarly approaches to these emphasized equally. But surely the methods of study help to determine the facts, and the world's musicians and ethnomusicologists have affected each other in various ways. Thus, the order of events on the ensuing pages is first to deal briefly with the initial contacts of non-Western cultures with Western music, then to survey the early history of ethnomusicology in order to try to determine why these contacts did not immediately become the objects of study, and finally to examine changes in attitude that caused scholars finally to take an interest in the exchange of musical ideas among cultures. It will be necessary also to look at concepts that were developed in order to make this kind of study possible, and at the ways in which the responses of the world's societies to the coming of Western music have been described and classified.

But first, just what do we mean by the term "Western music"? It is necessary to question the concept. Surely all non-Western societies were not introduced to the same kind of Western music. Are there even ways of defining the music of a culture unit so large and complex and vaguely delimited? Some answers: Western music is all music produced in Western societies; or perhaps all music with which members of Western society or its segments identify themselves; or perhaps all music regarded by the non-Western outsider as being "Western." Well, such definitions are possible, but they are too all-encompassing, or difficult to test, or just plain bland. Beyond these, however, there is the consideration of music as a system of sound as opposed to musical life or culture, a conglomeration of ideas, concepts, institutions, practices, all—but not always predictably—affecting and affected by the system of sound. It is evident that we are dealing not with a Western music but with a group of Western musics of great variety—"early," classical, recent; art, folk, jazz; central and peripheral; elite and vernacular; mainstream and experimental; and more.

And even so, despite internal diversity and complexity, it seems appropriate to regard Western music for certain purposes as a unitary concept, and to maintain this view even if it requires exclusion of important, though not central, elements of the musics of Western societies. In many of the world's cultures, the concept of a Western music is well established and in use, and the differences among various Western musics are regarded as trivial. Combining the many kinds of music labeled as Western shows a majority of them to share traits, principles, and ideas, and these have actually been prominent in those kinds of music that Europeans and Americans chose to use in first presenting their culture to the non-Western world. Perhaps the most obvious among these is the system of functional harmony along with the concept that in proper music, harmony must always be present. Then there is the idea that music is normally made by groups, the larger the better, with a form of dictatorial leadership. And further: the notion that planning is important, with the norm of the carefully composed piece, meticulously rehearsed, and performed the same way every time; the concept of radical innovation in musical content or style in composition, along with the need for precise repetition in performance; the principle of control as exhibited in notation; the concept of music as something sufficiently independent of the other domains of culture that times, venues, and contexts of performance are not rigorously determined by religious, ceremonial, or social constraints; emphasis on doing what is difficult and showing it off. These traits are present in a variety of otherwise stylistically and contextually separable musics, they help to justify viewing Western music as a unified system, and they also can be related to a variety of characteristics of Western culture at large. I suggest that members of non-Western societies, when they were introduced to Western music and culture, may have seen these relationships more clearly than did Western insiders.

But if indeed there is such a thing as Western music, its nature essentially unified, and if there was a pattern in its exposure to other cultures, it will be necessary to suggest explanations for the variety of responses in the assimilation and adaptation of the traditional music to it. Look only at the obvious: Japan is today dominated by Western music, its older traditions largely maintained as museum pieces, the purpose now being to preserve them unchanged. In India, Western music has barely penetrated and traditional music is maintained, but to a large degree within institutions that have been changed to a Western format. In sub-Saharan Africa, the mainstream of music is comprised of a stylistic mixture of Western and indigenous, in both the musical sound and its uses. Latin America, the most difficult area to comprehend in this kind of study, has a group of indigenous musics that are themselves ultimately of European origin—mariachi bands and marimbas, the *waynos* of the Andean highlands—acting the part of the non-Western and confronting the more recently introduced European musics, with the African-derived styles playing a counterpoint to the interaction. In the Middle East, Western music is prominent and the traditional music changed slightly to exhibit some elements of the West.

The roots of the variety seem to lie less in the character of individual musical cultures than in the quality of the relationships between cultures and between musics. They lie in the degrees to which a society was technologically and economically developed at the time of musical confrontation; the relative size of populations; the variant of European culture that appeared, North or South, Catholic or Protestant, economically exploiting, colonializing, missionizing with military occupation, and so forth. They lie equally in the relative complexity of musics, and even more, their stylistic, instrumental, conceptual, and institutional accordances. It is to these relationships that we must continually point in order to explain what has happened in Wiora's fourth age, the recent history of world music.

# REFERENCES

Walter Wiora, *The Four Ages of Music* (New York: Norton, 1965), 147–97. **Charles Hamm, Bruno Nettl, and Ronald Byrnside,** *Contemporary Music and Music Cultures* (Englewood Cliffs, N.J.: Prentice-Hall, 1975). **Curt Sachs,** *The Rise of Music in the Ancient World, East and West* (New York: Norton, 1943), section VII; and *The Wellsprings of Music* (The Hague: M. Nijhoff, 1962), chapters 3, 9, and 10.

# 2
# First Encounters

In many instances, the first intensive exposure of non-Western societies to Western music was through church music. Certainly this was true in the Americas, and although the sounds of military music may fleetingly have preceded, it was religious music that various groups of Indians were first persuaded to learn. Robert Stevenson, in his 1952 history of music in Mexico (p. 51), commented on the "amazing speed with which European music was taken up and mastered by the Indians immediately after the arrival of the Conquerors" and cited this as "convincing proof of the innate musicality of the aborigines." It is doubtful that such proof is needed, but if it were, the ability to learn Western music might not necessarily be a good criterion. Learning the music quickly was surely more a function of desire or pressure than simply of ability. But the speed with which Western music was added to the indigenous repertory, or replaced it, was indeed amazing, for Torquemada, the Franciscan chronicler, quoted by Harrison (p. 48), tells us that, within a few decades of the conquest, traditions had developed that included polyphonic singing of masses and Vespers—even in small settlements, and local building of European instruments, organs among them.

Many Mexican Indian cultures did indeed change greatly and quickly. Rather than ascribing it simply to talent, we may argue that this rapid expansion of a musical culture instead bespeaks some important areas of compatibility between old and new, or the important role that music may play in culture change, its significance in a system of worship, and its emblematic nature in a political system. Some of the new music, such as Gregorian chant, may have been perceived as compatible with the mainly monophonic Indian tradition. But the style of Spanish Renaissance polyphony was surely quite distant, and the rapid adoption of its strange sound is more easily ascribed to broadly cultural than to strictly musical factors.

The theme of the Mexican chroniclers was echoed elsewhere in the New World. Garcilaso de la Vega (cited by Stevenson in 1973, p. 5) describes a *Te Deum* performed by Spanish musicians as early as 1541 in Arkansas, and ambitious instruction in European music was a major factor in the conversion of the Pueblo Indians in the early seventeenth century. The *Jesuit Relations*, chronicling the history of missions in the French colonies of North America, similarly praises at length the ability of Indians to learn Western church music. But actually, the sources for uncovering the history of music in the newly discovered American continents tell us much about the teaching of Western music to the Indians, also something about the Indian ceremonial traditions then extant, but little about the ways in which the two musical systems affected each other. Most North and some South American Indian peoples maintained the two traditions separate and distinct. When it did occur, the development of mixed styles, forms, and uses—adoption of instruments and harmony into indigenous traditions, or intertribal repertories—appeared much later. To the American Indians, despite the probability of remote contacts with North Europeans and Oceanians, the coming of a totally different musical culture from the outside was probably something completely fresh, and perhaps a highly dramatic event. At the same time, if the advent of Western music in non-Western cultures during the nineteenth and twentieth centuries was a major historical watershed, we should also bear in mind that the musical contact between East and West has been going on for centuries.

For example, no doubt the musical culture of Iran has had contact with that of Europe since the Graeco-Persian wars, and opportunities for the adaptation of instruments, of attitudes about music involving composition and concert life, and of harmony and scale often presented themselves. But not until it was clear to the Persian ruling classes in the nineteenth century that they would somehow have to come to terms and compete with the Western cultural system was a specific effort made to introduce Western music. This event has usually been ascribed to the coming of a French musician, Alfred Lemaire, to Iran in 1868. But Lemaire's appointment to be the imperial director of music, with the assignment of modernizing military music and of developing a system of musical education that would establish a military music tradition, was actually, as described by Mojtaba Khoshzamir, the final step in a series of developments of the previous fifty years. Early in the nineteenth century, students who were to become officers were sent to Europe for a technical education, but occasionally they were also encouraged to study music and art. In 1856, a group of French military advisors went to Iran and recommended, among other things, the Westernization of military music. As a result, several musicians, including two Frenchmen and later an Italian clarinettist, successively took up residence in Iran, but their success in establishing their institutions was limited.

Lemaire, coming a decade later, was perhaps more imaginative, energetic, and talented; but also the time was evidently more propitious. He established a kind of military music still used in the 1960s, music more like that of the small-town American drum and bugle corps than the band of John Philip Sousa, but his services were also in demand for introducing French nineteenth-century musical culture in general, including training in harmony and composition. His most significant accomplishment may actually have been the teaching of Iranian musicians who believed that some aspects of Western music could be adapted to help the survival of the Persian tradition. This view was later taken up by Iranian musicians, especially Ali Naqi Vaziri, the person most responsible for the development of the strand of Iranian classical music that explicitly features stylistic elements taken from Western music.

And so, while there may have been some kind of intermittent association between Iran and Europe in the realm of music for many centuries, the first sustained contact, with tangible and lasting results, did not arrive until the nineteenth century. Ironically, when it did, it was through the medium of the military band, a European tradition that is itself widely believed to have been informed before 1700 by the musical practices of Turkish janizaries.

In the Middle Eastern cities closest to Europe, Cairo and Constantinople, contact must indeed go back for centuries, and Western music must have been heard in Constantinople throughout its history. We are told by Reinhard (p. 27) that Turkish traditional music changed greatly after 1800, and Western music itself began to play a major role about that time, as indicated by the appointment of the illustrious composer Giuseppe Donizetti as music director to the court, and the founding of an opera house in 1839. In Cairo, similarly, the adoption of Western practices (with opera as their most powerful emblem) culminated in the commissioning of *Aida* for the 1869 opening of the Suez Canal. Even so, in the nineteenth century, even some sophisticated Arabic musicians and music-lovers regarded Western music as strange and exotic.

An example at once parallel and contrastive to the experience of Iran is the history of Western music in Japan, described in Eta Harich-Schneider's comprehensive history of Japanese music. The first sustained contact took place in the sixteenth century, when Christian missionaries, mainly Portuguese, played a major role in Japanese life and even politics, and when a substantial proportion of Japanese were converted to Christianity. This "Christian century" ended by the 1630s with the widespread persecution of Christians and, by association, Western culture, including its music. But by then a considerable amount of Western music had taken hold in Japan. Though largely church music, the repertory must have comprised great stylistic variety, given its broad base in the European Renaissance. Harich-Schneider (pp. 445–85) describes a wealth of genres, musical practices, ensemble types, and instruments. It would appear that the musical practices of at least portions of the nation were at that time virtually Europeanized. A "blend of Japanese and European music," encouraged by the Jesuit Cosme de Torres, probably meant the combination of Western and Japanese works in the same social or performance context rather than the adumbration of Japanese pieces with Western style elements (or vice versa). If this interpretation is right, the entry of Western music into Japanese culture may have resembled that of Chinese and Korean repertories in other periods, for these are widely thought to have been adopted and then retained as more or less separate units within the national repertory. If the practice of compartmentalizing cultural phenomena is really, as has sometimes been suggested, a national characteristic of Japan, this may well explain the tendency in music to maintain separation among the various repertories according to functions and uses, instruments, schools of musicians, and places of origin. Even so, the combination of styles was probably much greater in fact than in theory. If sixteenth-century European music was simply one of a series of musical invasions, it did not, in contrast to Chinese-, Korean-, and Indian-derived repertories, remain part of the Japanese musical traditions; rather, it seems to have disappeared almost without trace after 1638.

The second introduction of Western music to Japan, in the nineteenth century, involved a very different style and social milieu. Shortly after Commodore Perry's renowned visit in 1853, military bands were introduced. Secular Western music, performed largely for ceremonies and impressing international visitors, gradually began to play a major role. Of special interest for the subject of this essay, however, is the requirement that court musicians be trained in traditional as well as Western models, a practice perhaps reminiscent of the incorporation of other foreign musics in earlier times. In 1872 a music education system based on Western music was introduced into the schools. Throughout the period to 1945, many musicians were evidently trained in both traditional and Western music. Only later did a much greater degree of separation take hold, probably as a way of maintaining authentic forms in the older traditions.

Harich-Schneider (p. 540) maintains that the "rapid spread of Western music was to a great extent due to the Christian hymns" introduced from 1850 on by missionaries, whose activities were being permitted again after 200 years of absence. The language of Western music had changed enormously between the Renaissance and the nineteenth century, and it is certainly not clear whether the two manifestations of Western music were perceived as being one and the same style. But it does seem possible that each of the two Western intrusions was at first treated as others had been in earlier times, given the remarkably consistent culture of Japan.

In some societies of sub-Saharan Africa and on the island of Madagascar, too, the main impetus in the introduction of Western music was the Christian missionary. And the speed with which accommodation between Western and African styles took place, as in the introduction of African rhythmic practices into church music, has been widely noted. There was also a military side to musical missionizing. A short newspaper account affords a rare glimpse of events as described in their own time, and of the contemporary Western attitudes. The article, from the New York *Journal of Fine Arts* (May 1, 1851), speaks of Radamo, "king of Madagascar," who "encouraged the intercourse of his subjects with Europeans, and especially with his neighbors of the Isle of France. . . ."

Radamo was passionately fond of music—as indeed appear to be most of his countrymen—and sent over twelve boys to form a band, under the instruction of the bandmaster of the 82nd regiment, who received 200£ a year for the undertaking. They attained considerable proficiency, when they were summoned to their own country to play the chefs-d'oeuvre of Rossini and Mozart in the forests of Madagascar. We may imagine the astonishment of a traveler at being welcomed at a native court, in an almost unknown country, by a band of half-naked savages, with some familiar overture, executed with the precision of a London or Paris orchestra. The great aptitude for music may be witnessed at all hours in the streets of Port Louis, where the airs played by the military band are taken up and whistled with extraordinary taste and accuracy by all the little black boys of the place. The regiment to which I had the honor of belonging was received with screams of delight on landing, from the number of black drummers kept up in that distinguished corps.

As elsewhere, the military band was an early point of contact, but we have here some evidence that these musicians of Madagascar also played at least some works from the classical concert repertory, or arrangements thereof, in addition to regular military music.

This is the characteristic first contact of the world's peoples with Western music: hymns and masses, and military bands. It is noteworthy and perhaps a bit ironic that some kinds of music most valued by large segments of the Western musical audience—the classical repertory, popular musics in their nineteenth-century urban guise, authentic traditional folk songs—were not introduced. In certain respects, the particular kind of Western music that was introduced may not have mattered. But phenomena such as the military-like bands that now play for weddings in Benares and the choral sound of some of the popular music of the New Zealand Maoris show that style, genre, and function did sometimes play a major role.

What now about the matter of patterns? Each society had its own first experience of Western music, and in each the response was conditioned by the quality of social, cultural, musical relationships. There was contact before 1800, but despite the fact that ancient Greece, that "cradle of Western civilization," was in its time an outpost of Middle Eastern culture, despite the well-known interchanges of the Middle Ages and Renaissance, that contact was neither intensive nor lasting. At that point, European and North American nations began the business of colonizing more extensively even than before, Western technology clearly gained the upper hand, and there developed a musical system obviously symbolic of this superiority but also adaptable to other musics. At that point, the dual approach of Western music through church and army began to affect many societies.

In a number of places the approaches of Western musicians had much in common. Everywhere we can read of the extraordinary musical talent of the "natives," who are able to learn Western music with little effort. We see the large ensemble and the concept of functional harmony introduced as hallmarks of Western music, idealized and imitated. And we can imagine Europeans and Americans introducing their military styles, hear them saying, in effect, "You cannot have an effective military machine without our kind of band." And perhaps also implying, "You cannot enter into the Christian kingdom of God without Western-style hymns harmonized in major and minor." It is this syndrome of events, attitudes, and sounds, of technology, religion, and politics, essential not to European culture throughout its history but rather to its nineteenth-century manifestation that characterize Wiora's "fourth age." The first encounters varied greatly and led to different reactions to Western music later on. But in a way, its coming around the world was really a unified event.

## REFERENCES

**Frank Harrison,** *Time, Place, and Music* (Amsterdam: Knuf, 1973).    **Robert Stevenson,** *Music in Mexico, a Historical Survey* (New York: Crowell, 1952); "Written Sources for Indian Music Until 1882," EM 17:40, 1973; and "English Sources for Indian Music Until 1882," *EM* 17:399–442, 1973.    *The Jesuit Relations and Allied Documents . . . 1610–1791,* edited by Reuben Gold Thwaites (New York: Pageant, 1959).    **David E. Crawford,** "The Jesuit Relations . . . Early Sources for an Ethnography of Music Among American Indians," *EM* 11:199–206, 1967.    **Ella Zonis,** *Classical Persian Music, an Introduction,* (Cambridge: Harvard University Press, 1973), chapters 1 and 7.    **Ruhollah Khaleqi,** *Sargozasht-e Musiqi-ye Iran* (Tehran: Chapkhané Ferdowsi, 1955–56), vol. I, 216–18; vol. II, 39–66.    **Mojtaba Khosh-zamir,** "Ali Naqi Vaziri and His Influence on Music and Music Education in Iran," D. Ed. diss., University of Illinois, 1979.    **Victor Advielle,** *La musique chez les persanes en 1885* (Paris, 1885).    **Kurt Reinhard,** "Die Türkei im 19. Jahrhundert," in *Musikkulturen Asiens, Afrikas und Ozeaniens im 19. Jahrhundert,* edited by Robert Günther (Regensburg: G. Bosse, 1973), 21–48.    **Eta Harich-Schneider,** *A History of Japanese Music* (London: Oxford University Press, 1973), chapters 14 and 16.    **Record:** *Valiha Madagascar,* Ocora OCR 18, 1964; notes by Charles Duvelle.

# 3
# Unchanging Music

While in the course of the late nineteenth and early twentieth centuries the Western musical world was presenting itself to other societies, in quite a different sense the non-Western world was also gradually being introduced to the peoples of Europe and North America. One result of this interchange was the interest taken by Western composers in the musical sounds of the world; but this is a subject for other authors and other essays. A second result was the emergence of ethnomusicology. In the second half of the twentieth century, these reciprocal introductions became the roots of interdependence.

The events that made Western music known elsewhere were also those that stimulated the beginnings of ethnomusicology. The precursors of this field of research had appeared by the beginning of the nineteenth century, and in the 1880s one could begin to speak of a discipline, or sub-discipline, or at least of a field whose main thrust was the descriptive, comparative, and to some degree historical study of non-Western musics. The task here is not to review this history but to examine briefly the ways in which ethnomusicologists viewed the world of music in this time of mutual discovery, just before and after 1900. This was the time in which ethnomusicologists conceived of the musical world as essentially static.

Not always explicitly, but by an implication evident in their work, they divided the world into a group of musics, each an independent and, with the one great exception of Western art music, an essentially stable unit. Every society had its own music that remained essentially unchanged, except when disturbed by the military and colonial expansion of Western society. To be sure, in a way this viewpoint still persists, but not in the extreme sense of about 1900. The belief that there is a difference *in essence* between Western music and that of the rest of the world supported a broad view of humanity widely held in Europe and North America, a view that pitted the West and its ideals and values against the rest. This essential difference justified some of the ways in which Western society was treating the rest of the world.

In music, one major difference, so it was thought, was the attitude towards change. That this should have been a major area of emphasis has much to do with the character of Western art music in the late nineteenth century, a period in which there was an extraordinary amount of style change and emphasis on innovation. Indeed, newness in the musical content, themes, harmonic and rhythmic motifs, manipulation of current formal principles, might all not be enough to justify composing, but there had to be, as well, as least the promise of radical innovation in matters of style. Other cultures, it was firmly believed, did not come close to this fondness for new-found principles and harmonic devices.

There were, of course, social and political reasons for the bifurcated view of world music, a view that accordingly became the foundation of a field of research that had certain basic assumptions. In the following paragraphs, it is necessary to take a respectfully critical view of one aspect of the comparative musicology that developed in and from the world of Carl Stumpf, Erich M. von Hornbostel, and their contemporaries and students. What is at issue is the concept of a static non-Western music, a concept both convenient and inevitable. Given the small and uncertain samplings, comparison could best be carried out with artifacts that might reasonably be assumed representative of a repertory that existed over a long period, providing more than a fleeting glimpse of a rapidly changing system. Cultural evolutionists were readily served by the notion that each of a number of societies with its music represented a historical stage valid over a long period. Consequently (and conveniently), Western approaches to music study could be based on examination of the artifacts rather than on the following of processes. The idea of cultures as separate units allowed one to avoid studying mixed or hybrid forms whose character flew in the face of academic musical values. And so, the early period of ethnomusicology may be depicted as one in which stability was considered the normal state of non-Western musics, and techniques of description and comparison were developed without regard to their changeable nature.

Anthropology, as established in the period around 1900 particularly in the U.S. and Germany, also perceived culture as largely static except when disturbed by outside forces, with equilibrium the normal state and change studied as a special phenomenon. But in the late 1930s, the investigation of processes of culture change and not merely of its results began its gradual ascendancy in anthropology until, by the 1960s, it became almost axiomatic in cultural studies. Meanwhile, however, ethnomusicologists continued to disregard what had become, by the middle of the twentieth century, the most prominent kind of music in the world's cultures, music in which Western and non-Western elements were combined, and in which the musical practices and concepts from the West were used in various ways to modify non-Western traditions.

A number of important concepts were developed in the period during which ethnomusicologists regarded stability as the norm. These continue to be factors in ethnomusicology, including its study of Western influence; and so it is appropriate to comment on them briefly. If the world of music was a group of relatively isolated musics, it followed that a non-Western music would be homogeneous, and thus a small sample would provide the essentials of the whole. This concept was applied to all, but particularly to tribal and folk repertories. The musics of the world were divided into three or four categories, in accordance with the presumed complexity of both style and culture, under such rubrics as "primitive," "folk," "art," and popular music. While these Western concepts are actually used by certain societies, such as Chinese and Asian Indian, ethnomusicologists made them into categories of presumed general validity capable of describing the stratification of world music.

These categories of course have their uses and are surely often appropriate. But to rely on them as a way of classifying all music at all times requires the assumption of an essential stability and diverts attention from intermediate categories and from change. Thus, the repertory usually designated in Western culture as folk music has, since 1950, come to share important traits of popular music. African tribal music, often classed as "primitive" because the societies involved are non-literate, has the professionalism and the great complexity of art music, to say nothing of the kind of stratification used to distinguish art music in Asia and Europe.

But if most ethnomusicologists before circa 1950 ignored popular music in favor of the other categories, the main reason seems to me to be its mutability and the fact that throughout the world, it comprises stylistic mixture, combining African and Latin American with European in the West; European, Middle Eastern, and Indian on the subcontinent, and so on. It is bemusing to see that a field dedicated to the study of all the world's musics could omit a major portion of this basic material because it did not conform to certain postulates about the nature of the musical world. Ethnomusicologists in the early part of the twentieth century seemed inclined to share the values of the European academic musical establishment. Western art music was supposed to change, but when other musics did, it might be cause for worry, perhaps even for criticism in the case of popular musics, for their supposedly characteristic faddishness has always been considered one of their weaknesses.

The way in which ethnomusicologists in the first half of the twentieth century (and, to an extent, later as well) described and analyzed music was likewise closely related to and derived from the view of non-Western musics as static and thus in essence different from Western art music. The method of description involved such things as a statement of tonal inventory or scale; the relationship among sections of a song or piece; meter and singing style; typical relationships between voices in a polyphonic texture. We can't deny the importance of these parameters for comparative study. But there is a strange neglect of those aspects of music that treat it as a dynamic phenomenon. Thus, identification of melodic or rhythmic motifs as subject to development was rarely attempted. The conceptualization of process, as exemplified, say, by identification of tune families or other tune relationships, classification of melodies, and other techniques that had become widely used in the study of folk music, hardly played a part in the study of non-Western music.

A further characteristic of stability-oriented ethnomusicology was a strong interest in origins. The origin of music per se was at least a subject of theoretical speculation, but even more, the belief that any phenomenon, style, piece, repertory could be traced to its origins, indeed, *had* an ascertainable origin is characteristic. By implication we might trace anything back to its roots because it came into existence as artifact and never underwent substantial change. A related concept is the periodization of history implicit in the thinking of the so-called *Kulturkreis* school of German anthropologists; in this view history was as a series of discrete periods, each represented by a cluster of culture traits with similar geographic distribution.

The early period of ethnomusicology gave particular stress to certain aspects of non-Western music: absence of notation and dependence on oral transmission; the absence of a system of harmony such as the functional system of the period circa 1700–1900; and its intervals incompatible with the

tempered chromatic scale. The prominence of these traits to ethnomusicologists may be derived from the importance, in the view of
musicians and scholars around 1900, of their opposites in Western art music.
What was dearest to the European music-lover of that time was precisely the
system of harmony. The intervallic structure of the basic tone material was so
fundamental that one could not really imagine intelligible music to be without
it, while on the other hand, rhythmic theory and feeling were far less sophisticated and therefore perhaps less specifically directed. The idea of a music
not written down would have been incredible to an audience thriving on
Berlioz, Brahms, Wagner, and Verdi. And separation of those who "understood" music from the rest was in the first instance based on the criterion
of musical literacy. To early ethnomusicology, harmony, equally tempered
scalar structure, and notation were among the most basic criteria for distinguishing Western from non-Western music.

Finally, among the characteristics of this early period of ethnomusicology,
we should mention the concept of comparability. If comparison has an
unbroken history in ethnomusicology, it has also had its ups and downs as a
tool for gaining insight; central to the field at its beginnings, it has since
declined but taken its place among other important weapons in the arsenal.
The purpose here is not to discuss or criticize comparative study. But it is important to recognize that the comparative approach developed by early ethnomusicology was influenced by the conception of the world as one group of
musics from which Western art music stood out. Accordingly, its methodology
developed frameworks for comparisons that would readily indicate similarities
among non-Western musics and differences between any one of them and
Western art music.

In all of this, it is easy to recognize the relationship of ethnomusicological
concepts to the ideas and circumstances of the culture in which its practi-
tioners were rooted. The purpose here is not to be critical; the emphasis on
stability probably had to come first. But a comparison of publications from
1900 to 1940 with those from 1970 on readily indicates the changes that took
place.

# REFERENCES

G.A. Villoteau, "De l'état actuel de l'art musical en Egypte," in *Description d'Egypte*
1:609–846, 1809. Carl Stumpf, *Die Anfänge der Musik* (Leipzig: Barth, 1911). Erich M.
von Hornbostel, see all of his works, but particularly those in *Hornbostel Opera Omnia*, edited
by Klaus P. Wachsmann and others, vol. I (The Hague: M. Nijhoff, 1975). Jaap Kunst, *Ethnomusicology*, 3rd ed. (The Hague: M. Nijhoff, 1959). Walter Wiora, *Ergebnisse und
Aufgaben vergleichender Musikforschung* (Darmstadt, Wissenschaftliche Buchgesellschaft,
1975). Marvin Harris, *The Rise of Anthropological Theory* (New York: Crowell,
1968). Mantle Hood, "Music, the Unknown," in Frank Harrison, Mantle Hood, and Claude V.

Palisca, *Musicology* (Englewood Cliffs, New Jersey: Prentice-Hall, 1963). **Bruno Nettl,** *Theory and Methods in Ethnomusicology* (New York: Free Press, 1964), chapter 2. **Albrecht Schneider,** *Musikwissenschaft und Kulturkreislehre* (Bonn: Verlag für systematische Musikwissenschaft, 1976).

# 4
# Concepts

   The typical ethnomusicologists of 1900 or 1920 were steeped in nineteenth-century classical music and its theory, and in ideas derived from the concept of cultural evolution, and they made contact with non-Western music largely through the missionary or colonization movements. By contrast, scholars of 1970 had a broader experience of Western music with its increased variety of styles, and also lived in an environment in which the sounds of non-Western music were readily available and no longer a shock. A more liberal theoretical system derived from styles developed in Western art music of the twentieth century, greater recognition of interest in jazz and vernacular musics, and a generally wider view of what may be included in the concepts of music distinguished the scholars of 1970 from those of several decades earlier. And also, in society at large, the concept of non-Western cultures had changed, from the barbarian tribes good only for colonization to underdeveloped and often poverty-stricken Third World nations. The scholars of 1970 had often experienced direct contact with non-Western peoples, through military occupation in World War II, Korea, and Vietnam, central and southern Africa, through organizations such as the Peace Corps, and, as jet travel increased accessibility, as tourists. The striking feature of "exotic" peoples and their cultures was no longer their pristine isolation, but the ways in which rapid change was taking place and the problems of coping with Western values and technology.
   It was therefore almost natural for ethnomusicologists to take much greater account of the world's musics as constantly changing phenomena, to become interested in the products of change, and to develop concepts for their analysis and comprehension. As direct objects of study and as issues for debate, these concepts may characterize the field of ethnomusicology as it

operates in the second half of this century. But they have become established in good measure because the orientation of scholars changed from a static to a dynamic view of the musical world.

Several of these interrelating concepts involve the description of musical sound. The world of music continued to be seen as a group of discrete musics, but whereas their mutual isolation once seemed to be their main characteristic, greater emphasis was now placed on their interrelationship. Thus, while classic studies such as those of the Thompson River Indians (by Hornbostel and Abraham), of Javanese music (by Kunst) and of South African instrument traditions (by Kirby) treated their subjects in isolation, one was now more apt to see research on phenomena such as the performance of "white" music by Plains Indians (by Witmer), the various interrelationships between Japanese, other Asian, and European musics (by Harich-Schneider), the measurement of change in fourteen years of the history of an African tribe (by Merriam). The notion of musics as analogues to languages took on changed significance in the perspective of music as system, with interlocking parts capable of responding selectively to a variety of stimuli from inside and out.

The concept of confrontation of musics required them to be seen as if they were organic wholes—with lives of their own, organisms whose separate subsystems interacted and responded independently to the outside. Thus, as Merriam suggested, a musical system would consist of sound, concept, and behavior; or, of the music itself (the heart of the matter) and the social context (a kind of superstructure); or it could be divided in a variety of other ways. The sound part of the spectrum, in turn, could be divided into repertory and performance practice; or into musical content (e.g., the tunes) as opposed to style (e.g., the scalar, rhythmic, formal characteristics), each capable of changing (to a degree) independently of the other. The idea of music as a complex phenomenon follows from the recognition of change as an ever-present component of musical life.

These thoughts are related to the idea of all music as something in which innovation and creation takes place. Students of Western academic music had taken this for granted. But the acceptance of individual creativity as characteristic of non-Western and especially folk and tribal music is somewhat newer; after all, the emphasis on their strong traditions, anonymous composition, and great age had long been juxtaposed to the constant innovation of Western music. Now, in order to show non-Western music as capable of interacting with the Western, it had to be presented as something not in essence so different. The study of creation, change, and innovation introduced to our view of these musics some of the major values of Western academic music.

The concept of Western music—now a single system—simply as one of many in the world, and not in essence different from all the rest, also belongs to the newer approaches. The idea of popular, folk, and art music all having enough in common to be treated as a unit would perhaps have been unacceptable to the typical urban music lover of 1900, but it was probably essential for the development of a study of musical confrontations. Western music may have been perceived as a unit by members of other societies who at first perhaps ignored the social and stylistic distinctions between oratorio, hymn tune, and dance piece. This leads us back to the consideration of music as something associated particularly with a population group. The older view of music as the sole property of a group of people who also shared a culture had to be altered as a result of the newly multi-musical character of societies everywhere. If for example an American Indian tribe once had its own music and knew no other, and could thus have been musically identified by its repertory, it might, by the middle of the twentieth century, have added to it the music of other tribes, some multi-tribal repertories, "white" music from church and radio, country music, and music of black Americans. But such a tribe may still identify the core of its culture with a particular musical repertory or style. And so, ethnomusicologists had to change their view of the relationship between a music and a society. Once, a people had its own music; more recently, it might "have" or participate in many musics, but perhaps only one with which it truly identifies itself. And from this also stems the strong interest of ethnomusicologists in the emblematic function of music, the emphasis on music as closely related to ethnicity, its immediately recognizable sound one of the most powerful symbols of the group. While earlier ethnomusicologists emphasized the undeniable fact that in most of the world's societies, many activities cannot be properly carried out without the correct performance of accompanying music, more recent scholarship has added a concentration on the importance of a particular kind of music to the group's identity.

The view of musics as entities changing and interacting with each other, internally, and with other domains of culture has resulted in the development of concepts to explain and describe several processes. The first area of cross-cultural interaction to attract widespread interest was the creation of various African-derived musics in all parts of the New World. Already long ago the subject of commentary by European scholars such as Hornbostel and Africans such as Ballanta-Taylor, this group of musics later became the subject of more intensive study by Melville Herskovits and his students, particularly Richard A. Waterman and Alan P. Merriam, who suggested the heuristic concept of syncretism, that is, the confluence of similar or compatible culture traits to create new, mixed forms. This concept requires the recognition that certain cultures or forms, or for that matter musics, are compatible (perhaps by being similar in central or significant facets). Waterman suggested that African and Western musics had such compatibility, and Merriam, comparing both to North American Indian music, went on to hypothesize that the smaller degree of similarity between Western and Indian denied them the necessary compatibility to create such mixed, syncretic styles of music. Having been used to explain the Afro-American picture, syncretism became the starting point and model for other examinations of the confluence of musics, and the first among several concepts which classified and described the processes resulting from the interaction of musics.

Syncretism assumes an approximate measuring of the degree of compatibility between musics, and prediction of the typical direction of resulting change. Somewhat related are the complementary concepts of Westernization and modernization, borrowed from the anthropology of culture change, which involve process as well as motivation and may explain the differentials of change in various parameters of one musical culture. Modernization may be described as the incidental movement of a system or its components in the direction of Western music and musical life, without, however, requiring major changes in those aspects of the non-Western tradition that are central and essential. Westernization is the substitution of central features of Western music for their non-Western analogues, often with the sacrifice of essential facets of the tradition.

The concept of musical energy is implicit rather than explicit in ethnomusicological literature. A theoretical construct, it results from the observation that when a non-Western society absorbs aspects of Western music, the older musical tradition must adapt itself in some way to the decreased attention that it now enjoys. Let's hypothesize that a society devotes a certain, and relatively constant and limited amount of energy to music—this means time and effort expended on performance, creative work, study, listening, and more—and that when some of this energy is channeled to a new musical system, less is available for the old one. Adaptation may involve reduction of repertory, or of the number of styles, or in number of musicians devoting themselves to the older tradition. It may bring about combination of the repertories of the society's subdivisions and even of once-discrete culture units. It could also include increased efficiency in learning with the use of notation, recordings, and other technology; standardization of instruments; substitution of recordings for live performance. Thus, the reduction of classical Japanese chamber music to a repertory of few pieces; the standardization of Plains Indian songs into a single predictable form; the adoption of Western notation to teach Persian music; reduction of the number of musicians available for the Korean classical repertory while the majority performs Western music; establishment of an intertribal Indian repertory in lieu of several individual tribal ones; all of these may be interpreted as shifts in musical energy. The term may not be ideal, but it is surely useful to have some concept to indicate that, when a people is faced with the addition of a second music to its life, something inevitably happens to the first.

The concept of centrality is equally tenuous and also to be seen simply as a theoretical abstraction of heuristic value in analysis. It suggests that in any musical style, one or several features are more central than others and function as hallmarks. They can be identified by their ubiquity in a repertory, also by the fact that they symbolize the style itself to its own society as well as to outsiders. These central features have a special effect on other parameters of the music, playing a kind of guiding and integrating role. In Western music, the most obvious central feature is harmony; and in West African music the rhythmic character of the percussion ensemble, performing alone or as accompaniment. There are probably greater and lesser degrees of centrality among the features of a musical repertory; and the concept can be extended to aspects of musical behavior and conceptualization. For example, in Western culture, the concept of music as art, difficult to learn, create, perform, is important; among the Blackfoot Indians, it was once the concept of music's relationship to supernatural forces. Of course Western culture has religious music, the Blackfoot had notions of musicianship, but in each culture different ideas enjoyed centrality. The point is that, when undergoing change, a society may treat central and non-central facets of its music differently and also distinguish central and non-central features in absorbing a new musical system.

Of similar importance is urbanization, a concept not used differently in ethnomusicology than in other fields, especially social sciences and history, from which it came. While much of the music that ethnomusicologists have studied all along has been of urban provenience, the particular effect (on music) of change from rural to urban environment, whether through change of the environment itself or through migration of song or singer, has only recently begun to be studied. Cities have existed in non-Western societies for centuries, and urbanization is not in itself an effect of Western culture. But the kind of rapid urbanization that has taken place in the twentieth century is associated with the development of Western technology, Western-style nation-states, large-scale immigration. It has been customary to look at urbanization in distinct stages or phases, the primary involving the establishment of cities within individual cultures, and the secondary, the growth of cities as large intercultural or multi-cultural units in which a confrontation of cultures takes place. Thus the inclusion in ethnomusicological study of communities that are in themselves multi-cultural is also a conceptual change bearing on the problems discussed in this essay.

Industrialization, a process generally but not necessarily an effect of Western culture, is closely tied to urbanization. Beginning in the late Renaissance but becoming more concrete and intensified in the nineteenth century, it bears on all of the kinds of culture contact we are discussing. The acceptance of industrial principles of instrument construction, printing of notation, electric means of dissemination all have had enormous effect, and their currency in the Western system has led to their introduction to other cultures. The centrality of industrialization in the Western cultural system and its indirect association with principles of economics, politics, and even religion may make it a legitimate subdivision of the process of Westernization. On the other hand, it can also be a vehicle of modernization that enables a traditional system to survive without incorporating central features of Western music. There is no question as to its significance to our subject.

As one might expect in surveying what has been learned, the various parts of the world have been subject to different kinds of treatment in research. Rough characterization is possible. The area perhaps most prominent in these studies is sub-Saharan Africa, together with African-derived societies in various parts of the New World, with literature going back to the 1920s providing detailed assessments of the interaction of African and Western traits. Considerable research has also been done in South and West Asia. The influence of Europe in the Arabic, Turkish, and Persian world usually forms a final chapter in the long music history of these nations, but broader approaches to the study of change have been suggested for Israel. In India, research on Western influences has concentrated on the "behavior" part of Merriam's music model—performance venues, attitudes towards musicianship, teaching, social structure. For North American Indian cultures, a combination of historical, ethnographic, and musical interests has brought about comparison with Black Americans, discovery of newly created genres and styles of Indian music, and analysis of music as an emblem of ethnicity in changing societies. For the Far East, studies have concentrated on the decline of traditional music and its partial resurgence as a result of the growth of modern Western-style nationalism.

Latin America is an example of a culture area in which many of the concepts introduced here must be modified in order to make sense. The musical styles which many of the populations used in pre-Columbian times are largely gone or unknown, and cannot be really extrapolated from what is now performed. On the other hand, traditional musics combining Western and non-Western elements long ago merged into a kind of indigenous tradition. The mariachi music of Mexico, the marimba music of Southern Mexico and Guatemala, the music of the *charangos* and panpipes in the Andean highlands themselves interact with later forms of Western music, playing out the game of confronation which is elsewhere reserved for specifically non-Western versus Western music. The point is that the line between Western and non-Western musics, a fundamental assumption in this essay, is in fact often quite blurred—and probably nowhere so much as in Latin America.

The number of case studies bearing directly on the interaction between traditional and Western music, still small, is beginning to grow rapidly, and the conceptual framework of ethnomusicology since about 1950 has been changing to accommodate the new direction of studies.

# REFERENCES

Erich M. von Hornbostel and Otto Abraham, "Phonographierte Indianermelodien aus Britisch-Columbia" (originally published in 1906), in *Hornbostel Opera Omnia*, edited by Klaus P. Wachsmann, vol. I (The Hague: M. Nijhoff, 1975), 299–322. Jaap Kunst, *Music in Java*, 3rd ed. (The Hague: M. Nijhoff, 1973). Percival Kirby, *Musical Instruments of the Native Races of South Africa* (Johannesburg: Witwatersrand University Press, 1953). Robert Witmer, "Recent

Change in the Musical Culture of the Blood Indians," *Yearbook for Inter-American Musical Research* 9:64–94, 1973. **Eta Harich-Schneider**, *A History of Japanese Music* (London: Oxford University Press, 1973). **Alan P. Merriam**, "Music Change in a Basongye Village (Zaire)," *Anthropos* 72:806–46, 1977. **Nicholas Ballanta-Taylor**, *Saint Helena Island Spirituals* (New York: Schirmer, 1925). **Alan P. Merriam**, "The Use of Music in the Study of a Problem of Acculturation," *American Anthropologist* 57:28–34, 1955. **Richard A. Waterman**, "African Influence on American Negro Music," in *Acculturation in the Americas*, edited by Sol Tax (Chicago: University of Chicago Press, 1952), 207–18. **Bruno Nettl**, "Persian Classical Music in Tehran: The Processes of Change," in his *Eight Urban Musical Cultures* (Urbana: University of Illinois Press, 1978), 146–85; and "Some Aspects of the History of World Music in the Twentieth Century: Questions, Problems, Concepts," *EM* 22:123–36, 1978. **Adelaida Reyes Schramm**, "Explorations in Urban Ethnomusicology: Hard Lessons from the Spectacularly Ordinary," *YTM* 14:1–14, 1983. **Kathleen L'Armand and Adrian L'Armand**, "One Hundred Years of Music in Madras: A Case Study in Secondary Urbanization," *EM* 27:411–38, 1983. **Klaus Wachsmann**, "Criteria for Acculturation," in International Musicological Society, *Report of the 8th Congress, New York* (Kassel: Baerenreiter, 1961), 139–49.

# 5
# Responses

The illustrations that follow this introductory section show the non-Western musical world to be highly diverse in the configuration of its responses to the coming of Western musical culture. Numerous factors play a role: general character of a culture, its complexity, geographic proximity to Europe or North America, relative similarity to that of the West; relative complexity and similarity of a musical style and of its system of musical conceptualization, institutions, behavior, transmission processes in relation to the Western; a society's attitudes towards music, towards change and cultural homogeneity; type and length of exposure to Western music; and much else. Each society has handled Western music in its unique way. But our task is to look for commonalities and regularities, and while that is a more appropriate consideration in the final section, entitled "Regularities," I wish in this section, by way of preparation, to mention previous attempts to classify responses to Western music and processes of musical change resulting from cultural interaction.

How does a musical system change? Early ethnomusicological publications (by Wachsmann, in 1961, and Nettl, in 1958) distinguish between intercultural contacts and intracultural events and conditions as causes, and delineate levels of change in piece or song, repertory, style, genre, et cetera. Separating musical sound and cultural context, Blacking in 1980 suggested further refinements, involving amount and nature of change. Thus, a society can substitute one musical system for another; the wholesale adoption of Western music by most of the population of Korea may be a case in point. Or, a society may add a musical system; modern or "new" music has been added to Western culture, which nevertheless holds on to the older, so-called common-practice tradition. Change accepted and even required in a musical system may be distinguished; take the conception of the new composition which gradually changes or expands a musical style as a major value in Western academic music. The performance of a folk song in variants which do not necessarily indicate gradual change in style illustrates the category of allowable variation. Blacking also distinguishes true change of a music (which he calls "musical change") from other kinds of alteration or modification of a system and its parts, and further, change perceived as such by the society concerned from that only evident to the outside observer, as well as change in the music from change in social context. The juxtaposition of these dichotomies and continuums provides a broad group of classes for comparative study. Only certain kinds of change can be considered responses to Western culture, and Blacking does not try to separate them, nor to give examples that explicitly involve that particular relationship.

Somewhat earlier a similar but simpler statement appeared in Merriam's classic *Anthropology of Music,* which in the first instance distinguishes change caused by contact from outside from that resulting entirely from forces inside a culture. Although the kinds of change with which we are concerned are almost by definition from the "outside," there are different kinds of "outsideness." Changes resulting from contact among various non-Western cultures which in itself results from military or economic pressure on the part of a European nation, but which do not themselves involve Western musical practices, may be distinguished from adoption of elements of Western style. One may study relationships between ethnic groups living together in a modern nation-state and between more and less Westernized segments of a society. In a world in which it is difficult to find any society not affected by others, change totally devoid of outside factors can hardly be imagined.

The literature dealing specifically but holistically with Western influences in non-Western music is relatively recent. A small group of articles is devoted to distinction among and enumeration of the many different responses. Without taking account of a specific group of cultural or musical parameters, but pointing out the great variety, I suggested in 1978 that there were at least eleven such responses. Eight of them could easily be noted in individual situations or musical works, while three others may also apply to entire cultures or music systems—syncretism, modernization, and Westernization. Old friends by now, they need only a few more comments. Syncretism, a process depending on a particular kind of compatible relationship between cultures or musics, can only be identified through consideration of whole repertories or large samples. The difference between modernization and Westernization has been criticized; there is a qualitative and perhaps patronizing side to the term "modernizing." The word may indicate interaction with Western culture but also with others. Westernization on the other hand is much more specific in its directionality. Yet in some reference works (e.g. the *International Encyclopedia of the Social Sciences*) the two are defined almost identically, whereas anthropological literature usually makes them the labels of contrastive situations.

But the two concepts may be used not only to designate simple opposites or extremes of a continuum, but sometimes also successive stages in a sequence of developments. A further difficulty is that their application requires knowledge of motivation and, in the absence of such knowledge, may confuse products and processes. Is a group of people really trying to become a subdivision of the West, or is it trying to keep its central values? Can one tell from the resulting products such as musical works? Yet, while searching for better alternatives, I would still maintain that the two concepts are useful if applied with care, that they should indeed be seen as ends of a continuum along which societies, contexts, events, and pieces can be placed for comparative study, that most non-Western societies in the twentieth century partake of both but may on balance find one or the other more appropriate to their needs, and that analysis sometimes allows extrapolation of motivation.

This question of motivation, however, leads us to touch very briefly on the ever-broader problems of determining values, judgments, intentions of a society. Anthropologists and to some extent historians have habitually done this, sometimes using the statements of one native consultant in a brief field experience to draw wide-ranging conclusions. All of this seemed to make sense in the study of presumably homogeneous societies and of musical styles that were thought incapable of rapid change. The difficulty of establishing satisfactory field methods increased as scholars turned to complex societies with greater internal variation, to such venues as cities in which many culture units may interact, to loci of rapid change. In this essay we are forced to face such complexity, as our illustrations show the interaction of musicians in one society with greatly differing views of innovation (see "Innovators" within the Illustrations section) and the number of musics interacting in one record store of a city ("Streets"). In the face of generalized judgments such as those presenting fundamental differences between Madras and Tehran ("Two Cities"), the reader is perhaps justified in asking who, in the population, determines whether the motivation is modernization or Westernization. But surely there is such a thing as culture, upon which a society always develops a concensus, and it can, whatever the difficulties, be discovered through observation and the statements of sufficient numbers of thoughtful informants.

Among other responses that I suggested in 1978, two are opposite sides of a coin. Consolidation is the combination of style elements from diverse parts of a native repertory into a musical style with broadened cultural significance. An example is the establishment of a relatively simple and compact intertribal or "pan-Indian" North American Indian style to replace a group of separate tribal styles; or the combination of North American Plains, Southwestern, and European elements to establish the intertribal Peyote song style (see "Powwow"; "Old-Time Religion"). Diversification, on the other hand, is the combination into one performance context of musics from the gamut of a non-Western repertory, a combination that could not have been made in earlier times—dances from a variety of tribal ceremonies in the repertory of a national African ballet company, for example, or songs from tribal, folk, and classical sources on the soundtrack of a single Indian or Iranian film ("Streets"; "'Pop'").

Some of the other responses represent points along a continuum. Complete abandonment of a musical culture by a society still extant actually seems to be very rare, but there are instances in which there is no more than a vestige ('Migrants"). If more remains, the response may well be reduction (I called it "impoverishment" in the 1978 article) of a native musical culture, its personnel, style elements, internal diversity, complexity, uses ("Macuma"; "Duck Dance"; "Americans"; "Ethnomusicologists"), in a shift of musical energy. Some non-Western cultures respond more aggressively, as in the practice of artificial preservation, the conscious separation of the older tradition from those aspects of culture that are being Westernized ("Treasures"). Further removed from abandonment is the exaggeration of the distinctive traits of a non-Western style ("Emblems"; "Powwow") for underscoring ethnic identity, and further, reintroduction of non-Western materials in a new form after a period of perhaps virtual abandonment or great reduction, where compatibility permits syncretism ("Compatibles"; "Indigenizers"; "Juju"). Peaceful coexistence of styles may bring with it some rather specialized phenomena such as the presentation and juxtaposition of traditional and Western music in a single social context, for the purpose of making the contrast explicit, the effect intended by music makers to be humorous. Examples are the satirization of American songs sung in Asian Indian styles, in Indian films; or the performance of European classical masterworks in mariachi style.

In an article published in 1981, Margaret J. Kartomi suggested a way of designating responses that result from musical culture contact, refining, sometimes paralleling, and also going somewhat beyond the list in my article of 1978. At one end of a continuum is "virtual rejection of an impinging music." "Pluralistic coexistence of musics" is a broad category that would include my "diversification" and "reduction." "Musical compartmentalization" is seen as a sub-category (see, e.g., "Pianos"; "Notes"). "Nativistic musical revival" (e.g. "Juju"; "Duck Dance") is a special form of my concept of artificial preservation. The "transfer of discrete musical traits" (as in "Harmony";

"New-Time Religion"; "Concertos") is suggested as a special response, but is also present in several of the responses suggested in 1978. The concept that dominates her article, however, is that of transculturation, in which emphasis is on the crossing of cultural boundaries by complexes of culture traits, not alone of individual discrete traits. Recalling Blacking's distinction between change *of a* music, and change *in* music, Kartomi maintains that "transculturation occurs only when a group of people select for adoption whole new organizing and conceptual or ideological principles . . . as opposed to small, discrete alien traits" (p. 244). Of interest also is her suggestion that "aesthetic tastes and standards, together with the many extramusical meanings attached to music, have tended to cross cultural boundaries with far greater difficulty than have tangible objects such as musical instruments" (p. 244), but the illustrations in the present essay do not really support that view.

Dealing with a more restricted set of instances in only one nation, Israel, Amnon Shiloah and Erik Cohen in 1983 examined the influence of a Western-oriented mainstream culture upon various repertories of "Oriental" (i.e., Sephardic and Yemenite) Jewish musical tradition. Citing a wealth of responses in this one culture, they present a set of concepts applicable elsewhere. Concentrating on music as a system of sound, but with reference also to types of sponsorship and audience, they propose what is in essence a continuum of the following nine responses. "Traditional" includes continuation of pre-immigrant musical forms, a kind of music that might also result from Kartomi's "virtual rejection of an impinging music," but is not really reflected in any of my 1978 categories. "Conserved" music is the deliberately preserved traditional pre-immigration repertory, edited and adapted for a new, external audience; and "museumized" music is the same kind of material, collected and preserved in "authentic" form by ethnographically trained outsiders. Both could be partially subsumed under my category of "artificial preservation." Shiloah and Cohen (S & C) then move to musics termed "neotraditional" ("innovative continuation of traditional music styles . . . absorbing some outside influences"), "transitional" ("the bulk of contemporary ethnic musical production . . . with . . . many extraneous elements"), and "pseudoethnic" ("artistic transmutation of ethnic musical forms by producers and performers from outside the ethnic group for an external audience"). These kinds of music are probably more typical of European nations than of the non-Western world at large, but they occur under conditions described by Kartomi as "pluralistic coexistence of musics" (see also "Harmony"; "'Pop'"; "Mahour"; "Violins") and, in the case of pseudoethnic, may sometimes be the subject of nativistic musical revival (see "Concertos"). Kartomi's "transfer of discrete musical traits" is also explicitly involved in these three types of S & C, which also intersect with several of my 1978 categories such as consolidation and diversification. They are of course likely to be the object of impoverishment or reduction, although S & C do not speak to this issue directly, evidently taking the universal reduction of repertories for granted. One might also see neotraditional, transitional, and pseudoethnic musics as manifestations of modernization, and perhaps of syncretism.

The last three types of S & C are strata of the modern urban musical culture and, perhaps more than the other categories, involve urbanization. Labeled "popular," "ethnic fine," and "fine" (derived from Charles Seeger's term, "fine art" for classical or art music), they are also part of the continuum. Popular music, through audience and styles, is a bit closer to the "traditional" end. The fine art music, which may go no further than using ethnic thematic elements, is close to the category of virtual abandonment and may be illustrated by some of the works described in "Concertos."

The three groupings are not coordinate. S & C present a continuum. Kartomi's scheme approaches a continuum but includes other classes. Mine of 1978 includes overarching concepts as well as instances of specialized behavior, and in other respect, categories of greatly varying magnitude. In several instances the three groups agree. S & C's "traditional" ethnic music is a result of Kartomi's "virtual rejection." My "artificial preservation" is close to S & C's "conservation and museumization," and its musical forms exist in the context of Kartomi's "compartmentalization." S & C's "fine art" music sounds like an instance of my "abandonment." My categories of "reduction," "exaggeration," and "reintroduction" may be manifested in S & C's "pseudoethnic" music, and may involve Kartomi's "transfer of discrete traits." Kartomi's "pluralistic coexistence" of musics might well be accompanied by what I call "diversification" and "consolidation," and her "nativistic revivals" would presumably be called "neotraditional" by S & C. Syncretism would likely apply to the middle parts of S & C's continuum, could include popular music, and might involve the "transfer of discrete traits" fromKartomi's categories. Modernization, in general, would involve conserved, museumized, neotraditional, and perhaps transitional musics from S & C's group; Westernization certainly includes the "fine" and "ethnic fine" categories, and perhaps the popular and pseudoethnic as well.

But of course the three groupings were established with a variety of aims, and they attack the subject from different sides. Even where they coincide, they speak to different facets of music, and in the end, they cannot do more than to suggest some of the kinds of things that occur and interpret the role of different musical processes and products in their respective cultures. A piece, event, person may be categorized individually. At the same time, one may characterize the responses in any one culture by their configuration, and thus determine, for example, that in one instance, it is preservation that is most desired, while elsewhere, it is modernization; here, transculturation in toto while there, the creation of a carefully honed combination of elements from both sides of the musical fence, to create a symbolically significant balance.

Two strands of history gradually come together: the introduction of Western music to non-Western cultures and the resulting musical turmoil resulting in many forms, concepts, sounds, contexts; and the gradual discovery of the powerful role of these culturally mixed musics by ethnomusicologists who were at first loath to recognize them. No doubt many scholars of non-Western music, given their training as musicians and as members of the Western musical culture with its love of clear categories, would rather have stayed with a group of discrete musics in which interaction was exception rather than rule. But they have recognized that instead of producing the cultural greyout widely foreseen as the outcome of Wiora's fourth age, cultural interaction, however offensive its roots and methods, have actually diversified the musical world.

## REFERENCES

Klaus Wachsmann, "Criteria for Acculturation," in International Musicological Society, Report of the 8th Congress, New York (Kassel: Baerenreiter, 1961), 139–49. Bruno Nettl, "Historical Aspects of Ethnomusicology," American Anthropologist 60:518–32, 1958; and "Change in Folk and Primitive Music: A Survey of Methods and Studies," Journal of the American Musicological Society 8:101–9, 1955. John Blacking, "Some Problems of Theory and Method in the Study of Musical Change," YIFMC 9:1–26, 1978. Alan P. Merriam, The Anthropology of Music (Evanston, Ill.: Northwestern University Press, 1964), chapters 14 and 15. Bruno Nettl, "Some Aspects of the History of World Music in the Twentieth Century: Questions, Problems, Concepts," EM 22:123–36, 1978; The Study of Ethnomusicology (Urbana: University of Illinois Press, 1983), chapters 13 and 27; and "Transplantationes de musicas, confrontaciones de sistemas y mecanismos de rechazo," Revista Musical Chilena 34(149–50): 5–17, 1980. Margaret J. Kartomi, "The Processes and Results of Musical Culture Contact: A Discussion of Terminology and Concepts," EM 25:227–50, 1981. Amnon Shiloah and Erik Cohen, "The Dynamics of Change in Jewish Oriental Ethnic Music in Israel," EM 27:227–52, 1983.

# ILLUSTRATIONS

# 6
# Powwow

*Dearborn, Michigan, 1962.* Walking into the small suburban stadium, I was greeted by a booming voice speaking rapidly through the microphone: "Isn't this great? Indian people and white people singing together, dancing together, having a good time together, celebrating the great heritage of America! Look at us!" The patter went on, and as I arrived at the top of the stairs I saw a small podium on which an American-Indian-looking man in jeans, boots, and cowboy hat was speaking and gesticulating with much animation, the volume turned high. Near him, on folding chairs, sat a small circle of men huddled around a bass drum, beating it in unison and singing in the style of North American Plains Indian music. Two of them, including the leader, appeared actually to be Indians; the rest might have been white men and boys. They were less heavily amplified and their song provided a sort of background to the continuing banter of the master of ceremonies. They were situated on the outskirts of a roped-off circle within which some twenty people were dancing, four or five Indian men, two Indian girls, a couple of presumably white men and a dozen white girls. All were wearing costumes of brightly colored cloth, feathers, beads, some rawhide, and other decorations, with the exception of the Indian girls who wore longish beige dresses and in contrast to the vigorous jumping of the others were dancing in a subdued style. The dancers moved individually, turning and changing position in relation to each other, but the entire group moved slowly clockwise around a pole in the center.

The event had been billed as an American Indian "powwow." To be sure, most of the participants didn't appear to be Indians, but the styles of singing and dancing were dominated by Indian elements and of course did not fit into any conception of Western music and dance I knew of.

The audience for whom this was all being done was almost exclusively white Americans. The performers were both Indians and whites, but it was not simply a matter of whites joining in and taking Indian roles. The Indians maintained two styles of dancing, men's and women's, and two types of costume, by sex; but all of the whites, men and women, joined in the men's style and wore costumes derived from those of Indian men. Even within the Indian component of the event there could be confusion. The music was clearly in the Plains Indian style, with its falsetto beginnings, its harsh, tense, pulsating way of singing, its terrace-shaped melodic contour and characteristic stanza structure, its texts typically comprised of vocables. But the Indian participants themselves were, as I later learned, not of Plains but of Midwestern

Algonquian, Eastern Iroquois, and Southwestern Pueblo origin. It might be difficult to pin down the cultural identity of this event.

Ethnomusicologists of an earlier day would have written all this off as Plains Indian music and dance presented in thoroughly unauthentic fashion. But in the 1960s, much of what we might (carelessly) call Indian music was actually presented substantially in this way, once discrete Indian cultures combined and mixed with the culture of the whites, one of the many results of cultural interaction, acculturation, transculturation.

The powwow at Dearborn showed the effects of Western culture on a Plains Indian event that was quite different before whites came into the lives of the Indians. Modern powwows are not merely the latest version of one particular traditional type of event, but one of its ancestors must surely be the Plains Indian Sun Dance, the principal public religious ceremony of a number of tribes in the nineteenth century. Without going into detail, let me say that the Sun Dance normally took place in the summer, was the focal point of a meeting of the entire tribe (which during winter may have lived divided into several separate bands), and consisted of a number of simultaneous events of which the most important was the dancing of young men around a pole to the accompaniment of a circle of singers beating a drum in unison. Descriptions of the Arapaho and Blackfoot Sun Dances around 1900 indicate a complex ritual not too rigorously prescribed. A few songs had to be sung at specific points, and others were generally associated with the Sun Dance, but songs from the repertories of social dances might also be heard. From early and recent recordings, one gathers that their style was not highly distinctive. Various social events including dances and age-grade ceremonies took place at the time of the Sun Dance, as did athletic contests and gambling games.

Taken as a unit, the old Sun Dance seems to have functioned as a religious emblem of tribal identity as well as a social symbol of tribal unity. On some Plains reservations, and in some tribes substantially influenced by Plains culture, it continued in recent decades to be celebrated, but largely as a memorial, a somewhat artificial reconstruction of a tradition interrupted, usually presented by a small number of persons for an audience mainly of Indians.

But at the same time, the Sun Dance also has a more vigorous successor. On reservations in the Western Plains and Rocky Mountain States, in Western Canada and in Oklahoma, tribal get-togethers in midsummer, lasting several days and incorporating the social if not the religious aspects of the Sun Dance, have been established since the 1940s. The "North American Indian Days" of Browning, Montana, is typical, an event descended from the Blackfoot Indian Sun Dance suppressed in 1887, and from attempts to keep it in existence by moving it to July 4, thus associating it with a major white American festival. By the late 1960s, it had attracted a number of characteristics of Western musical life evidently because it was carried out in a milieu really belonging to Western society and performed by people whose lives were in most respects part of Western culture.

Older practices seem to have been adapted to modern conditions. For example, while the entire Sun Dance ceremony took some nine days, its central activities required four; and North American Indian Days in 1966 was also a four-day affair. In earlier times, the various bands of the tribe joined together; today, residents of communities throughout the reservation as well as Blackfoot people living elsewhere, as far as Minneapolis and San Francisco, use the occasion to visit. Athletic and other contests among members of various bands took place in the nineteenth century. While athletics did not play a part, gambling games and contests among singing and dancing groups were held representing various villages on the reservation and elsewhere, perhaps replacing the bands as social units.

But what was once a specifically tribal event had by the 1960s become, additionally, an exhibition for whites in the area, including tourists from nearby Glacier National Park, who were encouraged to participate as dancers but were mainly spectators, and for members of other tribes on nearby reservations, who participated fully. The music had changed from a heterogeneous mixture of ceremonial and social dance music to a much more unified repertory of social dances, mainly the Grass or War Dance of late nineteenth-century origin, sung without meaningful texts and in highly standardized form, but unmistakably in the Plains manner. Along with these one might hear gambling songs accompanying a nearby traditional game, in an old style traditional and peculiar to this genre. Amplification, the patter of a master of ceremonies speaking in English, prizes for good dancing and costumes, commercial fast-food vendors, and patronage by local white-owned businesses all showed the influence of the Western environment. And so did, at a different level, the tendency to sing in especially high falsetto, in a style as contrastive as possible to Western singing of whatever kind—opera, church choir, country-and-western. Perhaps this exaggerated Indian-ness was intended to impress on the white spectator the genuinely exotic nature of this culture, with only its music and dance left to symbolize its special character. The fact that Western music is widely heard on the Blackfoot Reservation has not caused the songs of the powwows to sound more Western, but it has had significant indirect influences—exaggeration of the non-Western vocal style, standardization, loss of Indian texts, and of course a multitude of effects on the social context of the music.

The North American Indian Days powwow in Browning may therefore be interpreted as a modernized form of the Sun Dance, whose ceremonial aspects it abandoned while keeping many of the social ones. In a variety of ways it was a response to the realities of Western cultural surroundings. Adopting Western musical technology and aspects of the Western concert formats, it used the English language and abandoned Blackfoot as a medium of song texts, permitting members of other tribes and whites to participate. At the same time it exaggerated certain traditional elements of musical style in its general sound, if not in the details of musical structure. This illustrates the way in which the complex interrelationships within a musical event can be manipulated to symbolize various aspects of cultural interaction—compliance, adaptation, and preservation.

If the traditional Sun Dance and North American Indian Days in Montana seem far apart, it is only a short way from the essentially tribal Blackfoot powwow to the intertribal event in Dearborn. The latter has added a broadly Indian orientation, permitted wholesale participation and even virtual domination by whites, and emphasized further the audience–performer dichotomy. The use of the Plains musical style by Indians not from the Plains culture area reveals the need for a general Indian idiom, seizing upon the Plains style precisely because it is so different from Western music and thus quintessentially Indian. The three way stations in the history of the powwow show three responses—attempts to preserve, adaptation of tribal culture, development of a general Indian and urban society. In each case, American Indians used music to make a statement about this relationship to Western culture.

## REFERENCES

James H. Howard, "Pan-Indianism in Native American Music and Dance," *EM* 27:71–82, 1983.   Samuel W. Corrigan, "The Plains Indian Pow-wow: Cultural Integration in Manitoba and Saskatchewan," *Anthropologica* (n.s.) 12(2):253–77, 1970.   John C. Ewers, *The Blackfeet: Raiders on the Northwestern Plains* (Norman: University of Oklahoma Press, 1958), 174–84, 310–11.   Clark Wissler, "The Sun Dance of the Blackfoot Indians," *American Museum of Natural History Anthropological Papers*, vol. XVI, part 3 (1918).   Robert Witmer, *The Musical Life of the Blood Indians* (Ottawa: National Museum of Canada, 1982), 23–31, 41–42.   William K. Powers, "Contemporary Oglala Music and Dance: Pan-Indianism versus Pan-Tetonism," *EM* 12:352–72, 1968.   Alfred L. Kroeber, *The Arapaho*, Bulletin of the American Museum of Natural History, no. 18 (New York, 1902), 279–308.

# 7
# Harmony

A quick survey of a few recordings. The first is a performance of the mode, or *dastgāh,* of *Chahārgāh* by an Iranian *santour* player. It is from the *āvāz* section and thus improvised. The first subdivision, *darāmad,* takes about two minutes. It is monophonic, but implies a semblance of Western harmony in the emphasis of tonic and dominant, though Western harmony in its full and proper sense is not feasible; the second and sixth degrees of the *Chahārgāh* scale are each a quarter-tone lower than they would be in Western major. The player proceeds in traditional Persian style, but after about one minute at the end of a principal section, an arpeggio on the tonic major triad suddenly rises over two octaves. Then, after a second minute of traditional sound, there is a stretch of emphasis on the fifth degree of the scale, and a brief but dramatic ending using alternation of fifth and tonic. These two instances remind one, slightly and subtly, of the Westernized environment of this essentially non-Western music.

The second piece is performed by Vadya Vrinda, the orchestra of the Madras station of All India Radio. Throughout most of its course it is monophonic (with tonic drone as one expects in Indian music) but there is also some antiphony among groups of instruments resulting in overlapping, one group holding a tone, drone-like, while the other moves through a tetrachord or a pentachord. Occasionally, two melodic lines move in parallel thirds over the drone on tonic or fifth degree, thus giving an impression of triads and seventh chords with passing tones. Basically, such music is melodic; or presents a melody in parallel thirds. But the drone adds to the impression that Western harmony is indeed present, that in order to make the older tradition sound modern, allusions to Western functional harmony are essential. Here the harmonic material appears throughout the piece, not only in isolated spots as was the case in our piece from Iran.

The third piece is a Navaho song (recorded by Willard Rhodes), monophonic of course, immediately repeated by the singer on his harmonica. Now, many songs of the Navaho (and Apache, too) have triadic scales, some of them using only what sounds like a major triad. This is such a song, and the harmonica rendition is restricted to the pitches in the tune. There is Western harmony of sorts, but we hear only a tonic chord. Western harmony or simply drone? There is reason to believe that the Navaho singer used the harmonica as a way of producing his song in a Western musical context.

In Zaire, Alan Merriam recorded a song entitled "Jose de Lux," with words that praise the singer and his homespun wisdom. The melody could fit neatly into a traditional African context, consisting as it does of two short musical lines continually repeated with variations. The second line, a kind of answer to the first, recalls the characteristic antiphonal singing of many African peoples. The singer accompanies himself on the guitar, using only two chords, the first line moving from tonic to dominant, and the second, returning from dominant to tonic. This is of course Western harmony, but it barely goes beyond the drone.

From the same town and on the same disc is a recording of a kind of barbershop trio, a group of Bangala men singing in a tavern. One of them also plays guitar. In close three-part harmony, they sing a short song, two phrases, statement and response, over and over. The harmonic scheme is like that of the solo song, "Jose de Lux," except that the subdominant chord is used as transition from tonic to dominant and again from dominant to tonic, but very briefly, rather as if it were an ornament, thus: Phrase A: I I I IV V V V V / Phrase B: V V V IV I I I I. A bit more complex than "Jose" in terms of functional harmony, but not really quite right or conventional. Traditionally, the subdominant does not follow the dominant. Is this experimentation with the Western system? Or is it a matter of using harmony, but not being quite sure how it works? At any rate, this song uses three chords, and incorporates the basic Western cadence.

Different from all these examples, yet still derived from Western functional harmony, is the chordal accompaniment of Andean highlands songs, executed on the guitar or on the charango, a guitar-like instrument that has become traditional in the area. In a large proportion of these songs the harmonic pattern modulates from major to relative minor, as from C major to A minor, using tonic and dominant of the major and then of the minor key. Actually, the line is characteristically in major, and only near the end comes the almost inevitable shift to minor. Western harmony, but in a pattern that has become unmistakably Andean. Possibly the characteristic anhemitonic pentatonic scale of the melodies, which includes a minor third above the tonic, is responsible for this peculiar and consistent harmonic pattern.

But there is also harmony by monophonic implication alone. Faromarz Payevar, a famous Iranian santour virtuoso, begins a lengthy traditional performance of Persian classical music with an Alpine tune that alternates tonic and dominant arpeggios. A modern *tasnif,* performed monophonically in the Iranian mode of *Māhour* (which is much like major), is introduced with a tune emphasizing triadic pitches, and readily harmonizable with functional harmony. But while both pieces initially emphasize the major mode and its chords, both proceed through modulations that require accidentals, introduction of three-quarter and five-quarter tones, moving through the *dastgāh* until, at the end, the triadic sound in major reappears. In these recordings, Western harmony doesn't dominate, but its importance is symbolized by its appearance at key places, beginnings and endings.

The presence of Western harmony in non-Western music is in many instances limited and symbolic. A chord here and there, alternation of two harmonies, triadic melody. Sometimes there is more. West African highlife music gives you all that jazz and rock might offer by way of harmony, along with typically West African percussion ensemble patterns. Central African church music has developed works, such as masses, in which the parallel thirds, found all along in the African tradition, are tamed to produce cadences of functional harmony. A mass in Madras, composed at least nominally in accordance with South Indian ragas, has chordal accompaniment on the harmonium, and while the harmonic style departs a bit from the older Western tradition, there are cadences of three chords, IV V I.

A few Iranian pianists have taken to playing Persian classical music, and while most of what they perform is monophonic, or in octaves, or at most heterophonic, there is some music in which the left hand is essentially accompaniment comprised mainly of tonic chord arpeggios. Sometimes the dominant-tonic cadence also appears, but more interesting is the frequent use of the Neapolitan sixth. Probably the Neapolitan relationship is seen as appropriate for the characteristic cadence of several Persian modes, moving from the second degree, a three-quarter tone above the tonic, to the tonic. As in the Andean highlands music, the characteristics of melody here provide the background for harmonic selection.

There are many ways of using Western harmony in the world of non-Western music, but in each case it functions as the central feature of Western music and its use is a technique of associating the traditional with the modern.

## REFERENCES

**Records:** The first example is taken from a recording made by the author in 1968, and not issued; but similar material can be heard on *Traditional Persian Music*, Festival of Arts, Shiraz-Persepolis, 1970 (Tehran: Āhang-e Ruz). No commercial recordings of the Madras Vadya Vrinda are available; the piece discussed here was recorded by All India Radio ca. 1980, and kindly made available to the author. Other recordings specifically discussed here: "Navaho Song of Happiness," on *Indian Songs of Today*, edited by Willard Rhodes, Washington: Library of Congress AAFS L36. "Modern Congo Songs," on *Voice of the Congo*, edited by Alan P. Merriam, Riverside Records RLP 4002. Several songs on *Le charango des hauts plateaux andins*, Arion 30 T 143. Other recordings containing music in the styles and with the characteristics specified here include *The West African Highlife Scene*, London International SW 99498; and *Master Performers of Persian Traditional Music*, Tehran: Āhang-e Ruz ARTMS 11 (Payvar, santour) and ARTMS 2 (Maroufi, piano).

# 8
# Two Cities

Tehran (ca. 1970) and Madras (ca. 1980). The two cities have much in common. At the times given, each had a population of between three and four million. Both are centers: Tehran, the capital of Iran, and for a century its cultural hub, the Paris to Iran's France; Madras, the capital of Tamil-Nadu, center of Tamil culture, and also the largest city of Dravidian-speaking South India, a distinct cultural unit of the subcontinent. Both cities have assumed this status within the last 100 years, superseding earlier culture centers such as Tanjore and Mysore in India, Isfahan and Shiraz in Iran. Each has also become, in the twentieth century, the definitive center of its classical music culture. In both cases, the classical musics had sustained contact with European music, musical thought and behavior, and had to face the demands of the competitive domineering Western culture.

There are also ways in which these two cities are not at all alike. Take for one thing the difference in the value of music. Broadly speaking, it is high in Hindu South India and much lower in Shi'ite Muslim Iran. While this statement could bear thorough discussion, let me simply illustrate by pointing out that classical music plays a major role in Hindu temple worship and other religious events, while Shi'ite Islam looks down on music and musicians, keeping classical music out of the mosque, drawing a conceptual line between it and liturgical music such as reading the Qur'an and the call to prayer, for which a separate terminology is maintained. In the total musical picture of Tehran in 1970, it was Western popular music, a Westernized style of Middle Eastern popular music, and Western classical music that were dominant, while Persian classical music was known only to a few. Those individuals who admitted to a love and understanding of any music as a great art were typically members of the Westernized sector of society and identified with the Western classics, public concerts of which outnumbered those of Persian classical by perhaps five to one. The majority of the intellectual elite did not place the two classical systems on the same level; the Persian was regarded as closer to popular entertainment. The two government-sponsored conservatories, Western and "national," reflected this inequality in the number and quality of their clienteles. By the late 1960s, Persian classical music was considered a dying art, even though the 1970s saw something of a revival. Various light and popular forms of classical music were developed after 1950 and promulgated on the radio and in government-sponsored concerts. At the same time, the achievements of Iranians in Western classical music were considerable. So, what we say about Persian classical music must be understood as referring to the music of a handful of distinguished performers, perhaps two hundred amateurs, and a couple of thousand occasional listeners.

By contrast, Carnatic classical music appears to dominate the musical culture of Madras, especially if one includes the accompaniment of dance dramas. On an average day in November or February, both "off months," there are two or three public concerts of Carnatic music and *Bharat Natyam* dance. But during the so-called music season of December and early January, there is a sudden and almost incredible escalation of classical music activity, as many as twenty-five public concerts in one day, in some dozen concert halls, spread through afternoon and evening. In addition to these public events, there are any number of other occasions for the performance of Carnatic music—private concerts, "felicitations" in honor of musicians and public figures, weddings, special celebrations such as the anniversary of the founding of a publishing house. At the same time, there are a few concerts of popular and film music, but in the course of a month, only one or two concerts of Western classical music (usually sponsored by a foreign consulate).

Among the institutions that support and organize Carnatic music performance, the most important are societies or "music circles" called *Sabhas,* which own or rent halls. In 1982, there were some thirty-five *Sabhas* in Madras, about ten of them devoted exclusively to classical music and dance, the others also involved although their major activity might be drama or film. *Sabhas* may vary according to function or to task—conservative or progressive. Some devote themselves to Carnatic music in general while other specialize in featuring young musicians or promulgating a particular instrument or genre (e.g., music for the oboe-like *nagaswaram,* once exclusive to temples, or concerts of devotional songs), promoting acceptance of North Indian music in the South, or preserving the most traditional forms. Apart from the *Sabhas* there are four large recognized music schools, which sponsor concerts, and a host of smaller ones. All India Radio also provides daily concerts, most of them live but expecially tailored for broadcasting; and there monthly television concerts.

The city of Madras, large and sprawling, with well-defined districts, has areas in which classical music is particularly prominent. The stronghold is the old district of Mylapore, on which site the city was first settled. There are six concert halls featuring Carnatic music and three large music and dance schools. Walking along the streets, one constantly hears the sound of Carnatic music, practicing, music lessons, radio. There is nothing like this in Tehran. Mylapore has a large population of conservative Brahmins for whom Carnatic classical music is a major symbol of cultural and social identity. By contrast one might encounter Hindustani (North Indian) music where the intent is to "be modern"—at performances of contemporary dramas in English, in hotel restaurants, and in movie houses.

On the whole, Carnatic musicians maintain that Western music has had little impact on their system and actually has less now than in years past. If one pointed out the Western-style concert life, radio, and the rest, they might say, as did one musician I met, "Of course, we got a lot of good ideas from the English, and besides, we use Western instruments, but our music is Carnatic music and these things just make it possible for us to maintain it. When we see that some ideas from the outside world are useful to us, we take advantage of them. But clearly, Carnatic music is the music for us, and perhaps it would be best for everyone else if only it were propagated."

Of course, there have been attempts to introduce Western musical style elements into Carnatic music. Some of the great composers of the nineteenth century occasionally set Telugu texts to English tunes such as "God Save the King," and also composed some music in imitation of that style. Today these songs are only curiosities, and the only Western tune regularly heard is a spritely instrumental waltz called "A Note" or "English Note," used to end performances. It is said that the violin, when first used, was played in a style more closely approximating the Western than now. But the Western influences of the nineteenth century were evidently absorbed, and the Carnatic system consolidated, while the rest of life continued to Westernize.

But if Carnatic music seems to have been little touched by Western styles, this circumstance may stem in part from the fact that, in certain respects, it is *like* Western music, though not, of course, in its sound. It would seem that Carnatic musicians, when confronted with Western music, saw that they could compete effectively simply by insisting on what they already had: a music of great complexity, with its great composers and large repertory and even—they frequently mention it—a seven-tone system and a solmization scheme rather like the Western. From Western musical culture they took certain principles such as notation (the *idea* of notation, and some of its practices, but not the Western system in toto), the idea that all music can be performed at any time, discarding the time and season restriction on ragas, and most important, various Western social contexts for performance. South Indians sometimes appear to have an unshakable belief in the superiority of their cultural system, life style, philosophy, and of course, their music. And so, if they adopted Western technology, they did this to maintain their traditional values. The classical music public of Madras confronted Western musical culture, took what amounts to its technology, notation, amplification, and instruments, and placed it at the disposal of a modernized society. The fundamental values of musical style remained intact.

How different the state of Persian classical music. If by the late 1960s one could hardly say that it had been thoroughly Westernized, style elements of Western music had made definite inroads. In contrast to its use in Indian music, the violin brought with it a Western playing style and sound ideal. Western harmony cropped up on occasion. Orchestras gave concerts of modernized forms of Persian music, using both traditional and Western instruments and a physical arrangement like that of the symphony orchestra. The significance of improvisatory sections had been replaced by greater emphasis on the composed portions of a performance. Those modes that coincided with the Western ones became more widely used, and meters not found in Western music, such as $\frac{7}{4}$, were gradually being abandoned. And other minor changes moved the musical system gradually in the direction of the mainstream of the Western musical style.

About 1970, the social context of music in Tehran had been somewhat less Westernized. As major institution, the public concert had not really taken hold, and the small private concert was still the main musical venue. Women did not participate as full members of the audience. Despite greater purchasing power, Iranians had far fewer records of their own classical music available than did South Indians. The cultural tradition of looking down on music kept it out of the public eye, allowing it to flourish in private only, and emphasizing amateur musicianship.

The sound of Persian music has changed greatly; the social context remains. It is the opposite of Madras, whose musical life has changed fundamentally while the sound remains quite essentially Indian. Each society has allowed aspects of the traditional culture to change, in order, we may guess, to preserve what it regards as most central. It is indicative of the value of music in the two societies that Tehran has held on to musical attitudes and institutions while Madras has kept its sound. In another respect, what has happened in Madras comes down to modernization, and in Tehran, to Westernization.

# REFERENCES

**Bruno Nettl,** ed., *Eight Urban Musical Cultures* (Urbana: University of Illinois Press, 1978); especially Kathleen L'Armand and Adrian L'Armand, "Music in Madras: The Urbanization of a Cultural Tradition" and B. Nettl, "Persian Classical Music in Tehran: The Processes of Change." **Mohammad Taghi Massoudieh,** "Tradition und Wandel in der persischen Musik des 19. Jahrhunderts," in *Musikkulturen Asiens, Afrikas und Ozeaniens im 19. Jahrhundert,* edited by Robert Günther (Regensburg: Bosse, 1973), 81–91. **Bruno Nettl,** "Attitudes Toward Persian Music in Tehran, 1969," *Musical Quarterly* 56:183–97, 1970. *Iran Alamanac and Book of Facts,* 7th ed. (Tehran: Echo of Iran, 1969). **Milton Singer,** *When a Great Tradition Modernizes* (New York: Praeger, 1972). **Kathleen L'Armand and Adrian L'Armand,** "One Hundred Years of Music in Madras: A Case Study in Secondary Urbanization," *EM* 27:411–38, 1983.

# 9
# Compatibles

About 1950, in what is now Zaire, three men were singing in a bar; one accompanied on guitar, and another struck an empty beer bottle with a knife. A short phrase (would you believe it required scarcely more than three seconds?) over tonic harmony moving to the dominant alternated with its melodic answer that was accompanied by harmony moving from dominant to tonic. The guitar kept repeating the same alternation of two chords, and the two phrases kept coming back, but in a slightly different way each time. The singers moved in close harmony, though one or two might spin off in a variety of directions here and there. The guitar provided a regular oom-chuck rhythm. The man on the bottle unerringly repeated a short syncopated phrase: eighth–quarter–quarter–eighth–quarter.

The description suggests an African style, but in fact the song sounds very European—four-part harmony, dominant–tonic, guitar, a tune in major with characteristic jumps from dominant to tonic on the pickup. What then was African about it? First: if there is a "Western" music, is there also an "African" music? As a matter of fact, there are more "African" musics than Western; Africans are less prone to regard their musical language as unified by some fundamental feature than are Europeans and Americans. But African musics have enough in common to allow us to determine principal characteristics, and some of them were present in our little song: short phrases combined in what is essentially a set of variations improvised on a very short theme, a simple rhythmic cycle in the tune and guitar juxtaposed to a rather more complex pattern on the bottle which sounds like the bell that gives the characteristic pattern in West and Central African percussion ensembles. Even the role of the guitar can be related to the accompaniment patterns of the *mbira,* or thumb-piano, an instrument also capable of harmonic effects. If this piece does not sound typically African, it nevertheless has, in the abstract, traits typical of African music. But also, you may say, a measure of four beats and a bit of syncopated rhythm, that's nothing so terribly African, it's long been possible in European folk music, popular music, light classics. As for variations of a short theme, a lot of European instrumental folk music works like that.

Obviously we've stumbled on a piece that incorporates characteristics of music common to Africa and the West. No great surprise, that. It's not difficult to imagine this kind of compatibility of traits. For example, the fact that African rhythm is often vastly more complex than European may be disposed of by using something just barely complex enough for the African and just a little more difficult than the usual Western folk and popular rhythm. African forms often have short phrases with responsorial performance. But this arrangement can well fit into the four-line scheme, ABAB, found in hymns, folk songs, and popular ditties of many European countries.

The fundamental similarities of certain traits of African and European music are thought to underlie the successful combination of styles in various parts of the New World and modern Africa; they permit syncretism, the fusion of elements shared by two musics into something new that is also compatible with both systems. The resulting exchange of ideas includes the introduction of African-derived rhythms into Western music and the intrusion of Western functional harmony into African music on both sides of the Atlantic. On the other hand, the fact that North American Indian music has not developed a similar combination of elements probably results from the much greater stylistic distance, and a lower degree of compatibility, between it and Western music.

But is similarity, with the resulting musical compatibility, necessarily a major factor in determining whether stylistic fusion will come about? Let's look at alternatives. We could argue that North American Indians have been isolated from white culture and its music for a long time, while African slaves had closer contact with their white masters. Moreover, a look at the social and political organizations of the peoples involved shows the typical African society considerably closer to the European than that of American Indian cultures. And then again, what are the results of musical interaction in other cultures with styles more or less compatible with Western music?

The art music of India is similar in scalar structure, in general formal principles, in certain aspects of rhythm. It has no harmony, but at least the foundations for something like Western harmony in its emphasis on tonic and fifth. And yet, there has not been much real exchange of ideas in the classical music. Harmony has, it is true, been added in certain specifically light or popular styles of the music, usually in a simple form using only two or three chords, rather as in the African example cited above. The classical music allows itself to move a bit in the direction of Western sounds—witness the use of certain Western instruments, or the increasing popularity (so musicians say) of talas (metric cycles) with eight or sixteen beats, and of ragas compatible with Western major. And yet no combined form of classical music has appeared. In Indian film music, we come closer to a syncretic style. Western harmony is used substantially although other Western elements have penetrated less. To put it very broadly, in India we don't find the kind or degree of exchange of ideas as in Africa; nor as much use of common elements to produce combined styles. Instead, there is avoidance of the obvious Western counterparts of Indian musical elements such as melody types and melodic formulas. So what we hear are characteristically Indian melodic and rhythmic structures sometimes accompanied with Western harmony. Perhaps the distance (musically speaking) is too great.

Persian music has even less in common with the Western than does that of India. In the older tradition, there is no harmony, no emphasis on ensembles, rather scales with intervals incompatible with those of the West. But unlike Indian culture, which seems to have held itself as aloof as possible, Persian culture seems to have tried to become in some respects a part of the West. And so, as we have seen, bits of Western harmony find their way into cadential points in Persian classical music. The concept of harmony, if not its substance, is found in the octave-like treatment of melodies by popular music ensembles. Three-quarter tones sometimes shrink to semitones to produce scales reminiscent of Eastern European folk songs, legends of the Levant, sad gypsy tunes. A lot of music in Iran sounds like a combination of Western and traditional elements. It's more like the African experience than that of India; and yet, the similarities between Indian and Western music would lead one to expect results more reminiscent of the African developments.

This does not mean that syncretism and compatibility, as concepts which will help us predict, have no usefulness. But if the results of musical interaction are in good measure determined by the type of relationship of musical styles, the social and political relationships of cultures and the attitude that a society holds toward its culture and towards cultural change also play major roles.

# REFERENCES

Melville J. Herskovits, *Acculturation: The Study of Culture Contact* (New York: J.J. Augustin, 1938); and "Problem, Method, and Theory in Afroamerican Studies," *Afroamerica* 1:5–24, 1945.   Richard A. Waterman, "African Influence on American Negro Music," in *Acculturation in the Americas,* edited by Sol Tax (Chicago: University of Chicago Press, 1952), 207–18.   Alan P. Merriam, *The Anthropology of Music* (Evanston: Northwestern University Press, 1964), chapter 15.   Record: Alan P. Merriam, *Voice of the Congo,* Riverside RLP 4002, 1953.

# 10
# Violins

The idea of bowing a string did not originate in Europe. The ultimate ancestor of the bowed violin may even be the musical bow, used in sub-Saharan Africa and among some South American Indians, with its string activated by the beating of a stick. Using a bow of horsehair may have originated in Central Asia, whence it moved to the Far East, resulting in instruments such as the Chinese *hu-ch'in,* to the Middle East and India (producing instruments such as the Persian *kamāncheh,* the Indian *sarinda* and *sarangi*), and to Europe. Thus in a sense the violin is itself the result of influences from outside Europe. But once developed and, by the seventeenth century, established as a primary instrument of Western art music, it penetrated a number of other cultures and became one of the world's most versatile instruments. This versatility can be seen in the widespread use of the violin for light and popular music of the West, and in the folk fiddling of North America, and in the rural ensembles of Central and Eastern Europe and Scandinavia. And changed slightly, if at all, the violin has also become a major instrument in the traditional music of Iran, South India, and perhaps of the Amazonian jungle in Ecuador. But very different kinds of music have resulted.

By the 1960s, the violin had become perhaps the most popular instrument for performance of classical Iranian music. It is held just as it is in the West, under the chin, and the bow is held European-style, hand on top. It may be tuned as in the West, e–a–d–G, but other tunings, such as e–a–d–A, d–a–D–G, e–a–E–C, all derived from tunings of the traditional Iranian lutes, are also used. Sitting on chairs or standing, players perform the same music also played on *santour, tār,* and *setār,* and the bowed *kamāncheh,* but produce a somewhat different sound.

It is interesting to compare the classical improvised music of the *kamāncheh* with that of the violin. The *kamāncheh* is played in a low-key, quiet manner with no vibrato and little dynamic contrast. The violinist often takes from European classical music a more heroic style of playing, using vibrato, moving rapidly through the wide range of the instrument, playing now softly, now loudly, contrasting quick passages with long tones, building crescendos, using pizzicato and a variety of bowing techniques. He is typically a person who has also studied some Western music and plays some of it (and sometimes also Persian popular music), along with the Iranian classical material. He often employs the adaptation of Western notation that has become widely used in Iran. More than his colleagues playing traditional instruments, he tends to alter the traditional scales, with their $\frac{3}{4}$ and $\frac{5}{4}$ tones, in the direction of the closest Western equivalents. In effect, he is using the violin to demonstrate compatibility between the Iranian and Western traditions.

The violin was not introduced into Persian classical music until the late 1800s, as a result of the coming of European musicians. In South India, on the other hand, the history of the violin goes back about 200 years. It is believed to have been introduced, or at least first widely used, by the prominent musician Baluswamy Dikshitar, brother of the famous Carnatic composer Muttuswami Dikshitar (1775–1835). Today it is almost ubiquitous as an accompanying instrument for vocalists, flutists, even *vina* players and for performers on seldom-used instruments such as guitar and mandolin. But it is played in a peculiarly Indian way. Holding it against the shoulder, not under the chin, the player sits on the floor, cross-legged, and supports the scroll of the violin with his right foot; the instrument slants downward at a 45-degree angle. The left hand supports the violin but little and is thus free to slide up and down, constantly shifting position. Thus, ornaments are produced by sliding the finger, and the fourth, little finger is rarely used. Normally there is no vibrato.

The sound of South Indian violin playing is very different indeed from that of the West, whether it be gypsy cafe music, nineteenth-century violin concertos, or American folk fiddle playing. Instead, it imitates the sound of Indian singers and Carnatic musicians praise its adaptability to that style. It has actually turned out to be more successful in approximating singing than other Carnatic instruments, and it has probably become so prominent because Carnatic musicians regard their music as fundamentally vocal, and their entire music system to be based on singing. Even in the last twenty years prominence of the violin has evidently increased and its use expanded. It has become a solo instrument, accompanied in its turn by a second violin, and violin trios also appear occasionally. Its versatility has made it not only a part but a major component of Carnatic music. In music schools it is the instrument most widely taught.

Carnatic musicians do not ordinarily cross stylistic boundaries. A few singers perform popular music, particularly for films, but, with a couple of notable exceptions, Carnatic violinists do not perform Western music, and only a handful also perform Hindustani music. Unlike Iranian musicians, who often come to the violin by way of studying Western music first, they seem hardly aware of the Western violin repertory. Some of them find it hard to believe that the violin is not a traditional Indian instrument.

In a way, of course, these uses of the violin reflect the broader role of Western music in the two cultures. Iranians have permitted various aspects of the Western sound to penetrate their music, and they have sometimes used Western instruments to achieve this change. South Indians have avoided the introduction of the Western sound; they have adopted Western technology and concert format to maintain their system, but in general they have not allowed the style of the music to become Westernized. At the same time, the violin functions as a symbol of the relationship between traditional and Western. The Indian says, in effect, "We have our own, superior kind of music, and if we can find ways of improving it on its own terms, we will do so with anything that is handy." The Iranian's reply is, "Our music is viable because it can be made with the same devices as can Western music, it is in a way capable of becoming a kind of Western music, compatible and competitive with it."

And yet, the violin can also be a symbol of something that troubles the Indian music lover about the relationship of Western and Indian music. An Indian music critic (*The Hindu*, January 3, 1982) accuses Indian violinists of being sloppy, of allowing the bow to touch several strings at a time, and believes that South Indian violinists will not be taken seriously until they stop doing this, despite the fact that what they do is intentional and reinforces the drone so essential to the system. This critic is representative of South Indians who wish their music to be taken seriously on an international scale. They believe that it could have a great deal of impact internationally and look somewhat wistfully at the fame of the North Indians Ravi Shankar, Ali Akbar Khan, and Bismillah Khan in Europe and North America, a fame never quite shared by South Indian music. Some South Indian musicians seek for ways to give their art greater scope and impact than it now has, and one way as yet not widely used may be the Westernization of violin technique. Critics assert that one famed violinist, L. Subramaniam, plays "more cleanly" and is therefore appreciated in the West, but it is hard to know whether this is really the basis of his success. Indian violinists have been so generally relegated to an accompanying function that few of them have much experience in the role of featured soloist. In Iran, by contrast, while the violin may accompany, it is ordinarily the leading instrument. It is interesting also to see that the violin, originally introduced into North India as well as the South, plays an incomparably smaller role in Hindustani music than in the Carnatic. In part this may be due to the widespread use in Northern India of other bowed instruments, particularly the *sarangi* and the *sarinda*.

While India and Iran use the Western violin in its standard form, modifying only tuning and method of playing, some other cultures have changed the instrument very considerably. Sometimes, one can only guess that a string instrument has been derived from the violin, as, for example, in the case of the so-called Apache fiddle or Navaho violin, an instrument with one string of horsehair stretched over a tubular box, played with a horsehair bow shaped like a small hunting bow. Considering the fact that it is really quite unlike a violin in appearance, the instrument's sound is surprisingly similar to that of the violin. But if the Apache fiddle is indeed a descendant of the violin, it may also have been influenced by the musical bow traditionally used by certain American Indian peoples.

A more obvious derivative of the Western violin in aboriginal America is used among peoples of the interior lowlands of Ecuador, played by shamans of the Shuar and Canelos Quichua. It looks very much like a Western violin but is quite heavy, carved out of one piece of wood to which is added a belly of thinner board. Its two or three strings are not fingered, and it is held vertically. It is used to play music consisting entirely of short repeated motifs and, in overall sound and repertory, produces music very much like that of the traditional Shuar musical bow. Recordings show only the remotest resemblance to Western violin sound.

Of course there are many other uses of the Western violin in non-Western societies. Here it may be used in its original form, and there changed; one society uses it as a way of introducing Western music, another adapts it to traditional styles and sound ideals. At least until the advent of the electric guitar, it was probably the most widespread and surely the most versatile instrument brought from Europe to world music.

## REFERENCES

R. Rangaramanuja Ayyangar, History of South Indian (Carnatic) Music (Madras: author, 1972), 321–23. L. Shankar, "The Art of Violin Accompaniment in South Indian Classical Vocal Music," Ph.D. diss., Wesleyan University 1974. Bonnie C. Wade, Music in India: The Classical Traditions (Englewood Cliffs, N. J.: Prentice-Hall, 1979), 101–3, 201–3. Ali Naqi Vaziri, Dastur-e Violon (Tehran, 1933). Bruno Nettl, ed., Eight Urban Musical Cultures: Tradition and Change (Urbana: University of Illinois Press, 1978), 119–23, 128–29, 164–66. David P. McAllester, "An Apache Fiddle," Ethno-Musicology Newsletter, no. 8: 1–5, September 1956. William Belzner, "Music, Modernization, and Westernization Among the Macuma Shuar," in Cultural Transformations and Ethnicity in Modern Ecuador, edited by Normal Whitten (Urbana: University of Illinois Press, 1981), 731–48.

# 11
# Pianos
## by Steven Whiting

The violin is not only portable but musically adaptable; it is easily retuned, and its fretless neck permits unlimited microtonal inflection. By comparison, the piano is unwieldy in every respect. Costly to produce and to transport, it is not just an instrument but a bulky piece of furniture susceptible to lavish, nonstructural ornament. In the court of any nineteenth-century Oriental potentate it made an effective display of quantitative luxury and of political contact even without being played. And if it was played, the piano imposed the restraint of equal temperament, or whatever vestiges of that remained after transit.

Yet the impact of the piano as a manifold cultural symbol went far beyond this. No other Western instrument, it seems, is so charged with musical and social associations. Placing unrivaled sonorous resources at the command of a single person, the piano nourished at once the polar extremes of individual virtuosity and of musical democratization, for ability to manage the keyboard was an indispensable component not only of academic musical training but in the attainment of social polish. And, more than most other Western instruments, the piano is a machine. Because of its "manifold, intricate structure—and especially . . . its abundance of serially related parts" (so Arthur Loesser puts it) its quality did not suffer but actually improved through factory production. The spread of the piano has indeed depended on industrialism, so that, in countries eager to Westernize, local piano production is an act of cultural behavior as revealing as the construction of a concert hall or the establishment of a conservatory. Japan's first piano manufacturers went into operation fewer than two decades after the Meiji restoration of 1868; by the 1960s they had surpassed American production.

Not just a symbol of technological superiority, the piano also embodied that central trait on which rested the supposed musical superiority of Occident over Orient—harmony. If for Rousseau it was only another symptom of Europe's cultural decay, harmony appeared quite otherwise to most non-Europeans: a sign of aesthetic progress to be emulated as any other facet of Western life. Thus, Raouf Yekta's harmonizations of Turkish classical melodies (ca. 1920) sought to accommodate the characteristics of maqams to the limitations of the piano. So habitual did the tendency become to think in terms of piano score that even scholars of Oriental music who condemned the harmonization of indigenous melodies would still publish them (well into the twentieth century) in piano arrangements set in parallel octaves.

In Iran the piano was taken up into the classical instrumentarium in an effort to modernize musical traditions rather than to see them go under in the rising tide of Westernization. Not surprisingly, it first entered Persian society as an exotic luxury item, a status symbol in royal and aristocratic households eloquent beyond the need for anyone to play it. In Persia, as previously noted, the first attempts at academic instruction in music along European lines involved the training of military bandsmen. The study of the piano was introduced (significantly along with that of Western harmony) only in the sixth year of an eight-year curriculum. The French director of the school, Alfred Lemaire, at the turn of the century dabbled with the transcription of Persian classical melodies into Western notation with keyboard accompaniment. Although they retained the designation of indigenous genres (such as *darāmad, āvāz, reng*), these arrangements adjusted all microtonal pitches to the closest half-step and, whenever possible, rendered the music in a *tempo di valse*. Lemaire's Persian students imitated this procedure. When these students transformed the bandmasters' school into a Western-style conservatory, the piano assumed in that rarefied atmosphere much the status it enjoyed in Europe, with the difference that it did not become an instrument for the masses.

A different course was pursued throughout the period between the world wars by Ali-Naqi Vaziri, the champion of musical modernization, who strove to steer Iranian musical culture between complete abandonment of tradition and its artificial preservation. From the start these efforts induced two developments of particular importance and interest. The traditional Middle Eastern concept of music as a private, even secretive affair was gradually transformed into one more amenable to public instruction, public performance, even electronic dissemination. This in turn has involved the rapprochement of an "acquired" instrument—the piano—with its indigenous counterpart, the *santour*. The result has not been displacement, as of the *kamāncheh* (spike fiddle) by the violin, but rather reciprocal influence. The first development is a fairly common adaptive strategy of the sort found in many cultures. The second development, admittedly conditioned by the first, seems unique and worth special consideration.

Curt Sachs has described the piano as a large, mechanically struck zither, recalling the influence of an 185-string hammered dulcimer (devised by Pantaleon Hebenstreit ca. 1700) on several early makers of pianofortes. The *santour*—conversely a miniature piano struck by hand-held plectra—has seventy-two strings set in eighteen courses of four across two sets of bridges. The bridges stop the strings at nodes, so that three octaves of any given pitch class are adjacent. This permits quick shifts of register between phrases and between individual tones, resulting in three characteristic textures—split-plane figuration, drones, and tremolandos. The *santour* has a wide dynamic range. Struck with force, its strings produce considerable volume, brilliance, and carrying power—all qualities, be it noted, that the cloistered performance of traditional music seldom required before this century.

But the *santour* shares one limitation with the piano, as opposed to fiddles and lutes. Tones cannot be inflected in performance any differently than they have been tuned before the performance. If more than one inflection of any pitch class is desired—say D-natural and D-half-flat—they must sound in different octaves. In Persian music this is usually not a problem; shift of register accommodates.

In recent decades the piano has inspired at least three experiments in physical alteration of the *santour*. It has been built with five extra string courses in each octave, corresponding to the piano's black keys; this eases not only solo performance of Western and Western-style music, but also ensemble performance with chromatically flexible indigenous instruments. Occasionally, a *santour* is fitted with a pedal. More widespread is the practice of swathing the plectra in cotton batting, felt, or rubber to produce a softer tone quality like that of a piano without dampers.

That modern *santour* performance has acquired some characteristic turns from the vocabulary of the piano is evident from recent recordings. Arpeggiated flourishes at cadence points and the volleys of broken sixths are idiomatic keyboard figurations easily managed on the *santour*. An even more significant impact may well be the *santour*'s change of status within the traditional instrumentarium. The positions of *santour* and violin in classical Persian music have become much like those of the piano and violin in nineteenth-century European music. They eclipsed the delicate-sounding *tār* and *setār* for the same reasons that English pianos gained prominence over Viennese, and violins over viols: their increased range of dynamics, articulations, and timbres, and their ability to offer sudden contrasts in these parameters, favored an extroverted playing style that well suited the twentieth-century transition in Iran from a private to a more public musical life. The tone of the *santour*, especially when struck with bare plectra, has sufficient brilliance to carry in large halls. Swaddling the plectra allows performance with softer instruments. In this solo and chamber instrument, Iran indeed has its own piano.

But this is only half of the interaction. The first attempt to accommodate the piano to the *radif*, rather than vice versa, is credited to a *santour* player, Mohammed Sādeq-Khān, who altered the piano's tuning for a reportedly one-finger performance. An accompanied solo in Vaziri's 1921 method for learning *tār* is further evidence of early efforts to incorporate the piano into Persian music. The Western-style piano march, standing in place of the *pishdarāmad* (a section in metered rhythm introduced ca. 1900); the *santour*-like accompaniment of the solo sections, replete with heterophonic doubling and tremolandos; the treatment of the *dastgāhs* of *Māhour* and *Homayoun* as key-areas in the Western sense; the key signature using half-flats, requiring a retuned piano—all these explicitly demonstrate the syncretic thrust of Vaziri's efforts. When Vaziri became director of the government conservatory in 1928, he hired his student Javad Ma'roufi to teach piano "with emphasis on Iranian music." At the private Conservatory for National Music, founded in

1949 by another Vaziri pupil, Ruhollah Khāleqi, the piano was offered as a major instrument (again with Ma'roufi as instructor) even before the *santour*.

As a case in point, Ma'roufi's *dastgāh* music for piano, available in recordings by the composer and in print, suggests the flexibility of the interplay between piano and *santour*. Not surprisingly, the Western imprint is strongest in metric sections, for which Ma'roufi draws on such familiar accompaniment patterns as the "oom-pah" bass or waltz bass or, at slower tempi, nocturne-type arpeggiation. In the *āvāz* sections, the features of non-metric improvised *santour* performance prove to be the dominant influence—evident in the sharp appoggiaturas, the tremolandos, the unornamented doubling at the lower octave, the overall impression of motion by fits and starts. Frequently, though, such passages are adorned with rolled chords, which impose a Western tonal perspective, as do the familiar cadential patterns at points of melodic repose.

When Vaziri embraced the piano in the 1920s as an emblem of musical progress, he attempted a rapprochement with its indigenous counterpart, both by transferring *santour* idioms to the keyboard and by retuning the piano, thereby sparking a prolonged interaction that has effected changes in both instruments. The *santour* has undergone physical adjustments to liken it to the piano, and certain pianistic figurations have entered the vocabulary of *santour* performance. Even more significant has been the *santour*'s rise to the same kind of prominence—as vehicle of individual virtuosity and as ensemble instrument—accorded the piano in nineteenth-century Europe. At the same time the piano, too, has taken on a similar status within the context of Persian classical music. From the 1920s on it has been an integral part of efforts to sustain the classical tradition through modernization, and it has been accepted as a legitimate instrument of specialization for "national musicians."

# REFERENCES

**Arthur Loesser,** *Men, Women, and Pianos: A Social History* (New York: Simon and Schuster, 1954).   **Cyril Ehrlich,** *The Piano: A History* (London: Dent, 1976).   **Raouf Yekta Bey,** "La musique turque," in *Encyclopédie de la musique et dictionnaire du Conservatoire,* edited by Albert Lavignac (Paris: Delagrave, 1920–31), 1/5: 3063–64.   **Mohammad Taghi Massoudieh,** "Tradition und Wandel in der persischen Musik des 19. Jahrhunderts," in *Musikkulturen Asiens, Afrikas und Ozeaniens im 19. Jahrhundert,* edited by Robert Günther (Regensburg: Bosse, 1973), 73–94.   **Mojtaba Khoshzamir,** "Ali Naqi Vaziri and his Influence on Music and Music Education in Iran," D.Ed. diss., University of Illinois, 1979.   **Bruno Nettl,** "Persian Classical Music in Tehran: The Processes of Change" in his *Eight Urban Musical Cultures* (Urbana: University of Illinois Press, 1978), 146–85.   **Ella Zonis,** *Classical Persian Music: An Introduction* (Cambridge: Harvard University Press, 1973).

# 12
# Emblems

Here's an LP record with several kinds of music, all performed on one type of instrument, the *valiha,* a tube zither made of a thick length of bamboo along which are stretched varying numbers of strings. It's from the Malagasy Republic. Actually, *valihas* come in several sizes and a few different shapes, some round, some rectangular, but all have the same rather simple principle of design. The player holds the instrument between the legs, rests it on the ground, and plucks with both hands. The arrangement of the strings varies. On some instruments the pitches alternate, and in others each side has strings with one segment of the scale. The strings, from a dozen to some twenty, are arranged in one unbroken sequence, but each hand is responsible for plucking certain ones. The playing technique is not all that different from that of the *mbira,* the "thumb-piano" widespread throughout sub-Saharan Africa. Tube zithers, on the other hand, are not very prominent in Africa but more widely used in Southeast Asia. In Madagascar, however, the *valiha* has become sort of a national instrument. Some of its music is very African in sound, some more distinctive of the Malagasy cultures. Sounds seemingly from Western music of the early nineteenth century alternate with others reminiscent of twentieth-century popular music. A few of the pieces on this record are attributed to composers of the nineteenth century who were members of royal families, or even kings; others are anonymous. The record is a good illustration of the many things that can be done with one simple instrument.

The concept of a national instrument, that is, of an instrument that a society regards as most representative of itself, is quite widespread. What does it take to be a national instrument? For one thing, widespread use. But that isn't enough, for perhaps the fewer instruments of any kind a culture has, the more widespread each will be within it. A "national instrument" must also enjoy prestige, value, importance. Yet the concept must be more restricted. It seems unlikely that a society came up with the idea of a "national instrument" until it began to compare its culture with that of others. And of course the most immediate object of comparison in the twentieth century has been Western culture. Thus we might well look at the emergence of certain national instruments (using the concept and term "nation" very broadly) in the context of Western influence.

A concept similar to that of national instruments has certainly existed in various cultures for a long time. In traditional China, the *ch'in,* instrument of the scholars and literati, had higher prestige though not provenience than others. In Japan, the *koto* was fundamental in illustrating the theoretical system of music, occupying a role similar to that of the piano in the West. Thus, when classical music became the property of the Japanese middle class, the *koto* was selected as the instrument for tradition-minded amateurs, especially young ladies, rather in the fashion of keyboard instruments in the West from the eighteenth century on. In the Middle Ages, the Arabic *oud,* having frets at the time, also served as the exemplar in theoretical treatises. In South India the *vina* was long depicted as the instrument held by the goddess of wisdom, Saraswati, and in the twentieth century it had a history of middle-class use like the Japanese *koto.* In various African societies, drums symbolized the royal presence and in this way maintained a kind of national instrument status; and they remain important as symbols of African music in the modern world.

One instrument of particular interest in the intercultural interface is the Central American (Guatemalan, Mexican) marimba. Although its origin is sometimes ascribed to American Indian cultures, most of the evidence points to an origin in Africa; and more properly, perhaps, it is the result of the further development, in Middle America, of an instrument originally brought from Africa by Negro slaves. Once established, it seems to have become an instrument symbolizing the specifically American character of the culture which used it, of the instrument of people of mixed Indian, Hispanic, and African descent. But its repertory was probably never to any great degree derived from the aboriginal music of the area; rather, in terms of musical style, it is an instrument of Western and Western-derived music.

The marimba appears to have acquired the status of national instrument of Guatemala, where it had been established in the seventeenth century. It became the instrument most widely used for a great variety of contexts and functions. In Mexico, its prominence is rivaled by other instruments and ensembles such as mariachi bands, but there too it may in some respects also be regarded as a national instrument. Its repertory is extremely eclectic, encompassing almost any of the music desired by Mexicans, from indigenous popular songs to foreign hits and on to arrangements of Western classical music. What characterizes both *valiha* and marimba is the breadth of their repertories, in each case including European or European-derived pieces and styles.

In the Middle East, the concept of national instruments is more problematic. After all, as political and cultural entities most of the nations are of very recent origin, and a large number of instruments are widely and internationally distributed through the Middle Eastern area. The onset of modern Western-style nationalism in the twentieth century, however, may have brought about some changes in the geographic distribution of certain instruments. For example, the Iranian *tār,* one of a number of long-necked lutes in the area, was once found rather widely distributed, but more recently, its use has declined in Turkey, where the major instrument of its type, thought to be specifically Turkish, is the *tanbur.* The impoverishment of the classical music culture of Turkey after 1920 resulted in a concentration on a few principal instruments. At the same time, the *tār* became more prominent in Iran, where other instruments such as the *oud,* a major symbol of Arabic culture, declined in prominence. In the 1960s the *tār* was designated by some Iranian musicians as *the* national instrument.

In several parts of the world, the twentieth century has seen instruments that were prominent in a non-Western context acquiring greater status and increased use, eventually becoming symbolic, internally and to the outside, of cultures and nations. The tendency for traditional instruments to decrease in number as Western music enters the scene may result in increasing prominence for one of them. The establishment of modern nation-states of multi-ethnic complexion may play a role in the assumption on the part of instruments of roles similar to those of flags and national anthems.

## REFERENCES

Paul Berliner, *The Soul of Mbira* (Berkeley: University of California Press, 1978), chapter 2.   Vida Chenoweth, *The Marimbas of Guatemala* (Lexington: University of Kentucky Press, 1964), chapter 5.   Theodore Solis, "The Marimba in Mexico City: Contemporary Contexts of a Traditional Regional Ensemble," Ph.D. diss., University of Illinois, 1983.   William P. Malm, *Japanese Music and Musical Instruments* (Tokyo and Rutland, Vt.: C.E. Tuttle, 1969), chapter 7.   Record: *Valiha Madagascar,* Ocora OCR 18.

# 13
# Orchestras

The audience spoke softly and read their programs as they do in Carnegie Hall or the Avery Fisher, ready to hear a concerto for *santour* and orchestra. It was a unique institution in Tehran, this orchestra of the Conservatory of National Music. The instrumentalists were assembling on stage, tuning up and practicing short phrases in the usual manner of symphony musicians. But by the time all had arrived and were seated in their sections, I realized that this was indeed a unique group. There were the equivalents of the string sections—some fourteen violins on the left, and six cellos, but on the right, eighteen players of the *tār,* the curiously waisted, long-neck lute with frets, and in front of them, two smaller, softer *setārs*. Behind these groups, where one would expect to find woodwinds and brass, there were yet more string instruments in groups of two and three: *santour* (hammered dulcimers), *qanun* (plucked zither), *oud* (large short-necked lute), *kamāncheh* (spike fiddle), and a couple of end-blown flutes (*nei*). Also three goblet-shaped hand drums (*zarb*) and two tambourines. The solo *santour* was set up in front of the group so the performer could stand up as he played, next to the conductor's podium. After a bit these two principals appeared, bowed, and began. The concerto, though written circa 1967, sounded melodically rather like a late Baroque work for harpsichord, but in other respects more traditionally Middle Eastern. The orchestra played mainly in unison, or rather, in octaves, particularly emphasizing the large sound of a melody progressing rapidly in four octaves. Occasionally, near the end of a phrase or section, a bit of Western harmony could be heard.

There was only one such orchestra in Iran, and it served as a vehicle for experiments in the combination of styles. It was also important as a symbol, a way of showing that Iran, and Iranian music, could do anything of which Western music was capable. Iranians understood the symbolic importance, in Europe and America, of the large ensemble, in which many instruments or voices sang or played the same melody. This ensemble was a fine illustration of that central principle of Western music, but when created, it had no repertory. Special music had to be composed for it.

Other kinds of large ensembles could also be found in Iran. For example, in the 1960s, the national radio had an orchestra of *gheichaks*. A bowed fiddle, mainly rural, found in a variety of related shapes in Eastern Iran, Afghanistan, Pakistan, and Western India (where it is known as *sarinda*), the *gheichak* might have once been regarded as the instrument least likely to become standardized. By 1960 it was brought to Tehran, made into a single, easily recognizable artifact with four strings, fitted with a new and more violin-like bow, and produced in different sizes—soprano, alto, tenor, and bass, the latter very large and held like a double bass. A group of some fifteen of these instruments played, in octaves, arrangements of traditional and popular pieces. Again, however, there was only one such orchestra.

Smaller modern ensembles more readily approximated in size such traditional groups as the *takht,* the ensemble of Arabic origin used to accompany belly dancing: flute, *santour,* some kind of lute or violin, and two drums. Particularly prominent were those used to accompany popular songs on records and in night clubs; they typically included violins and even cellos along with the traditional *santours, tārs,* and drums, and sometimes a piano or accordion as well. Here too, the large size of the ensemble, the tendency to play in octaves, and the widespread popularity of its music as compared to solo or strict unison, all show that Western musical principles have had their impact.

These developments in Iran are parallel to and perhaps derived from certain musical practices in the Soviet Union. There the integration of folk traditions into a national and social network of unity stimulated the development of families of folk instruments in imitation of the violin family—for example, soprano to contrabass *balalaikas* and *domras*—and their combination into orchestras that play arrangements of folk, popular, national, and light classical works. But while the Iranian orchestra of the Conservatory of National Music restricted itself to works in some way associated with Iran—by Iranian composers or derived from the classical tradition—the Russian folk orchestras play a broad repertory that exhibits their great versatility. *Domra* and *balalaika*, in adapting themselves to national and international repertories, have assumed roles not unlike those of the traditional instruments that have assumed a national character—Guatemalan or Mexican marimba or Malagasy tube zither. In part, their job seems to be to demonstrate their ability to perform as broad a repertory as those central tools of Western music-making, piano, guitar, orchestra.

There is an important difference between cultures whose performance ideal has all along been essentially soloistic, but that wish to symbolize modernization through imitations or adaptations of the Western orchestra or band, and those in which large ensembles have traditionally existed but whose structure and repertory have been expanded by their knowledge of Western ensembles. In the Far East, where large ensembles had for centuries been part of the musical culture, newly established orchestras are actually less common than in the Middle East. In China, some orchestras of traditional instruments are not so much experimental groups for the purpose of competing with their Western counterparts as institutions to encourage communal labor and music-making in a socialist society. In Java, where the powerful and long-established gamelan principle has influenced the development of music-making groups of various sizes, we may ascribe to Western influence the establishment of the *anklung* ensemble. Here a set of tuned bamboo rattles played by a dozen or more people is used to produce harmonized Western music, in hocket fashion, with the use of notation in which each rattle is assigned a number in accordance with its pitch.

The concept of instrumental ensemble is almost a universal phenomenon. Yet in the Third World, the idea of the large ensemble, orchestra or band, looms large among the principal traits of Western musical culture. It recalls the nature of the first musical contacts—military bands, church choirs, and even attempts to produce large-scale works such as oratorios, whose magnificence was intended in part to convert, in part to intimidate. This characterization of Western music played a role even in sub-Saharan Africa, where the ensemble concept has been thoroughly developed and perfected in groups from five-man percussion ensembles and the playing of one xylophone by four men, to seven-horn hocket styles and ten-player drum chimes. In contrast to these small groups, the development of large and complex orchestras of xylophones by the Chopi people of Eastern South Africa and Mozambique is exceptional and perhaps a phenomenon of recent origin. These orchestras have forty to fifty players on xylophones of varying sizes and are led by a soloist who introduces pieces and indicates directions while playing. They play pieces by known composers, though in fact these are essentially themes that become subject for heterophonic improvisation, accompanying dances choreographed by specialists who consult with composers and leaders. The ensembles look a bit like gamelans, a fact that tempts one to suspect ancient contact between East Africa and Indonesia, and they thrive most in areas where men from different communities have been assembled for mining. If a recent phenomenon, it has been partly stimulated by social events—men were being taken from their families and needed to be entertained—perhaps also by what they may have known about the ideals of Western musical culture, but hardly at all by the styles of Western music.

The large ensemble concept has reached even farther, to the North American Plains, where organized and coordinated singing groups of eight to ten men have in the last three decades replaced smaller and more fluid organizations. And even in South India, steadfast faith in the integrity of the Carnatic system has nevertheless permitted the establishment of the orchestra-like *Vadya Vrinda*, which exists for experimentation, with Hindustani counterparts in Calcutta and Delhi. They are under the aegis of All India Radio, which has long nurtured conservative, liberal, and moderately radical movements in classical music, covering all bases, in a way similar to the practice of Radio Iran before 1978, though perhaps with less political intent.

The Madras *Vadya Vrinda*, founded circa 1976, consists of some six *vinas*, six violins, a couple of flutes, several *mridangams*, *ghatams*, and a mixture of other traditional instruments. It is a true orchestra in the Western sense. All *vinas* play the same melodic line, as do the violins of a section. Most of their music is composed by the conductor, M.Y. Kamasastry, it is written in Carnatic notation using the Indian tone syllables, and musicians use parts in rehearsal and performance. Although the music sounds barely Carnatic, it is cast in the traditional raga system. Harmony occasionally appears, but the Western orchestral flavor is more typically achieved by triadic melodies and devices such as antiphony, imitation, performance in octaves. Most Carnatic musicians do not take it so very seriously. But when asked about its value, they nevertheless insist: "Western nations have large ensembles, so why shouldn't we? European radio stations all have their orchestras, so why not All India Radio?"

# REFERENCES

**Johanna Spector,** "Musical Tradition and Innovation," in *Central Asia, a Century of Russian Rule,* edited by Edward Allworth (New York: Columbia University Press, 1967), 434–84. **Mark Slobin,** *Kirgiz Instrumental Music* (New York: Society for Asian Music, 1969). **Kuo-Huang Han,** "The Modern Chinese Orchestra," *Asian Music* 11(1):1–8,

1979.   **Hugh Tracey,** *Chopi Musicians: Their Music, Poetry, and Instruments* (London: Oxford University Press, 1948).   **Klaus Wachsmann and K.M. Trowell,** *Tribal Crafts of Uganda* (London: Oxford University Press, 1953).   **Ali Jihad Racy,** "Musical Change and Commercial Recording in Egypt, 1904–1932," Ph.D. diss., University of Illinois, 1977, chapter 2.   **Jaap Kunst,** *Music in Java,* 3rd ed. (The Hague: M. Nijhoff, 1973).   **Konstantin K. Vertkov,** *Atlas muzykalnikh instrumentov narodov SSSR* (Moscow: State Music Publishing House, 1963).

# 14
# Victrolas

In comparison with other cultures and other periods in history, what is it that best characterizes the twentieth-century musical culture of Europe and North America? Perhaps it is the ubiquitous impact of technology that fixes musical sound on cylinders, discs, cassettes, and film that has most significantly affected our musical life and our very conception of music. To this should be added the technologies for mass distribution, such as the pressing of records, duplication of cassettes, and the many later developments, but perhaps also radio and television; and then also the technologies for creating music directly onto the permanent record of sound—electronic, concrete, computer-generated composition. The character of twentieth-century music culture has been stamped by the possibility (or burden) of hearing a performance over and over without change, and by the composer's concomitant ability to produce and preserve sound as he or she wishes rather than being dependent on a human interpreter of the score.

With its predecessors and successors, the recorded disc—ten or twelve inch, 78 or LP—is at the heart of these developments. As an important feature of Western music it has of course affected non-Western societies, but the results are somewhat different from those elsewhere described in our illustrations. The violin, or notation, or the large ensemble concept, had long histories of development in Europe before being introduced to non-European peoples. In the case of recording, invented in the 1870s, the non-Western world followed closely on the heels of Europe and North America, whose cultures also continued to change as a result of the coming of disc, wire, tape, and all the rest. In India, Iran, or Egypt today, the contemporary forms of music owe much to the impact of recording. But already in the early history of records,

Asian and to a smaller extent other non-Western societies were quickly included in the market for recorded music.

In Europe and North America, recording began to make its mark as early as the last decade of the nineteenth century, first as a device for use in the home, where the owner could record himself and his friends, and play back; and shortly thereafter, as a form of mass distribution of music and speech on cylinders. Around 1900 began the production of commercial discs. Outside Western culture, at least in some cities, recording devices seem to have been introduced very quickly, and by the mid-nineties, some Egyptian singers, so Jihad Racy tells us, were already making private recordings. Beginning in 1902, some record companies, notably the Victor Talking Machine Co., Columbia, Pathé, Gramophone, and Carl Lindstrom, each representing one of the major Western industrial nations, were attempting systematically to develop markets for their technology—though not, indeed, particularly for recordings of Western music—throughout Asia, including Asian parts of Russia, North Africa, and Latin America. Sub-Saharan Africa, which was not yet participating in the Western-dominated system of international trade, was not to be included until the 1930s. But according to Pekka Gronow, who has traced this story in detail, recording spread almost with a vengeance all over Asia in the early years of the twentieth century.

What is particularly interesting is the very quantity of recordings that were made and marketed. According to Gronow, between 1900 and 1910, the Gramophone Company alone made about 4,400 recordings in India, almost 2000 in Turkey, about 1200 in Egypt, even 97 in Java and 44 in Tibet. The student of North American Indian music may be surprised at the number of songs in the early catalogs. But in contrast to these Indian recordings, which were made for the amusement of white audiences more than for Indian markets, the Asian recordings were made for local consumption. The size of the printings was never very large, as enormous volume was not needed to make this kind of recording profitable. The technology was relatively simple, could easily be transported, and production plants were set up in major cities in Asia. Rarely were musicians amply rewarded.

What kind of music was recorded in countries such as Egypt and India? There was of course a great variety, including arrangements of folk music, light forms and relatively short pieces of classical music, but also such Western-derived genres as marches and dances with some indigenous style elements, and some religious music. Eventually, the existence of recordings (and, thus, of radio, film, and television) was to provide the typical town or village resident an unprecedentedly large variety of styles for listening. But at first, the aim of the record industry was to provide each culture and subculture its own, local music, understandably following upon the idea that a talking-machine owner's first interest would be to record his own social circle, family, and self.

As to the effects of the record industry on the non-Western world, each culture had its own experience, but one can to some extent generalize. A small number of performers, some excellent, others selected for recording by the coincidences of life, have come to dominate the listening of a large public, while the average performer of music, perhaps a person of local significance, has declined. Further, music has decreased in its traditional, often religious function and become more associated with recreation. The connection of particular pieces or genres with specific times of year, or of day, has given way to a general use of music by anyone whenever he or she wishes to hear it. In this respect, of course, recording works in conjunction with other secularizing trends. Third, variety in musical style has tended to give way to unification. Traditional folk and classical styles, religious music, and Western imports have converged into a group of related styles comprising light classical genres (of both traditional and Western music), Westernized forms of traditional music, and arrangements of folk songs—a kind of musical mainstream. Records have also forced time limits on musical cultures unused to them, resulting in the emphasis on shorter forms in composiion, and, where the distinction exists, on composed genres at the expense of improvisation. In general, there is simply more planning.

The profusion of records sold to small local markets from circa 1900 on generally subsided about 1930, to be replaced by radio and sound film, media that made music more widely available at lower cost. And when the LP record came into existence in the late 1940s, it was at first seldom used to produce traditional music for non-Western consumers. In the1960s, the typical record store in Madras and Tehran had little Indian or Persian music on LPs. On the other hand it might have seven-inch 45-rpm records in great variety, though mainly of Westernized popular music and particularly short forms of indigenous classical music. By 1960, LP records of Iranian and Indian music were being produced in the U.S. and Europe, but they were largely for Western ethnomusicologists, educators, and students. Such a record usually included a series of short excerpts in a variety of styles, as many examples as possible on one disc. Typically it did not present traditional music as it might actually be heard in its own society. By about 1970, LPs more closely approximating traditional performances, mainly of classical music, were available in some Asian nations. But the kinds of changes already wrought on the musical system by the earlier period of 78-rpm records had at least temporarily taken effect.

Most recently, improved and lower-priced technology may have helped to reintroduce some earlier practices. Compare the typical LP record of American Indian music produced on a label directed mainly to teachers and students (Folkways, or the Library of Congress) with a record of Indian songs produced by one of the companies that has become prominent since 1970 in marketing to Indian customers (Canyon, or Songs of the Red Man, or Indian House). The former has a variety of genres and styles even if exceptionally the music comes from only one tribe. The latter may have sixteen songs of one genre, one function, one performing group—sixteen Peyote songs of the Kiowa, or sixteen Grass Dance songs of the Blackfoot. This kind of record presents the music more like the way it might have been heard in earlier times, when Indian listeners really did hear sixteen Grass Dance songs one after the other, and perhaps nothing else that day. It would seem that when the opportunity arose, at least some societies used records to turn to music that was presented in forms and sequences at least approximating the pre-Westernized traditional context.

## REFERENCES

Pekka Gronow, "The Record Industry Comes to the Orient," *EM* 25:251–82, 1981.   **Howard W. Marshall,** ed., *Ethnic Recordings: A Neglected Heritage* (Washington: Library of Congress, 1978).   **Jihad Racy,** "Record Industry and Egyptian Traditional Music, 1904–1932," *EM* 20:23–48, 1976.   **Bruno Nettl,** "Persian Popular Music in 1969," *EM* 16:218–39, 1972.   **Harold S. Powers,** "Symposium on the Status of Traditional Art Musics in Muslim Nations," *Asian Music* 12 (1):1–4, 1979 (entire issue includes articles by several authors relevant to this topic).   **Jaap Kunst,** *Ethnomusicology,* 3rd ed. (The Hague: M. Nijhoff, 1959), 16–24.

# 15
# Notes

In the culture of Western art music, the ability to read music is a major criterion used to set off the musician and the person who is said to "know music" from the rest of the population. The concept of musical literacy unifies our formal system of music education. Music notation has also become a symbol of the very concept of music; the G-clef and five-line staff are found on lapels, book covers, night-club marquees. And likewise, in certain Asian cities, debates about the benefits and evils of the Western musical influence often center on the real and symbolic uses of notation. The practice of notating music has long been known in many non-Western societies although, in fact, visual notation seems to have been developed only where there is also language literacy. But auditory ways of dealing with music that are related to the idea of notation, such as sets of tone syllables or rhythmic syllables to represent sound, also exist in Asian and African societies, including some that traditionally have no way of writing their language. Some Asian notation systems involve indications of tones in liturgical chanting with the notes tied to the verbal text, and tablatures which give finger, fret, string, or fingerhole to be used in the production of a particular tone. These Asian notations seem rarely to have been used during actual performance or even as teaching devices, but rather to have served more as archival sources for preservation and occasional reference.

"The coming of Western notation is the best thing that could have happened for the preservation of our traditional music," so one side of the great debate in Tehran (and elsewhere). The *radif* of Persian music, developed late in the nineteenth century under the partial influence of Western musical culture, was first notated in the early twentieth. Notations were made for various purposes. The great champion of modernization, Vaziri, wrote pieces for instruction and performance which were, in various ways, intended to show the vitality of Persian music, and the fact that he notated them at all seems to me largely a symbolic gesture, an assertion that Persian music *is* competitive with that of the West. In the 1930s his student, Abolhassan Saba, wrote pieces and published them; they include various sections of his *radif* and are presented as instructional materials for the conservatory, with efficiency of instruction perhaps the main purpose. The Ministry of Fine Arts published the *radif* of Musa Ma'roufi in 1963, the product (at least it was so intended) of an officially constituted committee, and it was presumably published in Western notation as a way of showing that here was *the* authoritative *radif*. Standardization was evidently the main purpose. The publication of Mahmoud Karimi's *radif* in 1978, with transcriptions of Karimi's performances by M.T. Massoudieh, provided a vocal counterpart to Ma'roufi. But in addition, Massoudieh was employing notation, in accordance with the principles of ethnomusicological transcription, as a descriptive rather than a prescriptive device. The various reductions of the Iranian *radif* to Western notation have a manifold significance as symbol, as aids to efficient teaching, as marks of standardization and official sanction, as tools of ethnomusicological analysis.

But, "with the coming of notation, some of the essence of our music has disappeared," the opposition would say. Traditional masters still insist that the music should be learned slowly while being contemplated. Each master should have his own version of the *radif*: standardization, while efficient, is not in essence Iranian. There are many things in the music that cannot really be expressed in notation. But the proponents of notation reply: The slow, contemplative way of learning just isn't possible when you have to rush from one end of town to the other three times a day for study, work, errands. There isn't time, we need all available tools for efficient study. In that case, a referee might suggest, why not use cassettes? They are closer to the oral tradition and you can study them, by listening, even while walking to work. The debate continues. But in the end, the most fundamental reason for the use of notation is its presence in the Western system, the need to feel that one must be just as skilled, as intelligent, as much in control of materials for the Persian music as for the Western. Even musicians who can't read music sometimes sit behind empty music stands. Of all things, notation may best show us that music can be more important as symbol than as system of sounds.

There is a similar debate in South India, but it is less shrill. In India generally, it is not the Western notation system that we find in use, but one based on the tone syllables of Indian music. Roughly equivalent to our do—re—mi, the Indian sa—ri—ga—ma—pa—dha—ni—sa and the name of the raga give the reader indications of pitches, intonation, and ornamentation. Non-metric materials are rarely notated, but composed songs, with *tala* or metric cycle, are found in manuscripts and publications going back to the nineteenth century. The rhythmic notation makes use of Western concepts—with periods, commas, semicolons, bar-lines, the underlaying of text.

South Indian music has a number of older traditional notation systems such as the pitch indications in Vedic chant and the oral and possibly written drum syllables indicating types of strokes and rhythms. The notation described above is a mixed system, using Western elements but incorporating such Indian elements as the raga concept, syncretically making use of those aspects of music that both systems have in common, particularly the scheme of tone syllables. In a few early twentieth-century publications greater complexity was attempted, with symbols prescribing ornaments quite precisely. But the last three or four decades have seen a return to a simpler kind of notation in publications of classical compositions and practice exercises. Some musicians notate large numbers of songs in manuscript, keeping in their homes a kind of archival repertory to be passed from fathers to sons. Of course, in all of this the verbal texts are as important as the music, but even a barely literate person can learn to read these notes.

In South India, this kind of notation has been widely accepted. It is recognized as a Western influence in part, but it is seen as help, not disturbance. Even conservative musicians admit that notation permits the use and control of larger repertories. The only real objections come from virtuosos with prodigious memories who feel threatened in this specialty by the ability of those less gifted to use notation to overcome their disadvantage; and from those who fear that, since notation is only partial, much of the traditional performance practice may be lost with time.

In China, notation systems have been around for centuries. But if traditional music, in spite of a recession after the 1950s, is still alive, the notations are giving way to Western-derived systems using numbers in lieu of a movable Do. And it is this newer notation that appears to be making possible the revival of traditional music. In Japan, traditional notation systems were also widespread and numerous schemes coexisted, some belonging to, and perhaps the secret property of, schools of musicians, some specific to genres and instruments. The traditional music, in some ways preserved in museum-like fashion, may actually have changed to oral tradition as a more typical form of transmission. While traditional notation systems are used less, Western notation has evidently not replaced them.

The introduction of notation into a musical culture with only oral transmission no doubt effects important changes, even where the tradition has all along espoused careful composition and precise memorization. But what does notation do to music in which improvisation is central—that is, not just music with ornaments and rubato introduced extempore, but major improvisatory genres such as *alapana* in India, *taqsim* in Egypt, *āvāz* in Iran. On the face of it, there would seem to be little cause for impact; improvisations had been performed alongside composed pieces all along, so why not alongside of music composed *and* notated?

But surely there are effects, caused in part by the coming of notation and in part by various other traits of Western musical culture and the way it is perceived. For example, in Iran's classical music improvisations play a smaller role than they did some decades ago; they are more frequently memorized, they are shorter and appear more predictable. The prestige of the notated piece as a Westernized phenomenon seems to have crowded improvisation into a position of diminished esteem and also to have made it more like a composition. Indeed, some Iranian musicians have composed pieces in the non-metric style of improvisation and published them, for use in place of the traditional improvised section of a performance. Such changes, however, are not universal. In South India, according to some older musicians, the attention given to the improvised parts may even have increased and in North India the concept of composition has not changed its role very much at all.

The way in which notation is used in the modern world tells us something about the interaction of Western and traditional music in a variety of cultures. At least in 1968 Iran had strong forces that wished to become part of the Western cultural system and thus adopted Western notation for its music. A major course of action in India is to take from the West only what will be useful for the modernized development of its own cultural system, and so musical notation develops out of the indigenous tradition, with some elements of Western notation added. Musicians in modern China, willing to obliterate stylistic lines and eager to use notation for the greatest teaching efficiency, use a simple system that is derived from Western theory teaching if not directly from the notational practices themselves. In Japan, musicians continuing the tradition of compartmentalizing musics do not use Western notation in their older traditions but find it difficult, in the atmosphere of rapid economic and technological development, to maintain the traditional notation systems in the vigor they once enjoyed. Whether adopted outright or with modifications, Western notation has had a great impact in world music, perhaps most strongly in its significance as a symbol.

## REFERENCES

Ella Zonis, *Classical Persian Music: An Introduction* (Cambridge: Harvard University Press, 1973). Mehdi Barkechli, *La musique traditionelle de l'Iran* (Tehran: Secretariat d'Etat aux Beaux-Arts, 1963). Mohammad Taghi Massoudieh, *Radif vocal de la musique traditionelle de l'Iran* (Tehran: Secretariat d'Etat aux Beaux-Arts, 1978). R. Rangaramanuja Ayyangar, *History of South Indian (Carnatic) Music* (Madras: author, 1972), chapter 27. Walter Kaufmann, *Musical Notations of the Orient: Notational Systems of Continental East, South, and Central Asia* (Bloomington: Indiana University Press, 1967). Fritz Kornfeld, *Die tonale Struktur chinesischer Musik* (Vienna: St. Gabriel Verlag, 1955). Han Kuo-Huang, "The Modern Chinese Orchestra," *Asian Music* 11(1):1–42, 1979.

# 16
# Migrants

*Well, my tribal songs and legends, I only know a few,*
*So I play country music on my ho'made didjereedoo.*
*And when I go to Fitzroy to have a drink or two*
*You'll find me sippin' Carlton draught through the*
*    ho'made didjereedoo.*

This is the refrain of an Australian song in country music style. The protagonist, an urban aboriginal, laments the loss of his cultural tradition, claiming to know nothing of his tribal songs and legends, and all he has left is his "homemade didjeridu," a hollowed-out eucalyptus branch which functions as a drone pipe in accompaniment of ceremonial songs. One can hardly use it to play country music. Many Australian aboriginal people have given up their tribal culture, forgotten most of it perhaps, moved to Melbourne, Sydney, Adelaide, where many of them constitute a downtrodden minority, working at menial jobs or unemployed, with a musical culture that is hardly distinctive. Or so it seems.

It's the kind of fate that has been shared by many millions. San Francisco, Phoenix, Seattle, Minneapolis, Chicago have all been the goals, often disappointing in the end, of American Indians. Mexico City has attracted millions from the countryside, as have Lagos, Calcutta, Cairo, Jakarta. The black inhabitants of South Africa have been willing to face humiliation and deprivation of all sorts and to work at low-paying jobs and suffer racial restrictions, in order to live in white cities: Johannesburg, Pretoria, Capetown. And in Europe we find Algerians in Paris, Turks and Arabs and Greeks in Frankfurt and Berlin, Pakistanis and Jamaicans in London, all there in order to make a modest living, congregating in ghettos of sorts, living in the cheapest dwellings, far from family, home, cultural tradition. If the urbanization of the non-Western nations results in one kind of contact between Western and traditional music, the movement of non-Western individuals, often in very large groups, to cities of the Western world in several continents, has provided another. Here are three short illustrations.

I met with a group of aboriginal people living in Adelaide. They wanted to speak with me because they had heard that I was interested in American Indian music, and they had also heard that the Indians had been much more successful than they in preserving their cultural traditions. They met me at an institution in which they could listen to tapes and records of their rural forebears. And they berated someone—they didn't quite know whom—for not having recorded and preserved more. I found their ignorance hard to believe and asked them if there was not *some* music with which they felt they could identify themselves. A bit of conversation yielded the suggestion that they indeed had such a music, and that it was their body of Protestant hymns, especially, perhaps, "The Old Rugged Cross." But, I countered, this song is sung by white people, from whom they had learned it. Yes, they knew that, but when they, the aboriginals, sang it, it was different. Did I want to hear? Of course.

A half dozen of them gathered around an old piano in that bare room, like an old gymnasium, and sang, four in unison, one on the alto part, with vigor and enthusiasm but moderate speed. I could not discern any fundamental difference between this performance and those I had heard from American whites. As the country song said, these people had lost their music and art, but the need persisted of identifying themselves, of having some musical symbol as an emblem of cultural identity.

I once attended a powwow in a high school gym in Chicago, whose American Indian population is some eight thousand. The people came from many places and cultures: Pueblos of New Mexico, Shoshone from Wyoming, Chippewa and Sioux and Winnebago from Wisconsin and Minnesota, Navajo from Arizona, Choctaw from Mississippi, Cherokee from Oklahoma. At the powwow one sees a lot of spectacular costumes, worn proudly by the

elderly men and by the children with the mischievous look of guests at a costume party. There is singing and dancing. It sounds very traditionally Indian;
there is no question that this musical sound is not the result of hearing a lot of
Western (or as some Indians would put it, "white") music. And yet? We are
hearing songs in a number of Indian styles, styles that some centuries ago
would not have been heard in the same social context or even in the same
part of the continent. Most of the songs sound like Plains Indian music, even
though Plains people are not in the majority here. But there is also the antiphonal Stomp Dance from the Oklahoma Cherokee; there are songs in the
singing style of the Midwestern Woodlands states, less tense and lower than
the Plains style though with the same form. There are the songs of the Eastern
Pueblo Eagle Dance. It is a musical event that could only be interpreted as
something urban and modern.

In an earlier illustration, the powwow was presented as an adaptation, to
modern conditions, of an important traditional Plains Indian ritual. But the
powwow concept fits into the Western conception of musical life in other
ways as well by involving performers and audience, newspaper ads, star
singers and dancers, a master of ceremonies, amplification. Moreover, it
doesn't matter who makes the music. A Crow Indian may sing a Pueblo song,
a Navajo may do the Creek Stomp Dance. What's important is that it be done
well. In those respects, a powwow is like the performance of a symphony
orchestra whose players are judged not by their cultural background but by
their talent and ability. And whether a piece was once intended to be performed in secret, only for deities, for victory in war, at sunrise, or to mourn the
dead, here it would be performed in public, and in the evening, just as readily
as a Mozart mass or a Bach cantata are performed in a secular concert on a
weekday, possibly by Jewish musicians conducted by a Zoroastrian.

Whatever the differences between these vignettes of aboriginals in
Adelaide and Indians in Chicago, the cities nevertheless have some important
things in common. Both were built by white people on what was once the
land of other societies; and the former owners of this land became outcasts
who eventually found their way into the city on the white people's terms.
Among other manifestations of this (actually rather curious) kind of relationship, the case of South Africa comes to mind, with Johannesburg an exemplar. Of its nearly two million persons, two-thirds are black "immigrants."
Members of a number of tribal groups whose repertories, while stylistically
related, were distinct, they established several musical genres which came to
characterize their culture, and which combined Western with indigenous
South African style elements. It is typically music that is performed at secular
neighborhood beer-drinking parties, events attended jointly by members of a
variety of African peoples—Sotho, Xhosa, Zulu. The music is derived from
South African traditions, which differ considerably from those of West Africa.
There is much emphasis on harmony, on antiphonal exchanges of choruses,
on rather sophisticated polyphony, but not so much on rhythmic complexity

and polyrhythms. The character of the beer-drinking music, essentially Western or at any rate easily compatible with Western popular musics, is thus also quite different from the African-derived popular music in the Americas, largely, it would seem, because of the dominance there of West African principles. It is also quite different from the highlife music of Nigeria and Ghana in which Western, Caribbean, and West African elements are combined. So, while the popular music of Johannesburg is on the one hand a blend of various South African styles and, on the other, yet another form of Western–African syncretism, in its regionality and its special configuration of traits it is also an accurate reflection of the urban culture of South African blacks.

How different, then, the musics and musical cultures of these three groups of migrants to cities that whites built on their land! Apart from differences in the cultural status of each as actual or virtual minorities, this divergence may stem from the relative complexity and compatibility of their musical styles. By Western criteria, at least, the Australian may have been too simple to survive except in vestige. The American Indian style has been strong enough to survive on an intertribal level but not sufficiently compatible with the Western to produce stylistic fusion. The South African, by contrast, has been compatible enough to produce a syncretic style despite the incredibly wide psychological gulf between the societies.

# REFERENCES

Song quoted from John Merson, ed. *Investigating Music* (Sydney: Australian Broadcasting Commission, 1978), 64. **David Coplan with David Rycroft,** "Marabi: The Emergence of African Working-Class Music in Johannesburg," in *Discourse in Ethnomusicology II: A Tribute to Alan P. Merriam,* edited by Caroline Card and others (Bloomington: Indiana University, Ethnomusicology Publications Group, 1981), 43–66. **Robert Kauffman,** "Shona Urban Music and the Problem of Acculturation," *YIFMC* 4:47–56, 1972. **Robert K. Thomas,** "Pan-Indianism," *Midcontinent American Studies Journal* 6(2):75–83, 1965. **Nancy Oestreich Lurie,** "An American Indian Renascence?" *Midcontinent American Studies Journal* 6(2)::25–50, 1965. **James H. Howard,** "The Pan-Indian Culture of Oklahoma," *Scientific Monthly* 18(5):215–20, 1955. **Fay Gale,** *Urban Aborigines* (Canberra: Australian National University Press, 1972).

# 17
# Music School

"Of course the music has changed; how could it help doing so when you look at the way people now learn it?" This paraphrases a statement made to me in different ways by musicians from Iran, West Africa, and India, in almost identical forms and with great emphasis. Doubtless, folk music sounds the way it does largely because of its transmission through oral tradition; and the Western violin virtuoso plays a huge repertory flawlessly because of the combination of rigid discipline imposed by a teacher and a system of transmission with the use of notation, along with the ready availability of audible performances, live and recorded, all of which increase the efficiency with which technique and repertory are acquired. And so it should not be surprising that musicians in non-Western societies, wishing to make their traditions competitive with those being imported from Europe and America, looked to the Western ways of teaching art music as a way of producing change. Those who do not like the results may well be right in blaming them on the teaching.

Each society has had its unique system of teaching and transmission. To label the latter simply "oral" or "written" is clearly insufficient. But very generally speaking, most of the world had partially (and sometimes substantially) abandoned old systems based on the handing down through demonstration, performance, and hearing of a tradition directly from teacher to student, the two often related to each other by blood, social class, caste, or ethnicity. The tradition encompassed techniques, repertory, and technical theory of music, as well as aspects of the philosophy of music, and much else, perhaps including history and mythology. The degree to which all of this was conveyed systematically varied greatly by culture; but on the whole, the music, with all of the mentioned components, was transmitted as one entity.

In comparison to the Western music then being introduced to other societies—classical, military, religious—this old way of teaching seemed inefficient—inefficient, that is, in the context of Western musical and cultural values. European teaching techniques characteristically involved the use of notation; the segregated instructon of instrumental and vocal technique, of repertory, theory, and history by specialists; wherever possible, teaching students in groups; the use of some music whose purpose is only to aid learning and practicing. The teaching process was abstracted from the musical culture. Thus, a teacher would present materials that would be incompatible in a concert, or he might extract units such as phrases, not acceptable as self-contained units in performance, for special pedagogical treatment. Western music teaching gives little if any attention to the relationship of music to the rest of culture.

For certain kinds of accomplishments, formal Western music teaching is very efficient indeed, and as such it probably stirred the envy of Third World musicians. It is not so efficient in other ways, such as ornamentation, techniques of improvisation, intonational niceties, in which some non-Western pedagogies excel. Even so, when Western musicians first came to Asia and Africa, they were evidently not impressed by the possibility of learning from the native teaching systems, did not feel, for example, that the establishment of a body of music such as the *radif* of Iran, which presents the student with an infinite variety of improvisatory techniques, could conceivably be helpful to them. On the contrary, they encouraged Third World musicians to learn Western music and to establish Western-style teaching institutions for more efficient instruction in their native traditions.

The result is that there are, in many parts of the world, educational institutions like those found in European cities that engage in the teaching of non-Western music in a largely Western fashion.

Take, for example, the University of Tehran, established in the 1930s by Reza Shah in accordance with French and German practices, a break with the long tradition of Islamic institutions of learning. The music department in 1968 had two sections, for Western and Iranian music. The history of officially established music schools in Iran actually goes back several decades and is rather complicated. Institutions that taught the traditional music, the modernized traditional music, Western music, and a combination of these alternated. Generally speaking, however, the history is characteristic of similar establishments in various parts of the world. Conservatories for the teaching of Western music were founded, and then their teaching and curricular methods were applied to sections within these schools, or to separate schools, devoted to traditional music. Thus, a student in Tehran would be attached to one of the two sections but also be required to take some work in the other. This requirement caused a good bit of resentment (as might a similar one in the U.S.) among students who felt that mastery of one musical language was enough to expect.

The curriculum of the Iranian music section was fluid, but the students were expected to study along a track that characterizes Iranian tradition as well as Western musical thought. For one thing, they were required to spend four years studying the *radif* of their professor Nour-Ali Boroumand, who guided them on his *tār* through this maze of repertory. The parallel but distinct vocal *radif* was not required. Classes took place twice a week, and Boroumand had some eight students performing a variety of instruments, all traditional except for the violin. His purpose was to teach in a style as traditional as possible; he taught slowly, without notation, insisting on time for practice and contemplation. As an additional approach to mastery of the *radif*, the basic theoretical and generative repertory, students would take a class in which they learned composed pieces of the Persian tradition. But the rest of the curriculum was less traditional. They took a course in Western music theory and history, some course work outside music, such as history, philosophy, and religion, and near the end of their baccalaureate studies they produced theses, which were usually modest pieces of library research. Except for the explicitly bi-musical organization, such a curriculum is compatible with that of an American institution.

Furthermore, in 1968 there were two government-supported conservatories in Tehran, one for Western music and one for "national music." The latter included in its purview the study of Iranian classical music and of traditional instruments—carried out with the aid of older Persian, Western, and mixed materials—and also some subjects perhaps intended to promote the modernization of Persian music, such as harmony, and in general, an intellectually Western approach to Persian traditional music. The conservatory for Western music, by contrast, made no attempts to include Iranian music. The fact that the student of Persian music was expected (1) to study in a teaching system derived from Western music, and (2) to absorb at least some subject matter relating directly to Western music is indicative of the approach to the two musics then followed in Iran.

Schooling similar to that of Iran was developed in a number of other nations, and characteristically embraced the idea of the binary conservatory —one part for Western music and one for a modernized form of the traditional. The modernization, however, might proceed along different paths. In Iran, it presented the classical tradition, in a manifestation that had been repeatedly refurbished throughout the twentieth century, as a national symbol drawing together the various ethnicities. In imitation of Western art music practice, other indigenous musical traditions, the folk and the popular, were not admitted. In Korea, on the other hand, some genres of court and rural tradition have been drawn together, while a number of other distinct repertories have been practiced and, in museum-like fashion, consciously preserved. In some of the intertribal boarding schools for American Indians in the Southwestern U.S., the closest things to an American Indian music school, choruses using Western vocal technique, complete with vocal blend and conductor, sing arrangements of songs from a variety of American Indian culture areas. The concept of a student body as disseminator of a national and thus intercultural repertory is found in African nations, as at the University of Ghana, where ensembles study and publicly perform music from several of the ethnic groups of the nation, much of the teaching being done with Western techniques. And since the maintenance of large ensembles is normally expected in Western conservatories, orchestras of traditional instruments have been developed for the purpose of performing modernized versions or arrangements of traditional music; much of their impetus has come from the class instruction of Asian, African, and Oceanian music schools.

If the emergence of bifurcated departments and modernized styles in national conservatories was widespread, the range of variation among individual cultures is exemplified in the contrast between China and India (in one significant year, 1927). In China, Western music was taught with completely Western methods, on the basis of the belief that this was not just foreign or international music that had to be learned, but that this was actually the new music of Chinese culture. By contrast, 1927 was the founding of the Central College of Carnatic Music in Madras, an institution that conspicuously avoided Westernization of musical style, although it did use Western teaching techniques. Thus, in Madras, one studied for three years towards a bachelor's degree with a prescribed curriculum: concentration on vocal music (in which case one "minored" in violin or *vina*), or on instrumental music of any sort, including *mridangam* and *ghatam,* the instruments providing rhythmic accompaniment (with minor in vocal music); courses in theory of Carnatic music, and some "musicology," which included history, general orientation to the musical culture, and a bit of attention to research and its methods in Indian music, as well as comparison of Carnatic music with others, including Western. Instrumental instruction with notation usually took place in classes of eight to thirty. This school became a model for many others in South India, and it developed syllabi of what was to be done in smaller accredited schools.

The point is that in many nations, schools teaching a Westernized approach to the traditional system, as well as those striving to preserve a more "pure" tradition, seem equally to have adopted aspects of Western conservatories and music schools: separate teaching of subjects, applied music majors and minors, teaching students in classes, and courses of study requiring relatively short periods resulting in the partial abbreviation of the system, something perhaps mitigated by the use of efficiency aids such as notation. The government-supported conservatories often have highly distinguished teachers on their faculties; the most prominent musicians of Tehran and Madras have made part of their living as professors. Yet these very artists tended also to question the validity of their schools and often maintained that the traditional teaching methods were more effective in the long run, that what was being produced in the schools was a class of amateurs, and that the changed form of teaching would eventually alter the system—not so much its sound perhaps as its fundamental values and concepts. But they also admitted that such changes might have to be accepted as a kind of tradeoff, if their musical traditions as repertories and in performance were to survive at all.

# REFERENCES

**Mojtaba Khoshzamir,** "Ali Naqi Vaziri and His Influence on Music and Music Education in Iran," D.Ed. diss., University of Illinois, 1979.  **R. Rangaramanuja Ayyangar,** *History of South Indian (Carnatic) Music* (Madras: author, 1972), especially chapters 25 and 26.  **Louis Ballard,** *The American Indian Sings: Arrangements of Authetic Tribal Songs . . .* (Santa Fe, N. Mex.: Ballard Music Co., 1970).  **Record:** Bala-Sinem Choir, *American Indian Songs and Chants,* Canyon Records C-6110, 1973; notes by Buford Wayt.

# 18
# Streets

*Beirut, 1971.* A record shop, small, a hole in the wall, but inside, lots of records of various sizes and speeds. Ask for any kind of music—it's there: music to belly-dance to, classical *taqsims* performed by a famous *bouzouq* player, the Beatles, the great Egyptian singer Umm Kulthum, an LP with old Glenn Miller hits, a symphonic suite with Arabic themes, some Chopin on a German label, and lots more. It's a microcosm of the modern Third World city and its musical life: music descended from the classical tradition of the old urban aristocracy; the music of the Westernized elite as well as various classes and ethnicities; music to reflect a great variety of attitudes about the cultural tradition, the incoming Western culture, and preferences for various combinations. Probably no one person listened to all these kinds of music, but the constituencies of all of them met in this shop.

In Madras, people are pretty exclusive musically. For example, those who listen to Western music don't like the Carnatic tradition while those who do like little else. Yet in the record stores of the Kilpauk district you'll find rock music, jazz, Carnatic classical and Hindu devotional music, film songs, North Indian sitar virtuosos. Or again, in Tehran of 1968, a walk around the business center would soon lead you past the Beethoven Record Store, which classified everything carefully, separated an "Iranian" section from the others, and was eager to sell you, on demand, and precisely identified, Western music of all types; Iranian classical, popular, folk; Armenian; Indian; and all else including prayers and singing of the Qur'an. The point is that such a store, within four walls, had all of the kinds of music that could be heard in the city, with all their gradations of style. It presented the culture's way of categorizing music. And it brought together the adherents of a large variety of music who would otherwise probably not be found under one roof.

Not that they were likely to speak to each other. But at that time a record store in Beirut, Madras, or Tehran was a fairly accurate reflection of the musical life of the city. Most Third World nations are still to a considerable degree rural; only some twenty to fifty percent are urban dwellers, compared to sixty-five to eighty percent in countries such as the U.S., Britain, France. Even so, Asia, Africa, and Latin America have vast metropolises, most of them only recently grown to their enormous size, comprised of people from the countryside with various cultural and linguistic backgrounds. Each group may settle in its own section, just as their predecessors in earlier times established Polish, German, Syrian, Mexican, Negro, and Jewish districts in the cities of Europe and North America. Each group brings along its culture and holds its music up as an emblem of its separateness, but also as something that it can use to communicate with and gain the respect of its foreign neighbors. And further, if this is a world-class city such as Tehran, Beirut, Lagos, Jakarta, or Bombay, the largely Western or Western-derived music of the international business and government-service community is also imported. And so it is that an enormous number of different musical styles dwell in the modern city, occupying radio waves, stereo speakers, and night-club and concert stages.

In some respects, each culture unit in such a city has its own configuration of musical experience, quite aside from the maintenance of ethnic identity. In Madras, the conservative Mylapore Brahmin may go to Carnatic concerts, hear a bit of Western music on the radio, and listen with some distaste to film songs when his children drag him to the movies. The medical student in Tehran may care only about rock and jazz, while the Iranian taxi driver plays indigenous popular styles on his car radio. A Lebanese author of my acquaintance attended piano and chamber music concerts, wanting nothing to do with Arabic traditions. A central European immigrant to Tel Aviv thought that there was not really anything that could properly be called music outside Mozart and Brahms and worked hard to introduce this view to his Jewish compatriots from Morocco and Iraq. But on the other hand, as time goes on, people in such cities do become conscious of the cultural diversity in which they live, and there is little doubt that the typical modern urbanite, because of the variety of musical experience available to him, has a different outlook on music than his rural forebear of 200 years ago.

But in all the diversity, there are institutions that bring together the musics of the city in a kind of cultural unity. Like record shops, instrument stores also symbolize the musical mosaic of the city. In 1969 the Delshad music store near Baharestan Square in South Central Tehran, characteristically operated by a Jewish family, had something for everyone: *santours,* instruments of Persian classical and popular repertories; *setārs,* for classical music alone; *dombaks* and *darbuccas,* the drums of Persian classical and Middle Eastern popular musics respectively; but also simple trap sets used equally in Western pop, jazz, and some modern Middle Eastern popular ensembles. The violin, prominent in several traditions, had an honored place. But there was also a *dotar,* used only by folk singers from Eastern Iran; a *chugur,* large, long-neck lute from Azerbaijan; flutes and oboes for rural weddings. Also a *qanun,* which you'd only expect Arabic and Turkish musicians to play; a couple of clarinets and an accordion; and out front, a small selection of electric guitars, not yet in the outrageous shapes of the punks, but obviously for a rock group; and more.

There are other such institutions. Go to the movies in Delhi. The typical Hindi film may be a lugubrious story of family loyalty, marital stress, white-collar crime. But at intervals the characters will break into songs (actually performed by famous vocalists called "play-back singers") that collectively illustrate, perhaps in one film, the multifarious musical experience of India. Some are outright Western with just an Indian tinge in the *tabla* accompaniment; others, based on light classical genres of North India; one sounds quite Arabic; one even affects the sounds of the exotic drum ensembles of Kerala folk music.

A visitor stopping in a Tehran night club in 1972 might have caught a series of four musical acts: a belly dancer with Arabic music; a *tār* player showing off his technique in a light classical *chahār mezrāb*; somebody singing *"Volare"* with accordion and trap set (not great but unmistakable); and a red-faced folk singer in costume from a village, with trained back-up chorus, playing the *dotar*. Later on, walking by Rudaki Hall, the main venue for public concerts, the visitor might have found this schedule of programs: an opera by an Iranian composer in Persian; the Tehran Symphony playing Beethoven and Dvořák; a mixed concert of Persian classical music with several prominent instrumentalists; an appearance of the Persian orchestra of the Conservatory of National Music playing its own concertos and suites as well as arrangements of *tasnifs,* traditional lyrical (and sometimes political) songs, under a baton-wielding conductor. And a jazz ensemble visiting from an American university.

Characterizing the musical life of a modern Third World city inevitably means confronting the great variety of musics, all living side by side, affecting each others' sound and performance context. The social groups that make up the city do maintain a degree of independence, as do the musics which are their emblems. But the city also provides some important institutions—record stores, film theaters, concert halls, night clubs, even the instrument shops—where they are thrown together in an almost helter-skelter way that reflects the processes of secondary urbanization.

# REFERENCES

Ali Jihad Racy, "Musical Aesthetics in Present-Day Cairo," *EM* 26:391–406, 1982. **Bruno Nettl,** "Persian Popular Music in 1969," *EM* 16:218–39, 1972.

# 19
# Concerts

It could be argued that the musical culture of twentieth-century Europe and North America is in essence a concert culture. Not that most music is actually heard in concerts—radio and records, film and TV all exceed in listening time. But it is probably true that most composers and performers would like to have their products produced in concerts, and not only in the classical tradition. This is the ideal setting for hearing music, so most typical consumers feel. The concert format celebrates the musical culture. Jazz, rock, and country performers whose regular venue is a bar or dance hall rejoice at opportunities to play in concert halls. Church choirs gladly leave their sacred surroundings for these as well. The marching band, after the parade, finds its grand moment in the bandshell. And beyond this, the many kinds of music that fulfill specialized functions such as the accompaniment of dance, marching, religion, opera, or musical comedy, can be transferred and variously combined in concerts, where music from a diversity of contexts —different historical periods, varied performing forces, options such as composition and improvisation—may all be united.

In contemporary Western culture, the concert may be the ideal locus of performance; but while it accommodates the universe of musical phenomena, it is a rather rigidly circumscribed social event. In Europe, the concept of performance for a passive audience goes back many centuries and public concerts have taken place since shortly after 1600. But not until about 1800 did the notion develop that all music should sometimes be heard in concerts, and that a broad cross-section of population should have the experience of hearing them. If the concert has become an institution of such importance in Western culture, we should consider how it has been adapted to other societies that have felt the impact of Western musical culture.

In 1906, a concert took place in Tehran which has since passed into legend. Sponsored by an association known as Okhovvat, its purpose was to bring classical music, then recently revived, to a larger audience, in a modern context. It is said to have lasted for twenty-four hours, and as a result, some things taken for granted in Western concerts did not apply: unity of performers, audience attention, characteristic structure. Performed by a number of famous musicians singing and playing alternately, it was thus perhaps really a series of separate concerts. Moreover, the *pishdarāmad* is said to have been invented for this occasion, a type of piece—metric, stately, of an introductory character—particularly suited to an ensemble. Several or all musicians present participated in it, presumably as a way of kicking off the event. It is known that ensemble pieces of this sort and even the term, *pishdarāmad,*

were already in use earlier. But it seemed to be important for the mid-twen-
tieth-century musical culture to have this concert, in its legendary status, stand
as a symbol of the ability of Iranian musicians to hold their own in the things
they conceived to be important about Western concert culture.

In the 1960s and 1970s, concerts of traditional music in Tehran were uncommon, but a few did take place, principally in Rudaki Hall, a fine audito-
rium built primarily for performances of opera, Western classical music, and
drama. The Iranian concerts were adapted to a Western framework.
Musicians sat in chairs, ensembles looked like string quartets or chamber
orchestras. And yet, the concerts of Persian music seemed to be presented as
something exotic to a segment of Iranian culture that saw itself as fundamentally Western. Musicians wore historical costumes while the audience wore
business suits and dresses. The concerts were rigidly limited in time,
improvisations were timed and perhaps rehearsed in advance, and a variety
of musics that once would not have been heard together in the same context
were combined. Where a traditional men's social gathering or an aristocratic
garden party might hear one *dastgāh* and two musicians, the Rudaki Hall audience heard several *dastgāhs* and a succession of soloists in one evening. It
was in part like a traditional symphony concert, with its short, long, and cli-
mactic pieces, and in part like a "new" music concert of the 1960s, with a
series of works each performed by a different ensemble or soloist.

In 1969, a concert in Rudaki Hall resembled a concert of Western classical
music in other ways, as well. There was the intermission with its familiar function of socializing—"see and be seen." There was a printed program with
notes. Seats were reserved and tickets purchased. After each number, there
was applause by clapping rather than with more traditional expressions of approval. Dress was formal Western; one did not see women in chadors or veils.
The audience was largely comprised of the thoroughly Westernized sector of
Tehran society, middle class, many academics, some students from the university music department or conservatories. There was a surprising number of
foreigners. Although there were obviously some people who seemed to feel
closely identified with the performance, on the whole, this audience gave the
impression of a group of people to whom the music was not something important, and who were not close to it. It was Persian music presented in a
Western concert. Hardly anything except the style of the music itself distinguished it from the concert of a string quartet.

The typical concert of Carnatic music in Madras is very different, even
though the concert format is also a relatively recent development (going back,
to be sure, to the beginnings of the twentieth century). Carnatic concerts also
share important characteristics with concerts of Western classical music—
public admission, tickets, sometimes printed programs, a middle-class audience, a stage, a length of two to three hours. There is a typical structure beginning with short numbers, building up in the second half to the long and

elaborately improvised *ragam–tanam–pallavi,* and ending with light pieces, in a plan compatible with Western concert procedures. But there are a number of ways in which the Carnatic concert format reflects traditional South Indian values.

The origin of this music in the temple tradition is not completely abandoned. There is usually a small altar and an oil lamp, and as they enter the performers bow to and greet the deity. The words of the songs are always devotional.

The relationship of musicians to audience is interesting. There is normally no intermission, and the audience does not arrive at the beginning, but drifts in gradually. This is not, as some might have you believe, the result of an Indian tendency to tardiness. Rather, the beginning of the concert is regarded as a warming-up period, especially the first piece, often a *Varnam,* a kind of etude whose function is more important in teaching than in the concert repertory. The audience expects the music to reach a technical and intellectual climax after the first hour or more, by which time everyone is present to hear what is normally the pièce de résistance. The Indian audience is visibly and audibly much more involved with the music than the Iranian. Statements of approval are heard at points of special virtuosity. Many members of the audience keep *tala,* the rhythmic cycle, with appropriate hand motions, following and sometimes reinforcing the vocal soloist. Musicians and other prominent members of the musical community, such as known patrons of music, are ushered to front-row seats reserved for authority. There is often a place for a "chief guest," a political or cultural figure, or a distinguished musician who may be listed as such on the printed program or in newspaper advertisements and has the duty to be present throughout and perhaps to garland the musicians at the conclusion of the performance. This institution may be related to the earlier royal and aristocratic patronage of music, in which a maharaja functioned, as it were, as "chief guest."

Applause, automatically coming after each piece in Western and Persian concerts, has a somewhat different role in Carnatic music. Some (but often modest) applause comes at such points and also at the end of a concert, but the audience reserves its greatest demonstration of approval specifically for those moments in which the performer's contribution is most pronounced, the improvisatory sections. One hears applause most typically at the end of an *alapana* preceding a composed *kriti,* or at the end of a rapid-fire responsorial exchange between singer and violin, *mridangam* and *ghatam.* In the first case, the applause rewards intellectual accomplishments in setting forth the nature of a raga imaginatively and movingly; in the latter, it is technical virtuosity. Not only sections, but individual phrases may be singled out for applause. Interestingly, the intellectual achievements are applauded most warmly and frequently. But there is also applause after compositions for which the performer of the moment is particularly noted, and a prominent

singer is likely to have a half-dozen favorite songs, one or two of which an audience will with special anticipation expect to hear at any concert. There is a
disparity in the application of criteria of musical excellence. In the abstract,
knowledge of the repertory of important composers and their songs is a major
criterion, but applause is given not so much to the performer's rendition of a
composition as to the ability to improvise, to make quick and effective musical
decisions.

There is a difference in Madras between the typical classical Carnatic concert, vocal or perhaps by a *vina* soloist, and concerts performed by ensembles
of the oboe-like *nagaswaram*. Even though they perform in concert halls, the
latter remain more a part of the temple tradition. Vocal and *vina* concerts
belong to the educated middle classes, largely Brahmins, and at least half of
the performers are members of Brahmin castes, while the *nagaswaram*
players are more frequently from traditional musicians' castes. As the culture
of South India urbanized, the priestly Brahmin castes became intelligentsia
and their concerts became the spearhead of musical modernization. But at
the *nagaswaram* concerts the atmosphere is much more traditional, one
hears less English, the dress of performers and audience is more old-
fashioned, men and women sit in separate sections, members of non-Brah-
min castes are more numerous, and the socio-economic level seems on the
whole lower.

There are other ways in which a Carnatic concert, essentially a Western-
style phenomenon, differs from the typical European concert. Take the practice of bestowing garlands on the performers after a concert. An Indian tradition, it readily fits Western conceptions of how musicians should be treated, as
witnessed by our practice of giving bouquets to female performers. However,
the order in which musicians are garlanded is indicative of recent changes. In
the earlier part of the century, musicians were garlanded in order of of their
musical function: soloist first, then melodic accompanist, and then mridangam
player followed by other percussionists. Eventually, as caste mobility
increased, caste identity became a factor, Brahmins preceding the members
of musician–barber castes, an order that tended to correlate with musical
function. The entry of women into concert life further complicated the criteria
of order, as males, especially accompanists of high caste, would object to following female soloists. The widespread popularity of certain musicians, as a
result of radio, records, newspapers, and widespread touring, has also
become a factor. There may now be a tendency to bestow honors first on a
famous percussionist while the somewhat less-known soloist may have to
wait. The role of Western musical culture enters into all of this through its tendency to promote social mobility, break down traditional roles of caste and
sex, and promote the star system; and also because of the interest of Western
and Western-influenced listeners in percussion, permitting greater freedom
and substantial solo work to mridangam players who thus develop independent reputations.

Where there are classical traditions, the concept of concert is easily adapted. Thus, in Korea classical music is being reintroduced to many city-dwellers who had lost touch with older traditions of court music, of folk songs and of narrative drama from the provinces, never accessible to most of the population. All of these are now presented in concerts, sometimes in mixtures and combinations that contradict earlier practices, but which may reflect the Western concert practice of combining in one performance the music of a variety of historical periods and nations, sacred and secular, music for the living room and for the stage.

In like manner a great variety of tribal styles and repertories which now contribute to a single national repertory in such countries as Mexico, Peru, Mali, and Guinea may be presented in individual concerts with an essentially Western structure. The Western concert format has been enormously adaptable in its European history and it has continued to show this flexibility more recently, throughout the world.

## REFERENCES

**Percy M. Young,** *The Concert Tradition, from the Middle Ages to the Twentieth Century* (London: Routledge and K. Paul, 1965). **John H. Mueller,** *The American Symphony Orchestra* (Bloomington: Indiana University Press, 1951). **Khatschi Khatschi,** *Der Dastgah* (Regensburg: Bosse, 1962). Concert programs of the Music Academy, Madras, published as "Souvenirs" of the annual conferences. *First Korean Traditional Music Festival 1981,* 8/20–25 (program booklet, Seoul, 1981). *The 5th Festival of Asian Arts,* October 16–November 1, 1980, Hong Kong (program book, published in Hong Kong, Urban Council, 1980). Issues of newspapers: *Kayhan International* (Tehran) and *The Hindu* (Madras). **Kathleen l'Armand and Adrian l'Armand,** "Music in Madras: The Urbanization of a Cultural Tradition," in *Eight Urban Musical Cultures,* edited by Bruno Nettl (Urbana: University of Illinois Press, 1978), 115–45.

# 20
## "Pop"

What about the music that most of the world's people listen to most of the time? It is the music disseminated by radio, records, perhaps film and TV, the music of the large urban populations, performed at myriads of tiny night clubs and a few vast stadiums. It is urban music, but also available in small towns and even villages. In the Third World, it's the music of great stars of the culture, the Egyptian Umm Kulthum and the South African Miriam Makeba, but also of imports from the West like the Beatles and Elvis. It's what we usually call popular music. Each culture has its own, but most share certain fundamental traits.

Take a record of American Indian rock music played by Jim Pepper and his group, some Indians and some whites, a record entitled "Pepper's Powwow." The style is rock-and-roll with elements of jazz and country music, but the tunes are actually borrowed from the modern Plains Indian repertory. One of them is a Peyote song sung in Indian style before and after the main part of the number which, in turn, consists of Peyote words sung to a single repeated pitch against a background of complex instrumental harmony. In another piece, two sets of words always sung in English to Indian tunes in the Pan-Indian powwow culture ("If you wait for me after the dance is over, I will drive you home in my one-eyed Ford" and "I don't care if you're married, I will get you") are combined ("I don't care if you're married, I will drive you home in my one-eyed Ford"), but they are set to yet a third familiar Indian tune (which is often sung with the words, "My sweetheart, she got mad at me . . ."). A creative but also symbolically significant combination of familiar materials. The music is harmonized but unmistakably derived from an American Indian repertory.

Or consider the large body of West African highlife. Its African sound comes through in the complex background rhythms of the percussion sections and its vocal tone color. The hemiolic beat of traditional rhythms such as *abadja* is likely to be there, hidden under the blaring of trumpets and saxophones, that otherwise produce North American big-band sound or the Caribbean flavor of calypso.

Or take Iran. Before 1978, many kinds of popular music were available on records and performed in traditional night clubs, everything from short versions of classical music, stressing virtuosity and a bit of Western harmony, to large ensembles, in octaves, playing lugubrious love songs in a Middle Eastern melodic style against a harmonium rhythmically repeating the tonic chord, and on to rural folk songs arranged with piano and modern drum set accompaniment. Or India: a vast body of music comes directly from the soundtracks of films, sung by the famed "play-back singers" using traditional as well as Western instruments, in styles occupying many points along the Indian–Western continuum. But, for that matter, also take the U.S., with its burgeoning popular music culture that has since 1960 been giving its listeners everything from folk-like country-and-western and blues to R & B, rock (with its many subdivisions), disco, new-wave, and what not, all musics that dominate other parts of the world as well.

If there is any trend in world music that might justify the fear of musical homogenization, it would have to be in this realm of popular music. All of these repertories do have a lot in common, aside from their dependence on the mass media. Everywhere there is Western harmony, though often in relatively simple forms, alternating a few chords or even confining itself to dominant–tonic interplay. Most of it is comprised of vocal numbers accompanied by an instrumental ensemble normally including a percussion section, and there are usually Western and traditional instruments performing together. Normally the numbers take from three to five minutes. They are almost always metric, in three, four, six beats, never too complex. And most significant, virtually every instance is a music symbol of an intercultural relationship.

In most parts of the world, the relationship involves the combination of Western and indigenous style traits. That is after all what we would expect: urbanization, the interaction of various culture groups, Western technology in music and elsewhere, secularization of musical culture—all of this came about because of the impact of Western culture, and so the music that might best symbolize this state of society would almost have to include Western and native elements side by side. But there are also combinations of various non-Western musics. American Indian and African elements come together in Brazil; Middle Eastern-sounding pieces find their way into the African–Caribbean–European mixes of East Africa; Indian film songs show influences from Iran and the Arabic world. The popular music of North America and Europe, as it now exists, is ultimately based on the adaptation of sounds of African origin, mainly in aspects of rhythmic structure and improvisation, but also in the variety of tone colors. In other ways, too, the popular music movements of Europe have thrived on imports from other cultures—India, Japan, of course Latin America, and more recently, a variety of practices from folk music. Likewise, in the popular music of Iran, there are Arabic, Indian, Western, Soviet Caucasian, and Turkish elements, and a variety of folk cultures, all combining to produce a repertory of extraordinary variety.

We think we know what we mean by "popular music," but in no culture is there a sharp line between it and other kinds. The term is used mainly in the West. In Iran, it is simply called "Iranian music," and it is the classical and folk categories that are especially designated. In India, it is usually and properly called "film music." In Africa, the various genres are classed individually. In Indonesia, the most "popular" genre, a combination of Portuguese and Indonesian materials with a modern general Western overlay, is designated simply by its name, Kroncong. In Western culture, the concept of "popular" is actually controversial and is, somewhat ineffectually, set off against classical and folk music; many regard it as emblematic of evils such as rapid urbanization, overpopulation, industrial dehumanization, to say nothing of sexual permissiveness, drug abuse, secularization, anti-Christianity, or at the very least, the breakdown of traditional values. Older Indians and Iranians share such opinions and stress the symbolic and substantive evil of cultural mix in music and life. Significantly, genres clearly outside the classical or folk—such as hymns from the Methodist hymnal and marches played by the high school band—do not share the dangerous ambience of the popular. Music from these genres may be beloved but are usually excluded from the "popular" category.

Categories such as "folk" and "classical" do not have universal validity. The kind of music usually called "popular" in the West is also the kind that, given its broad range of sound within a consistent framework of style and social context, and its tendency to cultural mix, has in the past suggested ways in which many of the world's cultures could move musically, when other musics failed. Evidently, they felt the need for a musical base upon which indigenous characteristics could be maintained within styles that could appeal to broadly national and even international audiences. Popular music was able to provide a context for such musical combinations more easily than the classical music system of the West which, despite some valiant efforts, has shown itself less amenable to intercultural treatment.

# REFERENCES

**Virginia Danielson,** "Traces of Tradition: al-Atlal as an Example of Modern Arabic Song" (unpublished paper, read at the 1983 conference of the International Council for Traditional Music). **Bruno Nettl,** "Persian Popular Music in 1969," *EM* 16:218–39, 1972. **Judith Becker,** "Kroncong, Indonesian Popular Music," *Asian Music* 7(1): 14–19, 1975. **Charles Hamm,** *Yesterdays* (New York: Norton, 1979), xvii–xix. **Charles Hamm, Bruno Nettl, and Ronald Byrnside,** *Contemporary Music and Music Cultures* (Englewood Cliffs, N.J.: Prentice-Hall, 1975), chapters 3, 4, 5, and 6. **Erik Barnouw and S. Krishnaswamy,** *Indian Film,* 2nd ed. (New York: Oxford University Press, 1980). **Firoze Rangoonwalla,** *Indian Filmography: Silent and Hindi Films (1897–1969)* (Bombay: Udeshi, 1970). **Records:** Jim Pepper: *Pepper's Powwow,* Embryo Records SD 731, 1971. Willard Rhodes, ed., *Indian Songs of Today,* Library of Congress AFS L36.

# 21
# Juju
## by Christopher Waterman

The Yoruba of southwestern Nigeria, who number about fifteen million, are one of the largest cultural groups of West Africa. Long an urbanized society, they have traditional music that displays a rich variety in terms of ensemble types, instruments, techniques, and style charcteristics. This diversity is underlain by a set of shared musical characteristics and aesthetic values that has provided a stable structure capable of absorbing and transforming new musical influences. Pervasive social change, stimulated in part by the political and economic incorporation of Nigeria into the British Empire, led to the emergence of a variety of syncretic Yoruba musical styles in the early twentieth century. Each of these musics was a unique confluence of musical materials—African, Middle Eastern, Afro-American, European—reinterpreted and integrated by musicians working in urban environments.

The locus of Western musical influence in the early twentieth century was Lagos, a bustling economic and administrative center located within the Yoruba homeland. The diverse population of Lagos provided urban musicians with unique opportunities and challenges. Among the major groups residing in distinct "quarters" of this major West African port city were the indigenous urban Yoruba, others from the towns in the hinterland, Nigerian peoples such as Edo, Igbo, Kalabari, Ibibio, Nupe, and Hausa; Afro-Brazilian and Afro-Cuban returnees from slavery, a Western-educated African elite composed largely of Sierra Leonan repatriates, African transients such as the Liberian sailors who frequented the nightspots along the Marina; and Europeans. It was in the socially heterogeneous and rapidly modernizing context of Lagos that the dominant genre of contemporary Yoruba urban popular music emerged in the period between the world wars, a vital, flexible, syncretic musical system called *juju*.

The roots of *juju* are to be found in the "palmwine" guitar tradition of the 1920s, which originated with the addition of the acoustic guitar to the pool of instruments used by Lagosian street musicians. The stereotypical "palmwine" guitarist wandered the streets of Lagos in the evening in search of informal social gatherings where he could perform in exchange for food, palmwine, beer, or a few shillings. His ensemble consisted of African, Afro-Brazilian, European, and perhaps other percussion instruments, along with the guitarist–singer. The guitar style itself was eclectic, drawing upon gramophone recordings of Cuban groups and country music pioneer Jimmie Rodgers, and strongly influenced by the guitar techniques of Kru sailors from Liberia.

According to elderly Lagosians, the first musician to play a style called *juju* in the early 1930s was Tunde King. Widely admired for his compositional abilities and clear falsetto voice, King fused elements from a number of musical traditions to create a new style. Chief among these sources were traditional Yoruba praise songs, guitar techniques from the "palmwine" tradition, Western instruments such as the tambourine, cymbals, and triangle, the banjo, and textual and melodic phrases from various other West African urban musical traditions. The average *juju* ensemble of the 1930s and 1940s was a quartet, consisting of a leader who played banjo and sang, a second vocalist who sometimes played cymbals or triangle, and tambourine and bottle-gourd rattle players.

In the 1930s as today, *juju* music was performed in two major types of social context: urban bars or "hotels" patronized by a predominantly male clientele, and neo-traditional Yoruba life-cycle ceremonies such as naming, wedding, and funeral occasions. Its popularity was further enhanced by dissemination via gramophone discs, produced by European companies such as Odeon, Parlophone, and His Master's Voice beginning in the 1930s. The primary audience for *juju* was ethnically heterogeneous and centered in an emerging African working class. It consisted less of the Westernized elite (who preferred European music) or the largely Muslim indigenous Yoruba (who opted for traditional and Islamicized drumming styles) than of "settler" Yoruba who had migrated to Lagos in search of work, and non-Yoruba transients such as the African and West Indian sailors who worked for shipping lines along the West African coast.

In the early lyrics of *juju,* musicians, like the traditional street musicians who were their predecessors, were expected to commemorate significant events, praise important individuals, and offer critical commentary on social trends. Most of their textual materials were derived from traditional Yoruba verbal genres such as proverbs, praise poetry, and praise names. Urban slang phrases in Yoruba were also common, as were phrases of other West African languages and English.

*Juju* music remained relatively stable until the late 1940s, when the convergence of a number of social and technological factors created the context for major changes in musical style and performance practice. The post-war period in Nigeria, as in much of the Third World, was a time of intensified political activity. The 1940s saw the rise of a political elite which consciously identified itself with traditional African cultural practices. By 1950, the nationalist movement had splintered along ethnic lines, and the cultural nationalism of the Yoruba involved Western-derived and newly discovered traditional forms and values.

Interestingly, the specific catalyst for what might be called the reindigenization of *juju* was the arrival in West Africa of an element of Western technology, electronic amplification. Portable public address systems and the electric guitar allowed *juju* musicians to utilize a wider range of traditional

Yoruba drums, drumming techniques, and rhythmic patterns, without upsetting the aural balance among voices, guitar, and percussion. This was a revolutionary change in a number of respects. First, it led to the incorporation of the small Yoruba hourglass-shaped pressure drum, reputedly first introduced by bandleader Akanbi Ege in 1949. Traditionally used as a "talking drum," in *juju* groups it usually plays the traditional role of "mother drum" which comments upon the sung praise lyrics and the social context, functioning also as a symbol of Yoruba ethnic identity.

At about the same time, the percussion section of the standard *juju* group was augmented to include a variety of conga-type drums, bongos, and claves derived from African-influenced Cuban popular music. The vocal component of the *juju* band was expanded from the leader-plus-supporting vocalist formula of the 1930s to a full responsorial chorus of two or three singers. The overall ratio of vocalists to stringed instruments to percussion instruments thus shifted fom 2:1:2 to 3:1:5 in the post-war period.

These changes constituted a basic revitalization and restructuring of *juju* music. The expansion of the percussion section allowed the incorporation of complex rhythmic patterns derived from traditional styles of social dance drumming. The Yoruba practice of grouping musical instruments into "families" with a "mother" was applied to the *juju* ensemble. Augmentation of the vocal chorus resulted in a renewed emphasis upon the call-and-response pattern typical of most traditional Yoruba vocal music. While the *juju* music of the 1930s and 1940s was a style prominently associated with Western influence and patronized by an ethnically heterogeneous audience, it became, from the 1950s on, a specifically Yoruba music. Yoruba politicians recognized its value, and *juju* musicians played at rallies, produced praise-songs in support of politicians, and were frequently identified with the specific political parties.

Contemporary *juju* music, a slick, commercialized style dominatad by an ever-expanding Nigerian record industry, has been influenced by such diverse traditions as Cuban-influenced pop music from Zaire, Indian film music, soul, reggae, country-and-western, and disco music. It is generally regarded by urban Yoruba as a Yoruba music which has incorporated foreign elements. There do seem to be theoretical limits to the perceived flexibility of the system, however. Most informants suggest that if the "talking drum" were eliminated, or if non-Yoruba lyrics became predominant, the *juju* tradition would be gutted. As one musician phrased it, "it might be good, but it won't be *juju-o*."

This short sketch of *juju* music over a period of some fifty years illustrates the complex interaction of such analytically distinct processes as Westernization, modernization, syncretism, and indigenization. The introduction of Western musical technology provides the means for reemphasizing core features of Yoruba traditional social dance music—call-and-response patterns, hierarchical organization of instruments into "families," combining or terracing of rhythms, and the "talking drum." On the other hand, continuity in traditional Yoruba concepts of musical sound and structure facilitates the incorporation of Western musical instruments such as the Hawaiian guitar and synthesizer. African-influenced New World musics such as mambo, rhumba, and samba returned to Africa via the gramophone, are reintroduced and syncretized with structurally similar Yoruba patterns.

The history of *juju* shows that Westernization may create the necessary conditions for indigenization; that continuity of indigenous ideas, values, and perceptions may facilitate Western borrowings; and that a musical style originally ridiculed by indigenes as an essentially foreign mélange may, through a series of transformations, become a powerful symbol of ethnic identity.

## REFERENCES

**J.S. Eades,** *The Yoruba Today* (Cambridge: Cambridge University Press, 1980). **Darius Thieme,** "Style in Yoruba Music," *Ibadan,* June 1967:33–39.

# 22
# National Music
## by Paul Wolbers

In Indonesia many contrasting cultures have been united under one government. Between 1512 and 1949, its history was dominated by Western influences; Portuguese, Dutch, and English colonizers conquered much of the archipelago and converted many of the inhabitants to Christianity, while Islam, also a foreign influence, diffused intensively and eventually became the most prominent religion. The economy became export-oriented. With the end of World War II, after centuries of foreign—and mainly Dutch—domination, Indonesia became an independent state. One of the government's many severe problems was the development of a cultural policy that would suit the variety of traditions. As Java was the seat of the government, had the largest population, and was heir to a very strong, old classical cultural tradition, there arose the fear among non-Javanese Indonesians that this culture would be imposed on them. One of its major symbols was gamelan.

The gamelan had always, both as concept and as musical ensemble, been regarded a symbol of power; the courts in the "feudal" period (ca. 1500–1800) had the best, largest, most beautiful gamelans; and the princes, though Muslims, did everything they could to maintain their magico-religious context that stemmed from the pre-Islamic Hindu period of history. But the orthodox Muslims and the intellectuals in the revolutionary movement had all along been opposed to the maintenance of the gamelan tradition, the first group because of their fundamental opposition to music in general, especially when sponsored by the ruling class, and the second, because to them gamelan was a symbol of the feudal society that they rejected.

To counter the fear that gamelan might become a Javanese symbol of all of Indonesian culture, the government, immediately after independence, founded Western-inspired conservatories with the assigned task of developing an all-Indonesian music. The first of these, however, were located in the principal bastions of traditional Javanese culture, Yogyakarta and Surakarta, and as the cultural power of the courts had declined, the schools, instead of creating a new musical system, took over their function as carriers of the classical tradition.

But already before World War II, Indonesia had developed something that could play the role of national music, Kroncong, a kind of music that had originated in the communities founded by freed Portuguese slaves in the sixteenth century, music in what was originally a Western style. In those so-called Mardika settlements, people used a small ukelele-like guitar and other instruments to accompany the Portuguese songs. Over a period of centuries this genre of song diffused to the cities, and in the course of its wanderings, it picked up elements of style from a variety of indigenous sources, including rhythms derived from the gamelan, pentatonic scales, and short, non-metric introductions similar to those of gamelan music. Today there are, incidentally, also variants of Kroncong that sound completely Western in the manner of big-band, ballroom orchestra, and modern Western "pop" genres.

The concept of Kroncong as a national music had developed under the Japanese occupation, from 1942–1945. Before that time, the popular Kroncong musicians were very often European or Eurasian. But these were imprisoned by the Japanese occupiers or went underground, and Indonesian singers came to fill the vacuum. This was the only Western-based music allowed by the Japanese, who actually encouraged it and used it effectively for spreading their propaganda. But when finally the Indonesian people recognized Japan as a new colonizing power, Kroncong songs began to be used against them, and their role as protest song emerged. The fact that the vast majority of Kroncong songs are in the national language, Bahasa Indonesia, is very important to their function as a national idiom. Between 1945 and 1949, Kroncong became associated with the revolution against the Dutch; the texts inspired the masses and contributed to their solidarity.

But to return to the cultural policy of the government. It would seem that the Indonesian people had already provided themselves with a genre of national music before the government drew up plans to create one. A survey from the early 1970's showed that many Indonesians did indeed regard Kroncong as a national music; but there no longer seemed to be a need for such a unifying repertory.

In this respect it is interesting to see, in the new cultural policy formulated shortly after 1970, that the government wishes the people to rediscover, preserve, and develop their cultural heritage, and would strive to enable them to avoid negative foreign influences while at the same time absorbing those that are positive. These developments, it is thought, should help to free cultural values from feudal restraints. In a statement clearly implying the desirability of a modernized musical culture, the government proudly stated that various genres such as the puppet theater, *Wayang,* are no longer restricted to religious or festive occasions, but are performed in regular theaters in the national language, so that larger audiences can enjoy them. The older classical tradition of Java has become national expression, and the authorities expect it to take an even larger role as an internationally valid art. But, the policy states, this can only be done if traditional and modern (i.e., Western) elements are combined: "The government encourages the pattern of using traditional art as the basis and source of further development which, it is hoped, will produce a harmonious blend of traditional and modern without losing a specifically Indonesian character. Such a style will thus be accessible also to foreigners."

An interesting contest: Kroncong, with its partially Western character, was a credible candidate for official recognition as national music; it had already fulfilled the expectations just stated. But it seems that the gamelan and its related arts—the great traditions of Java and Bali, of the dominant culture of Indonesia, with its large ensemble and spectacular theater and dance readily fitting Western ideals—may have won the day.

# REFERENCES

**Judith Becker,** *Traditional Music in Modern Java: Gamelan in a Changing Society* (Honolulu: The University Press of Hawaii, 1980), 34; and "Western Influence in Gamelan Music," *Asian Music* 3(1):3–9, 1972.   **Indonesian Department of Education and Culture,** *Cultural Policy in Indonesia* (Paris: UNESCO, 1973).   **Ernst L. Heins,** "Kroncong and Tanjidor: Two Cases of Urban Folk Music in Jakarta," *Asian Music* 7(1):20–32, 1975.   **Bronia Kornhauser,** "In Defense of Kroncong," in *Studies in Indonesian Music,* edited by Margaret J. Kartomi, Monash Papers on Southeast Asia, no. 7 (Melbourne, 1978), 104–183.

# 23
# Old-Time Religion

About 1950 two kinds of music were clearly delineated in the repertory of the Northern Arapaho people: Western or "white" music, and Indian. Insiders and outsiders to the culture could easily distinguish them. No doubt, the Indian part of this music must have been quite different from its form a hundred years earlier. Its set of substyles had become internally less diverse, but in a way it had also become more varied. The difference between recent and earlier states of the "Indian" repertory involves the addition of two styles which, though distinctly Indian, resulted from the coming of whites to North America. Though it is an oft-told tale, let me give a brief account of it here again, as it is one of the most interesting illustrations of the far-reaching and indirect effects of Western culture in non-Western music. It shows a society accepting new styles into its musical culture for reasons that appear to have nothing to do with music as sound.

As far as is known, before the coming of the whites the central repertory of the Arapaho approximated stylistically the more recently recorded songs of the Sun Dance, social dance songs, and songs of the Plains Indian powwows of contemporary America. After the arrival of the whites, the traditional religion of the tribe appeared to have ceased meeting its needs, and at least some of the Arapaho began to look for other kinds of spiritual solace: the teachings of Christian missionaries, and also new forms of old-time religions that were developing in other Indian cultures in response to the coming of the whites. The most dramatic of these religious movements came to the Arapaho as part of the last concerted military effort to oppose the whites. It was a movement that brought its music along.

Around 1870 Wovoka, a Paiute Indian living in inland California, began to preach a religion centered on a ceremonial dance that would bring back to life all dead Indians, remove the invading whites, and in general restore an idyllic form of Indian life, with its ancient songs, games, ceremonies. The songs of his ceremony presumably used the general musical style of Paiute songs. Until 1887, this "Ghost Dance" was evidently restricted to its original tribe, but then peoples from elsewhere, including the Plains, sent delegations to learn Wovoka's ceremony and teachings. Given the difficulties in which they found themselves, they must have been very much attracted to a religion that so promised to improve matters. Within a year or so, the Ghost Dance had been introduced to many tribes of the Plains and, with it, the musical style of the Paiute which was shared by other tribes of the area between the Rockies and the mountains of California. The powerful group of Sioux tribes, in particular, practiced the Ghost Dance vigorously and it became a focus of the so-called outbreak of 1890, which resulted in the infamous massacre of Wounded Knee.

The Arapaho learned the Ghost Dance in 1889, and continued to practice it into 1893. Many of their songs were collected by James Mooney and published in notation as early as 1896, and in 1935, in one of the classic ethnomusicological studies of musical change, they were compared with songs of the Paiutes and other Great Basin peoples by George Herzog, who made it clear that they constituted a distinct category in the Plains repertories. Although they shared certain traits of the old Plains style, the Ghost Dance songs had a small range (often a fifth or sixth), a less spectacular singing style, and a form in which each of several phrases (of varied length) was repeated. Despite the demise of the ceremony, some Ghost Dance songs were still sung in recent times. To the Arapaho they became a symbol not of the time of Wounded Knee, but of an earlier, more peaceful time, when humans and supernatural spirits were closer. The words of the songs ring powerfully:

> *My father, now I am singing it;*
> *My father, now I am singing it,*
> *The loudest song of all,*
> *The loudest song of all,*
> *That resounding song,*
> *That resounding song.*

But it was Western culture that made some Indian tribes seek the life of earlier times, with its simpler songs, words that reminded them of a distant and mythic past, and even instruments, such as the bullroarer and bone buzzer, that turned the tribe away from the changes that were taking place. The Ghost Dance became the focus of a kind of nativistic revival, a type of movement also found elsewhere. Societies may respond to forced change by facing the opposite direction, resisting, and stressing the integrity of the original cultural form through its earliest manifestations. But among the Indians, the development of an intertribally accepted musical style was also a sign of the latest times, and so, reviving ancient customs associated with a new old-time religion brought about some new musical developments, but not the creation of an actually new musical style.

Other musical repertories were introduced in North American Indian cultures under less dramatically charged political and social conditions. The Stomp Dance, a line dance accompanied by short musical phrases antiphonally thrown back and forth between leader and chorus, came from the Southeastern U.S. and spread throughout the Indian settlements of Oklahoma and elsewhere in the Southwest and Southern Plains. The "49 Dance," obscure in origin and nomenclature but with music in the Plains style, diffused to many reservations and settlements early in the twentieth century. And of course there is the widespread adoption of the Plains Indian style for modern intertribal powwows.

But back to the Arapaho. Their next musical adventure was the introduction of the Peyote style, which comes from another religious movement whose power, like that of the Ghost Dance, was so great as to have an impact on Indian societies throughout the United States. It also brought with it a unique musical sound. The roots of the Peyote religion are in ancient Mexico, but in the eighteenth century it diffused throughout the Southwest, slowly, at first, and then in the nineteenth and early twentieth centuries rapidly through much of the continent, particularly to the volatile and hard-pressed Plains peoples. Replacing the Ghost Dance in some tribes, it did not preach a return to older, pre-white times but sought for ways—some derived from Christianity—of accommodating the changes that had come about. Individuals converted from older religions or they simply added Peyote to their other belief systems. But like the Ghost Dance, the Peyote cult brought with it a distinctive musical style that contrasts in each tribe with the older styles already present.

Whether common to several tribes or specific to one, Peyote songs can almost always be recognized as such, for they all sound alike. Yet the origin of the style, unlike that of the Ghost Dance, is not so easy to determine. It is somewhat of a pastiche of Indian styles. The vocal sound, though distinct, seems most like that of the Navajo. The rhythmic structure is built on two note lengths (e.g., quarters and eighth notes), something common in Navajo but even more in Apache styles, but combines these units into complex metric cycles of up to seventeen beats, often in an isorhythmic arrangement. This procedure resembles Plains rhythm, but, on the other hand, the very complexity of the meters also relates the songs to the elaborate rhythm of Pueblo Indian music. The arrangement of sections in the songs is usually the one widely familiar in Plains Indian music—each stanza is comprised of two parts, the second an incomplete repetition of the first. But in Peyote songs the sections are longer (and more numerous) and often have particularly elaborate interrelationships. Often phrases are repeated in pairs, something reminiscent of the Great Basin and Ghost Dance styles. They are clearly demarcated, as in the music of the Eastern U.S. and Oklahoma. And characteristic meaningless words not in any known language, but possibly going back to the cult's Mexican origins, account for most of the texts.

In none of this do we find elements directly taken from Western music, although it is possible that the intonation of intervals, thoroughly compatible with the tempered system, may have been influenced by the Peyote users' acquaintance with "white" music, as may also the complexity of forms, the tendency to isorhythmic structure, and the strict adherence to meters. Meaningful words are occasionally in English. But it is the development of a style with elements from various traditional musical areas, and of a repertory that is in essence intertribal and crosses the borders of culture and music areas, that is actually the major effect of white culture.

The Arapaho began to practice the Peyote cult in the 1890s, just after the time of the Ghost Dance. Their people are among the most prolific composers of Peyote songs, but many of their songs have also come from the Kiowa and Comanche. In some respects, Indians responded to the coming of the whites by trying to be more "Indian," and this resulted in going back to what was felt to be an old Indian music, the simple songs of the Ghost Dance and its associated rituals and games. They also responded by forging a supertribal, broadly Indian culture which consciously borrowed from but reinterpreted that of the whites. The Peyote style is one of its musical manifestations. In each case, it was an old-time religion that brought about a new kind of music.

## REFERENCES

**George Herzog,** "Plains Ghost Dance and Great Basin Music," *American Anthropologist* 37:403–19, 1935.   **James Mooney,** *The Ghost-Dance Religion and the Sioux Outbreak of 1890,* Fourteenth Annual Report of the Bureau of American Ethnology, pt. 2 (Washington, 1896); the song text is quoted from p. 215.   **David P. McAllester,** *Peyote Music,* Viking Fund Publications in Anthropology, no. 13 (New York, 1949).   **Bruno Nettl,** "Some Influences of Western Civilization on North American Indian Music," in *New Voices in American Studies,* edited by Ray B. Brown and others (Lafayette, Ind.: Purdue University Press, 1966), 129–37; and "Musical Culture of the Arapaho," *Musical Quarterly* 41: 325–31, 1955.

# 24
# Indigenizers
## by Carol M. Babiracki

Over one hundred years ago, the Munda people and other "tribal" or aboriginal groups in India's east-central plateau region began converting to Christianity in large numbers. Conversion offered access to British colonial bureaucracy and power and the hope of recovering aboriginal lands from the area's Hindu and Muslim rulers and landlords. For these and other material benefits, the converts abandoned many of their beliefs, customs, and rituals. Traditional singing, drumming, and dancing in particular were forbidden by the missionaries because of their association with pagan rituals and with supposed licentiousness and other sins.

Today, the Christian descendants of those Mundari converts no longer sing Gregorian chant melodies or Western hymn tunes in four-part harmony. Their liturgical music is based primarily on Mundari melodies, and after a service an entire village may gather outside the church for night-long communal singing, drumming, and dancing. They say they are Munda first and Christian second. And indeed, to a non-Munda outsider, convert or not, the very fact that they are singing and dancing in a group identifies them as aboriginal.

Mundari non-converts, however, see very clear differences between their own traditional music and dancing and that of the converts. Apart from some experiments around 1900, the Christians began seriously relearning—or rather, reshaping—indigenous Mundari music only some twenty years ago and adapting it for dance just a few years later. Their songs and dances bear the same subtle traces of Western church music that can be heard in other aboriginal Christian music in the area, traces perhaps obvious only to other Mundas. The Christians now wish to be considered Munda, but distinct from the non-converts; they sing and dance neither with nor like non-Christians.

It is possible to account for the indigenization of Mundari Christian music purely in its own historical and social terms; to be a tribal in modern India brings economic and social advantages. The indigenization of Mundari Christian music, however, is also part of a larger movement of indigenization of Christian ritual and music throughout the non-Western world and in ethnic communities in the United States as well. In its many manifestations, the movement has been unified by similar histories and motivations and eventually by the official sanctions of both Protestant and Catholic church hierarchies. The early European missionaries carried their ideas of appropriate Christian music and ritual to the non-Western world. Proper liturgical music was based on Gregorian chant and European hymns, the words slavishly translated into vernaculars and set to European tunes. It was the incompatibility of these tunes with vernacular texts, in fact, that prompted the first calls for the indigenization of church music in Africa, some twenty to thirty years earlier than in India. Missionaries found it impossible to preserve the linguistic tones and thus the meaning of African vernacular texts. Despite this, indigenization was not accepted without decades of fierce debate. In reaction to the total rejection of indigenous culture by the established churches, thousands of independent, syncretic sects were formed in Africa in the early decades of this century, each worshipping with music and dance closely resembling traditional styles. These sects were seen as a threat to the established churches, and it is possible that their popularity even forced the eventual official sanction of indigenization by midcentury. Nationalism, the rise of vernacular language movements, and the shifting identities and allegiances of the post-colonial years certainly also have contributed to its acceptance. Today, indigenization is regarded as legitimate by all of the established churches.

The indigenization of Christian music has been a matter of recovering, relearning, and recomposing native music in a mixture of Western and native traditions. In both India and Africa, Christian missionaries and clergy wanted to adopt indigenous music without its non-Christian associations and with "prudence" and "good judgment." Suitably modified and "improved," indigenous music could help shape new musical idioms that were both Christian and African or Indian. Christian authorities have sought to reshape regional and language-specific sources into musical idioms that are to some extent pan-African, pan-Indian, pan-Polynesian, etc.

Although the underlying motives and goals of indigenization in Africa and India have been similar, the new Christian musical cultures themselves are extremely diverse. This has to do with the different musical and conceptual relationships to Western music and culture. In Africa, church musicians were able to legitimize their newly indigenized music and at the same time keep it distinct from traditional music and that of the independent sects by modeling certain aspects of its presentation on Western art music, a field in which African composers have been trained by European teachers and in Western-style conservatories. Their unique African "cathedral style" compositions, such as the famous *Missa Luba,* are intended not for congregational singing but for stage performance by choirs of trained, blended voices under the direction of a conductor. Many of these compositions are intertribal, using a mixture of traditional melodies and forms.

Christian missionaries and clergy in India, especially those in Hindu-dominated urban areas, also sought to legitimize their indigenization efforts, in other words to indigenize without losing social status. But Western art music has a low profile in India and tends to be segregated from native Indian traditions. Most non-tribal Indian Christian musicians have therefore looked to India's classical music for legitimization, but these, with their emphasis on individual improvisation and virtuosity, are clearly unsuitable for the congregational performance expected in churches.

Christian composers in India have solved the dual problems of legitimacy and congregational performance by constructing melodies based on the classical ragas but in styles of presentation and forms borrowed from Indian devotional music. The Christian hymns are even called *bhajans,* emphasizing their affinity with the communal hymns of the popular *bhakti* cult of Hinduism, a cult that stresses equal access to god regardless of caste.

Indian church music is more eclectic than its African counterpart. Melodies based alternately on South and North Indian ragas may be used in the same service, a North Indian drum accompanying a South Indian tune is not uncommon, and Indian *tabla* and harmonium may be played in the same ensemble with Western guitars and banjos. A vernacular service may also contain Gregorian melodies and hymns in English. The Christian Mundas (and other converted aboriginals of East-Central India) have been relatively isolated not only from influences of Western art music but also from those of the Indian classical traditions. Their liturgical music is largely based on Mundari melodies and forms, except that the melodic rhythm is typically in the "Gregorian style" of the urban churches. Mundari chants and hymns are accompanied by the traditional idiophones and drums—older drums, in fact, that are now out of favor with non-converts. This is perhaps another means for Christians, or perhaps alternately for non-Christians, to maintain their distinctiveness while presenting themselves as more traditional than the others.

In their para-liturgical singing and dancing, however, Mundari Christians, mainly young people, have chosen to incorporate those traits of Mundari music that we may consider central: antiphonal performance, communal dancing, a full set of traditional drums and other traditional instruments, and a tense, "shouting" vocal style. The more subtle non-traditional qualities of the songs—the short, symmetrical rhythmic patterns, equal subdivisions of the beat, and anticipation of the beat—are recognized as alien only by the area's non-Christian Mundas.

Despite the fact that African and Indian musics are so different from each other, compatibility of indigenous and Western musics was used by both Indian and African clergy as a justification for indigenizing. The compatibilities in sound between African and European musics probably allowed Christian composers to adopt more central traits from both African and Western music. Consequently, the indigenized music of the African established churches is more truly syncretic than that of the Indian churches.

Christian clergy in Indian urban areas found fewer points of contact in musical sound itself between Indian and Western music. Instead, they noted the scientific and spiritual qualities of both classical Indian music and dance and those of European art music traditions, and also the compatibility of Indian music itself with the modally based Gregorian chant. But because of the lack of compatibility in musical sound, fusion and syncretism have not been the expressed goals of the musical indigenization in India. Indian Christian composers have chosen fewer musical traits central to either Western music or to the Indian great traditions. Generally speaking, most Indian church music is less syncretic but also less profoundly indigenous than its African counterparts. Real efforts to indigenize Indian music have begun fairly recently, several decades after Africa, and Christian clergy in India tend to look to Africa, with its Western-style music schools, uniform standards of composition and performance, trained choirs, and sophisticated orchestras and stage presentations, as models.

Ironically, perhaps, indigenization of Christian music in Africa and India probably could not have achieved the momentum that it now has without the modernization and secularization tendencies of post-colonialism. These forces have allowed African and Indian Christians to separate indigenous music from its associated non-Christian rituals and beliefs. African Christians are able to look on music as a fine-art form. Indian Christians can assert that Indian music is neither Hindu nor Muslim, but simply Indian. And with Christianity firmly established in the modern nations of Africa and in India, the fears

of nineteenth-century missionaries that pagan associations are inherent in indigenous music no longer seem to matter.

## REFERENCES

**Josef Kuckerty,** ed., *Musica Indigena; Einheimische Musik und ihre mögliche Verwendung in Liturgie and Verkundigung* (Rome: CIMS, 1976).   **A. M. Jones,** *African Hymnody in Christian Worship: A Contribution to the History of Its Development,* Mambo Occasional Papers, Missio-Pastoral Series, no. 8 (Gwelo, Rhodesia: Mambo Press, 1976).   **Lazarus Nnanyelu Ekwueme,** "African Music in Christian Liturgy: The Igbo Experiment," *African Music* 5(3): 12–33, 1973–74.   **Isaiah Mwesa Mapoma,** "The Use of Folk Music Among Some Bemba Church Congregations in Zambia," *YIFMC* 1:72–88, 1969.   **Johannes Overrath,** ed., *Sacred Music and Liturgical Reform After Vatican II,* 5th International Church Music Congress, Chicago and Milwaukee, 1966 (Rome: CIMS, 1969).   **Keshari Sahay,** *Under the Shadow of the Cross: A Study of the Nature and Process of Christianization Among the Uraon of Central India* (Calcutta: Institute of Social Research and Applied Anthropology, 1976).   **Monica Thiel-Horstmann,** "Indian Traditional and Christian Folksongs," *Man in India* 58(2):97–150. (April–June 1978).   **Henry Weman,** *African Music and the Church in Africa* (Uppsala: Ablundequistska Bakhandelen, 1960).   **Records:** *Missa Bantu,* Philips Monaural PCC211; *Missa Koongo and Missa N'Kaandu,* Serenus SRS 12040, 1970; *Missa Luba,* Philips P 14023 R, ca. 1958.

# 25
# New-Time Religion

Using native elements in the missionary effort of the nineteenth and twentieth centuries was nothing new to the Catholic Church. Since ancient Roman
times it had succeeded in fusing pre-Christian rituals with the liturgy. In more
modern times, the pantheon of the West African Yoruba religion combined
rather readily with Catholicism and its plethora of saints, to develop unique
religious configurations in such places as Haiti and Bahia, with a musical style
largely African but also compatible with Western characteristics. Later, nineteenth-century North American Indians found themselves going to Protestant churches to hear choirs singing European music fitted to Indian texts,
and a bit later, early in the twentieth, English hymns translated into Kiowa
and Apache but sung to traditional Indian tunes. Yet it was not until about

1960 that the indigenizers began consciously and in large quantity to combine elements. We've looked at their motivations, approaches, and methods; how about some of the pieces?

The prototype of the modern African mass, the *Missa Luba,* was composed (or perhaps more properly, arranged) from traditional materials in about 1958 by Father Guido Haazen, a Belgian priest determined to keep traditional music intact. The mass is in Latin and sung by a company of musicians of the Luba people of Zaire. It includes the Ordinary of the traditional mass—Kyrie, Gloria, Credo, Sanctus, Benedictus, and Agnus Dei. Principal elements of both Western and African music—to the extent that one can talk about a general sub-Saharan African style—are present, and each of these elements is presented at a level of complexity sufficiently low so as to be compatible with both musical systems. Harmony, for example, is restricted to a few simple progressions. The rhythmic ensemble accompaniment avoids extreme levels of complexity, the staggered beginnings, and the breaking up of units into two, three, and four simultaneous subdivisions that one associates with Africa, yet it remains prominent, reminding the listener that this is, after all, African music. There is a good deal of responsorial singing, an African trait shared with Catholic liturgy. The tunes are short and repetitive, and thus have a certain African character, but with little variation and no improvisation.

But if a general mixed style is characteristic of this mass, another thing to be noted is the diversity of the sections. On the liner notes of an early disc recording, the mass is presented as purely and strictly Congolese, yet its most striking piece, the Sanctus, with its complex voice relationships and ample harmony is really quite Western with a bit of African flavor provided by the utterly simple drumbeat accompaniment. Some sections of the Credo have no Western sound at all, the only reminder being a tonic chord in the brief choral responses, something that might have been found in traditional Central Africa as well. The *Missa Luba* shows how a mixed style can be developed but also how a non-Western society can create, in one piece, music that exhibits greatly varying degrees of Western musical influence. In the latter respect, it is rather like an Iranian performance to be described later ("*Māhour*").

The idea of the *Missa Luba* is also found elsewhere in Africa. The *Messe Fang,* from Gabon, composed circa 1970 (following Vatican II) is cast in the native language of the Fang people. Accompanied by an ensemble of three xylophones, its sections alternate in style and give a less unified impression. Some use monophonic Gregorian chant, others are choral (accompanied by drums and xylophones) and use parallel thirds. Like the *Missa Luba,* the *Messe Fang* presents its materials in a style simple enough for fusion. The harmony is often Western by implication but uses the parallelism traditional in the polyphony at the eastern end of the Guinea Coast. The percussion accompaniment is kept at a decently uncomplex level.

That syncretic materials have been produced in Africa may be no surprise, but how does all this work in parts of the world whose music is not as compatible with Western? In Middle Eastern or North American Indian music there is hardly any church music that combines elements as does the *Missa Luba*. In North America, a few Indian tunes can, with a bit of change, be cast into a Western mold. In the Middle East, traditional Eastern churches maintain their liturgies with music that fits readily into Middle Eastern patterns, but like Gregorian chant, is hardly in a style now generally acceptable in Western culture. Otherwise, to the extent that Middle Eastern Muslims have been converted to Christianity, they usually sing American and European hymns.

In its compatibility with the West, the classical music of South India and the repertory of *bhajans,* Hindu hymns, may be intermediate between Africa and the Middle East. Some points of similarity are apparent in the classical tradition: drone on a tonic triad; emphasis on tonic, fifth, and often third degrees; diatonic scales; compositions with lines of equal length corresponding somewhat to the lines of Western songs and hymns. The Christmas mass of Madras, by the Indian composer Father Walter Albuquerque, and mentioned in "Indigenizers," was recorded in 1975, shortly after its composition. It is partly in Tamil, partly also in Latin and English, and sung by men's and boys' choirs accompanied by harmonium and in spots also the violin—present, no doubt, because of its importance in Carnatic music, yet in this case, played in Western style. Consciously based on or related to the classical Carnatic system, most of its sections are said to be cast in specific ragas. The *tala* concept is not used in the rhythmic structure, but the melodies have, one might say, a Carnatic flavor. So do the singing style and the ornamentation.

But there is also much diversity within this work, diversity of a sort that would be tolerated in neither traditional Indian nor Western music by itself. The early sections, including the Kyrie, are monophonic with harmonium accompaniment; men's and boys' choirs alternate. In one piece, the harmonium simply stays on the tonic triad; in another, it plays triads on tonic, second, and sixth degrees. The Credo sounds like true Gregorian chant, with harmonium accompaniment, and it is followed by a rendition of "Silent Night" in English, with harmonium and violin, and with choral singing of ordinary Western harmony, the tune rendered in octaves by men and boys. Sanctus and Agnus Dei follow the style of the Kyrie and are followed by a choral rendition of "Adeste Fideles" in English.

How about the Protestant churches? Let's look at a few other cultures. According to Christensen and Koch, the people of the Ellice Islands of Western Polynesia have a tradition of polyphonic singing, largely with the use of drones or alternating drones and overlapping antiphony. Moreover, a part of their repertory is comprised of triadic melodies. Given these characteristics, it may be expected that hymns with functional harmony would be readily accepted and come to be regarded as part of the tradition. They are after all relatively compatible. In transcribing performances of hymns, some of them composed by Ellice Islanders, Christensen found some with Western harmony but with odd departures: parallel fifths, curious kinds of doubling, unexpected octave parallels, dissonances. It would seem that the Ellice Islanders modified the Western harmony to fit some of their traditional expectations, or at any rate assimilated the harmonic practices imperfectly.

In Southern Africa churches of European affiliation as well as the independent, so-called separatist churches have large bodies of hymnody. When the separatists broke away from the European mother churches, they often took their hymns along. At the same time, the tradition of choral polyphonic singing in the culture of the Zulu and Xhosa could easily absorb four-part harmony. Sometimes hymnals combining older traditions with Western hymns appeared, as in the hymnal of the Shembe sect, a Zulu church, written in 1940. The tunes are partly from Baptist and Methodist hymnals, but others derive from old Zulu chants. According to Weman, the harmony, essentially Western, also has a lot of the traditional Zulu flavor. Evidently, in the preparation of Southern African hymnals, Western tunes were often used but modified. Modulations were avoided and changes of scale resulting from the minor scale were evened out so that only one version of any scale degree would be used. Yet in the hymnals of Southern Africa, the compatibility of Western and African music has syncretically allowed a rich harmonic practice to be developed.

It is different in North American Indian churches. In a Mennonite hymnal, *Tsese-Ma'heone-Nemeototse: Cheyenne Spiritual Songs,* the majority of the 161 hymns are from the European repertory, presented in four-part harmony, with Cheyenne words. Some twenty-five percent, however, are monophonic, and most of these are Cheyenne songs in traditional style with Christian words in Cheyenne, the tunes composed by (or attributed to) Cheyenne individuals in the late nineteenth or early twentieth centuries. Most of them have the general characteristics of Plains Indian music. A few are imitations of Western tunes, in particular children's songs. And a few tunes of European origin are presented unharmonized. Little is done to produce a combined style. Instead, the hymnal presents a cultural mix by giving the congregation Western and Indian melodies, all with the same fundamental purpose, between the covers of one volume. The worship music of new-time religion in non-Western cultures is subject to the same dynamic of syncretism as other realms of musical life.

# REFERENCES

**Josef Kuckertz,** ed., *Musica Indigena: Einheimische Musik und ihre mögliche Verwendung in Liturgie und Verkundigung* (Rome: CIMS, 1976). **Melville J. Herskovits,** "Drums and Drummers in Afro-Brazilian Cult Life," *Musical Quarterly* 30:479–92, 1944. **Dieter Christensen**

and **Gerd Koch,** *Die Musik der Ellice-Inseln* (Berlin: Museum für Völkerkunde, 1964), 180–82.   **Henry Weman,** *African Music and the Church in Africa* (Uppsala: Ablundequista Bakhandelen, 1960), chapter 5.   **David Graber,** ed., *Tsese-Ma'heone-Nemeototse: Cheyenne Spiritual Songs* (Newton, Kans.: Faith and Life Press, 1982).   **Records:** *Missa Luba,* Philips P 14023 R, ca. 1958; *Messe Fang,* Disques Vogue, LDM30110, 1972.

# 26
# Innovators

"There is no room for innovation in Carnatic music," thundered a distinguished concert administrator in Madras. "We need innovation, but because of the wide latitude for interpretation and the use of improvisation, we get it constantly and thus don't need far-ranging experiments," said a singer, expressing in his way an acceptable theory of the role of innovation in musical systems with much improvisation as opposed to those that have only set compositions. An opinion at the other extreme: "It's a good thing that we in Madras are having contact with other kinds of music, especially Hindustani and Western, because this will stimulate us to develop our music." And also: "The most interesting music is being made by young people because they are doing new things, unlike the old traditionalists." In 1982, musicians and music-lovers in Madras expressed a variety of attitudes towards innovation in Carnatic music. None was talking about replacing Carnatic with Western music. There has always been innovation of some sort in all musics, even one as solidly established as the Carnatic, but the degree to which a culture incorporates elements of Western music may be determined in good measure by its traditional attitude towards innovation. And conversely, the concept of innovation itself in the twentieth century must be affected by contact with Western musical thought.

In 1982, innovation clearly was an issue in Madras. Musicians were trying to further it, prevent it, channel it, but in any case, it was there. There is an awareness of the fact that Carnatic music has undergone what publications by Milton Singer and the L'Armands call primary urbanization, in which local and folk traditions have merged to create a classical "great" tradition of music. Secondary urbanization has also come, transforming the Carnatic socio-musical system into something very much like the Western-dominated international concert culture, with the associated changes in patronage, instruction, and secularization, and the participation of various castes and women. A further development of secondary urbanization would seem to be the confluence of several "great" traditions such as Carnatic and Western, and the internationalization of musical systems. What in all of this are the attitudes of individual musicians? Who permits himself innovative acts?

In the Carnatic musicians' strong sense of their own history, the concept of innovation plays an important role. Tyagaraja, a kind of musical culture hero whose shadow dominates this history, is revered not only because of the quality and number of his songs and the devout character of his life, but also because he is believed to have introduced various improvisatory techniques such as niraval and the technique of sangati in which a musical line, traditionally repeated many times, became the subject of systematic variations. Some major events in the history of Carnatic music are associated with influences from Western music. Baluswamy Dikshitar, brother of the famous composer Muttuswami Dikshitar, is remembered mainly for having introduced the violin into the South Indian tradition. In the nineteeth and early twentieth centuries, some attempts to set traditional songs to English words were made, and some Western tunes (e.g. "God Save the King") were adapted and imitated. M. Dikshitar himself, in the early nineteenth century, composed words to Western tunes. But in the twentieth century, the accommodation with Western music mainly involved the matter of social context.

A number of prominent musicians are discussed by the musical public of Madras as being innovators of some sort. The opportunities that exist for a large public to hear many musicians in concert, and the widespread availability of records, tapes, and radio performances, make it possible for people to hear and perhaps to expect variety. The concept of innovation is related to the interest in variety, and in the tendency of various musicians to develop personal styles and performance characteristics. On the basis of interviews with informed listeners in Madras, I am able tentatively to divide musicians into "conservative" and "innovative" groups. It may be that they themselves would quarrel with these designations. Certainly a majority are interested in maintaining a cohesive and homogeneous system, but certain important musicians stand outside it to varying degrees.

Among those often referred to as innovators is M. Balamurali Krishna, who is said to use his voice in novel ways prompted in part by the availability of amplification, who composes many new songs and also develops (or claims to develop, some critics notwithstanding) new ragas. He sometimes discusses and justifies these innovations between numbers in his concerts and he is criticized for this as well as for the fact that he claims to be self-taught and not the disciple of any distinguished musician. But M. Balamurali Krishna is highly successful; he makes records, performs on television, and commands some of the highest fees.

S. Balachander, too, adheres to no school, but has received the government's highest decorations for his accomplishments as a *vina* virtuoso. He is considered an innovator by virtue of having developed a style of improvisation and of *vina* technique that owes much to the Hindustani tradition and a bit to Western music as well. Conservative critics object that he makes overly elaborate gestures while performing. This highly personalized playing style, his broad popularity, and his image of separateness from the conservative center of the population of musicians make him a figure somewhat similar to that of Balamurali Krishna.

A third artist, Chitti Babu, in addition to participating in the traditional concert style, has formed with his students an orchestra of *vinas* and percussion instruments to perform his compositions. They use bits of Western harmony and adapt readily to Western rhythmic schemes that conform to Carnatic *talas,* resulting in a syncretic style that could be perceived as a rather simple version of either Western or Carnatic music. The vocalist K.V. Yesudoss performs film songs as well as legitimate Carnatic music, specializing in rapid-fire delivery of improvised passages, and is criticized for some "empty" virtuosity. Emani Shankara Shastry, a *vina* player, makes some use of Western harmony.

All of these musicians are regarded by the main musical establishment as belonging more or less outside the conservative center, and during the festival season of 1981–82 they were evidently not sought after by those music circles that tried to preserve the tradition in what they considered authentic form. On the other hand, they were among the most popular with record, radio, and television audiences, and when they did give concerts, they commanded large crowds and high fees. The less conservative listeners praised what they considered to be innovations and particular personal traits and styles. The criticisms that the conservatives leveled at these innovators involved non-musical behavior as much as musical style.

Another group of musicians, more generally accepted by the majority of traditionalists, are thought to be innovators who work more specifically within the system. M.D. Ramanathan is said to have a peculiarly personal vocal style, making use of a particularly low range of his voice and unusually slow tempo. S. Ramanathan introduces rare and rediscovered old compositions. T.M. Tyagarajan is said to have unusual and interesting ideas in improvisation particularly attractive to musicians in the audience. K.V. Narayanaswamy, similarly, is said to have special personal style and particular depth of intellect and imagination. These kinds of innovation within the tradition constitute the kind of variation the system has long allowed in order to maintain its stability. In a different kind of role, Seerkhazi Govindarajan, a singer of film songs, also performs classical music in a rather unconventional way, using special vocal effects, but is readily accepted by the conservative core of musicians, in part because he specializes in singing a large variety of devotional songs.

In such a complex musical culture, one might further expect to find a group of radicals who have given themselves the task of actually changing the system. There is little evidence of such an avant-garde, and change occurs more in the spirit of supplementing than of overturning tradition. New instruments are absorbed, the establishment of orchestras is limited to an experimental group sponsored by All India Radio, Western harmony is introduced by fleeting implication at most, one hears nothing of secular topical song texts, and attempts to introduce English words have gotten nowhere. The picture is quite different from that of innovators in Iran, who have introduced Western styles with the instruments, and used Western forms such as concertos. In Hindustani music, departures from tradition are more widespread. And even so, only performers with solid reputations in this tradition can permit themselves wide-ranging experiments; only a Ravi Shankar dares to compose concertos for *sitar* and Western orchestra.

In Madras, it is not hard to separate innovators from others; musicians and the audience make the distinction; but the reasoning is not always clear (to a Westerner). There appears to be a difference between what we may call the "informed" audience of music-lovers, many of whom have studied music performance, and a group less concerned with Carnatic music and more interested in a variety of musics. The former group make up the bulk of the concert audience in the main music circles, but the latter constitute the bulk of the record and radio market. If one seeks innovation, one may find it more readily on records than in concerts. The innovators working most closely within the system have few records and perform live music, appealing to an audience that may regard records themselves as something of an evil because of the change they inevitably bring about. Mylapore, the area of Madras with the greatest concentration of live music and the residence of many Carnatic musicians, has relatively few record stores.

A man who does not claim association with a recognized genealogy of musicians, or who claims to invent new ragas, who claims to make innovations, may be criticized as someone trying to bring down the system. Another experimentalist, even one who develops a revolutionary artifact such as an orchestra, might escape reprobation if he applies what he does to the older tradition and claims to work within the system. It is not only the interaction of Western influence, stability, and innovation within the tradition that is at issue, but also the innovator's evaluation of what he does, his posture toward the system. If he claims to be part of the tradition, the changes he makes, even those that come from Western music, may be accepted and absorbed.

# REFERENCES

R. Rangarmanuja Ayyangar, *History of South Indian (Carnatic) Music* (Madras: author, 1972). **S. Seetha,** *Tanjore as a Seat of Music* (Madras: University of Madras, 1981). **Daniel M. Neuman,** *The Life of Music in North India* (Detroit: Wayne State University Press, 1980) chapters 2 and 3. **Alan P. Merriam,** *The Anthropology of Music* (Evanston, Ill.: Northwestern

University Press, 1964), chapter 15.  **Bruno Nettl,** *The Study of Ethnomusicology* (Urbana: University of Illinois Press, 1983) chapter 13.  **John Blacking,** "Some Problems of Theory and Method in the Study of Musical Change," *YIFMC* 9:1–26, 1978.  **Milton B. Singer,** *When a Great Tradition Modernizes* (New York: Praeger, 1972), chapter 1.

# 27
# Americans

It goes without saying that in most respects, North American Indians today live in a style much closer to that of their white and black compatriots than to that of their direct ancestors two hundred years ago. That one can still hear music sounding so quintessentially non-Western as that of the Plains peoples is something of a marvel in what is otherwise a very Western atmosphere of motorcycles and trucks, hamburger stands, Methodist churches, cowboy hats, and English or Spanish conversation. One might expect that the older music, along with customs, religion, language would gradually be disappearing, and in some ways that is the case. Yet an examination of the life histories of some native Americans in the twentieth century shows traditional music playing an increasing role with age.

William Shakespear, an Arapaho Indian living for the first seven decades of this century on the Wind River Reservation in Wyoming, spent his early and middle years learning much of the culture of his people. This included some very old traditional ceremonial songs but, to a larger extent, the recently developed songs of the pan-Indian movement that one would hear at powwows. His main religious involvement was in the Peyote cult of recent vintage, whose distinctive songs he learned by the dozen and also composed. In 1950, he was sought out to serve as a professional consultant by a midwestern university holding a summer-long institute in linguistics and needing his help in research on the Arapaho language. There he also met a student of ethnomusicology who asked him to sing all of the songs he knew, and to tell what he could of his musical culture. He made important contributions to the understanding of the Arapaho language, patiently dictated texts, and helped develop methods for their analysis and for the explication of the musical culture. But in doing this he also came to realize that there was much about his own culture that he did not know, and he began to read the accounts of anthropologists such as A.L. Kroeber who had worked with his people around the turn of the twentieth century. He became an enthusiastic scholar in the Western sense, taking books out of the library and making interlibrary loan requests. He returned home to Wyoming a changed person. He made a project of teaching to his people the traditional culture, as he knew it and was able to learn it from books and older people. He taught songs, and in various ways revived what had been considered lost, and for this he became revered among his people. Shakespear used the tools of Western scholarship and the white American's interest in Arapaho culture to foster revival of older tribal tradition among his people. Indeed, it was the white man's interest that made him go back beyond pan-Indian songs and Peyote ceremonies to seek them out.

Calvin Boy was a Blackfoot Indian who never came to be especially respected by his fellow citizens of Browning, Montana. As a child, he lived with his mother and his stepfather, an influential man who urged his people to keep up tribal traditions, but also to learn to live in a Western economic, social, and political system, and after whom a village was eventually named. Calvin went to a Catholic school and played French horn in the band; in his early and teen years, he was in essence a participant in Western music. His contact with Indian music was restricted to a few songs, learned while listening surreptitiously to ceremonies taking place inside tents or houses. In adulthood, however, he became more interested in Indian traditions, not in the older, ceremonial material no longer much used and not widely known since 1900, but in the pan-Indian social dance songs of the powwow culture. He became a member of singing groups that sang Grass Dance, Owl Dance, Circle Dance songs in the Plains style, but without texts, and in highly standardized forms. This he continued from the 1940s into the 1950s. If in other respects, Calvin became a person who lived essentially in a Western style, he also knew that he was not accepted as an equal by the white people around him, and he soon lost interest in their music.

Becoming older, Calvin eventually turned to another musical repertory for his main interest. He did not abandon the modern intertribal songs but began also to learn those of the older, specifically Blackfoot repertory, particularly of the Sun Dance and of the traditional medicine cults which cured the sick, brought buffalo, and improved the weather. Calvin didn't really believe that these songs would accomplish all of this, but learned and sang them, of course, for other reasons. He kept up the older tribal tradition in two ways: by learning the songs at all, to be sure, but also by learning them when he was older. Thus he enlarged and expanded his personal repertory much as an old-time member of the tribe might have expanded his through successive initiation into several age-grade societies, or as the owner of a medicine bundle might have added to it throughout his life by learning songs in visions. These old Blackfoot songs symbolized for Calvin his Blackfoot-ness, more specifically and importantly than the pan-Indian repertory symbolized his general Indian-ness.

And so in the lives of both of these Americans, old tribal repertory reasserted itself, though its role had changed. In both instances, Western culture gave the impetus for threatened disappearance, eventual return, and changed function. Traditional music in its new role as major symbol of tribal identity came to Bill Shakespear through the inspiration of Western scholarship; to Calvin Boy, as a result of disappointment in the bigoted and ungenerous nature of white American society.

## REFERENCES

Paul Radin, *The Autobiography of a Winnebago Indian* (Berkeley: University of California Press, 1920: reprint, New York: Dover, 1963).   **Charlotte J. Frisbie and David P. McAllester,** eds., *Navajo Blessingway Singer: The Autobiography of Frank Mitchell, 1881–1967* (Tucson: University of Arizona Press, 1978).   **Bruno Nettl,** "Biography of a Blackfoot Indian Singer," *Musical Quarterly* 54:199–207, 1968.   **Bruno Nettl,** "Musical Culture of the Arapaho," *Musical Quarterly* 41:325–31, 1955.   **Loretta Fowler,** *Arapaho Politics, 1851–1978* (Lincoln: University of Nebraska Press, 1982).   **Malcolm McFee,** *Modern Blackfeet: Montanans on a Reservation* (New York: Holt, Rinehart and Winston, 1972).   **A.L. Kroeber,** *The Arapaho,* Bulletin of the American Museum of Natural History, no. 18 (New York, 1902).

# 28
# A Champion

Accounts of twentieth-century history are full of men of enormous energy who typically, we are told, brought nations out of their obsolete native traditions into twentieth-century modernity. Some of them are frightening figures. What they did can hardly always be regarded as incontrovertibly beneficial by their peoples; and at the very least, what they accomplished, if indeed accomplishment it is, was carried out at great economic and human cost. But it's hard to overestimate the impact of a Mao Tse-tung, a Kemal Ataturk, a Jomo Kenyatta.

Imposing culture change on their peoples, some of these leaders also introduced musical change. European-sounding music of a Russian sort came
to China in the wake of Mao's victory. Ataturk discouraged traditional Turkish
music. Western music was imposed on the military establishments in many
nations, African and Asian. Musical change is often seen as the result of
broadly based currents of culture; but sometimes it may also be the result of
dictatorial action by a small minority. If major political figures have had this
kind of effect, there were also musician revolutionaires, individuals who combined political, social, and musical activism to impose change on a musical
system. Like the legacies of the political leaders, the effects of their efforts
have sometimes been enormous, if in retrospect controversial to their own
peoples. Look at Ali Naqi Vaziri in Iran.

Born in Tehran in 1887, he was a member of a military family, learned
Persian music from a *tār*-playing uncle, joined his father's Cossack regiment
where he was attracted by the military trumpeters, seesawed back and forth
between careers in military life and as a musician. Finally, after World War I,
aged thirty-one, he decided to study in Europe in order to establish a modern
system of music and music education in Iran. By that time he had developed
a vision of a musical culture in which traditional Iranian elements were actually preserved and improved by the introduction of European notation, harmony, ensembles, and other borrowings from Europe.

Vaziri's background in Persian classical music was strong. In his youth he
had studied with major masters and had collected and notated the Persian
*radif* from the performances of its main protagonist, Mirza Abdollah. In an
orchestra of the Sufi Okhovvat society, he played *tār* under the leadership of
Darvish Khan, who promulgated concerts of Persian traditional music in a
slightly modernized style and context. When he went to Europe, it was with
the intention of modernizing, single-handedly, the musical culture of Iran. In
his studies in Paris and Berlin, he concentrated on theory, pedagogy, and
Western instruments and their repertories. But he also continued in his concern for Iranian music, working on textbooks for instruments and theory and
going on to publish his first book, *Dastur-e Tār* (Instruction Book for *Tār*) in
Berlin.

Returning to Iran in 1923, Vaziri became a whirlwind of activity pressing
for musical modernization. In the face of resistance not only to change but to
music in general, he had to steer a course among those who wanted to Westernize all music, destroying the older tradition, others who wished to keep the
older tradition unchanged, and of course also those who wished to exclude
music as much as possible from a devout Muslim society. He was trying to introduce a new music and a new musico-social and educational system in
order to keep the national tradition from disappearing. And as a member of a
society in which delegation of authority was not customary, he tried to solve
all problems himself, usually by direct action.

For example: he founded a music school for Iranian music, directed it, and taught most of the one hundred students. Without much success he tried to introduce Western ways of teaching, that is, separating theory and practice and getting students to understand theoretical and technical principles before taking up an instrument. He was successful in introducing notation, and gradually developed a Western, textbook-centered and standardized approach to music education. This school for Iranian music grew and was eventually organized into five grades, with a rather rigid and obviously Western-derived curriculum. But in 1928, when Vaziri became director of a government conservatory hitherto devoted to Western music alone, he quickly introduced an Iranian music requirement, which persisted in the official establishments teaching general—that is, Western—music into the 1970s.

The idea of an independent, modern, and secular Iran, as developed in the Pahlavi dynasty beginning in 1924, went hand in hand with the development of music as a nationalistic phenomenon in several ways. Western music institutions were developed. But on the other hand, military music was changed from a Western repertory, as developed before 1900, to an Iranian one, largely composed of pieces by Vaziri, in Western syle but indeed of Iranian origin. And also, music education was introduced in the schools. In all of this, Vaziri wanted to do two things which appear in a way to be mutually contradictory. He wanted to make Iran musically a part of the West, and he himself wrote music which could be regarded as Iranian but which was actually in a Western style. From the point of view of twentieth-century Western composers, he would have to be considered rather unsuccessful, as his works simply do not measure up to Western standards in any way. Yet he did achieve a combination of styles, so admittedly he made his point. But he also wanted to preserve the older Iranian music as a separate tradition, and he firmly believed if he was to succeed, the music had to change—to allow harmony, to take on new social functions, to be taught more efficiently, to be notated, to be performed by ensembles. Only thus could it remain competitive with the Western music. Vaziri was at once a Westernizer and a champion of modernization.

To accomplish all of this he wrote large quantities of music in various styles, and he founded and conducted an orchestra of Iranian and Western instruments that played both Western and Iranian music in the same concerts. He established societies for the furthering of a Western-like concert culture. He encouraged women to go into music, founded a women's music club, built a movie theater for women, and considering the time and place, generally championed modern feminism. He wrote articles and books, explaining music at large, both Iranian and Western music, to Iranian readers, in the manner of theory and music appreciation texts. He entered the age-old controversy of Middle Eastern interval theory, proposing the use of a quarter-tone scale as compatible with Western music and Western ways of musical thought; but unlike the earlier theorists of the Middle East, he put his ideas into practice, introducing a *tār* with twenty-four frets to the octave, in quarter-tones, and providing visual aids for musicians to convert from the earlier seventeen-fret arrangement. He also promulgated a different way of holding the *tār,* moving it from the player's chest to a position like that of the guitar, and thus making possible the playing of a large range, something appropriate to the broadening repertory that he proposed for the instrument and Iranian music in general. Vaziri's way of holding the instrument has been generally adopted.

Some of the changes he introduced have become part of the standard musical arsenal. More perhaps have been rejected. Vaziri hoped for the emergence of a modern, harmonized Iranian music; but this did not come about. He worked for a comprehensive system of music education for children, but succeeded only very slightly. He hoped for a Western-style social context for music, but its beginnings were wiped out in 1978. And yet, the shape of music and musical life in Tehran in the 1960s was to a large degree the result of the efforts of this man, who understood the importance of music as substance and as symbol in the culture of a people, especially at a time of rapid and perhaps forced culture change.

# REFERENCES

**Mojtaba Khoshzamir,** "Ali Naqi Vaziri and His Influence on Music and Music Education in Iran," D.Ed. diss., University of Illinois, 1979. **Ali Naqi Vaziri,** "Notation: Means for the Preservation or Destruction of Music Traditionally Not Notated," in *The Preservation of Traditional Forms of the Learned Music of the Orient and the Occident,* edited by William Kay Archer (Urbana: University of Illinois, Institute of Communications Research, 1964), 251–57. **Ella Zonis,** *Classical Persian Music: An Introduction* (Cambridge: Harvard University Press, 1973), 186–89.

# 29
# Visitors

In Western Europe or North America, one may sometimes hear it said that "only the Viennese can really play Schubert," or "white people don't really understand jazz." Such statements are not often taken seriously. Most classical music-lovers readily believe that Japanese violinists can master the Beethoven Concerto, and that Zubin Mehta can conduct a symphony orchestra in a Mahler work better than most others. In an important way, Western music has become the music of much more than the Western culture area, an international music accessible to all. To those involved in this music, it is not essential that a performer of Schumann have seen the Rhine. The grandeur of Berlioz can be perceived by one who knows nothing of the grandeur of Paris. To be sure, an interpreter of Mozart who has never had more than the printed page to guide him would surely sound wooden and mechanical, but recordings would help him more than a walk around the Burgtheater. It is accepted that anyone, no matter where his original home or what his native culture, given enough talent, hard work, and experience, can learn to perform Western music. If a slightly foreign accent persists, that may well be acceptable or even attractive. Western musicians regard their music as an essentially technical matter.

It is probably this view that has permitted Western students and scholars to dare try their hand at the performance of non-Western music. As ethnomusicologists, they have tried to gain entree through the study of performance, first to the music itself, and then to the society that owns the music. And as musicians, they have tried to increase the scope of their musical knowledge by entering non-Western musical worlds. They have studied with Indian, Japanese, Javanese, African, and other musicians employed as teachers on American (and some European) campuses. Many have also carred out their field research in large measure through the study of performance, often subjecting themselves to the same musical and personal discipline demanded of Asian and African music students. While the majority of these individuals have undertaken this study as an aid to specifically musicological research, there have been some whose aims have been primarily artistic. Their love of a particular non-Western musical form, instrument, or genre led them to try to become competent performers, on a par, if possible, with the accredited musicians of the respective culture.

But whether they can really accomplish this has been the subject of debate among both Western ethnomusicologists and thoughtful musicians of various cultures. Judgments include compliments: "He is very good, for an American, that is"; or, "She sings almost like a native." But, on the other hand, one may be told that no matter how much one studies, one will never learn the music in a way that will approximate the understanding of any untutored native, that an American might well learn its technical aspects, but not the emotional and cultural ones of deeper significance.

Whether Westerners can learn to perform like natives is not an issue here; rather, we are concerned with the willingness of musicians in other cultures to accept them as proper colleagues. The point is that in contrast to the West, where music has become essentially a conglomerate of technical features, in certain other societies it is something culture-specific. It is not only *how* you make music that matters, but when and where, and to a significant extent, even *who* you are. This is all a rather complex issue, as there are some societies (e.g. in the traditional Muslim Middle East), that, at least in theory, practically require music to be made for them by outsiders, and many cultures have been faced for centuries with the importation of foreign musicians. Twentieth-century changes in the attitude towards uses and functions of music may be accompanied by changes in the acceptability of foreign musicians.

The success of Western music in spreading itself throughout the world is perhaps partly due to Westerners' view of their music as an internationally valid system, a set of techniques, which could be learned by anyone. If we now look at those musics around the world that have maintained themselves most vigorously, we may find some among them that have similarly discarded certain cultural and personal constraints and can therefore compete with the Western system. Thus, if Southern India has managed to maintain its musical culture, I would argue that this is in good part because it has come to be regarded by a great many Indians themselves as internationally valid, to be performed by members of all societies. In adopting this attitude, Indian musicians have had to give up certain traditional ideas about who may perform music, when and where it may be performed. This change is surely not the result of the coming to India of a large number of Western students of Indian musical performance; but the picture of musical life in a cultural center such as Madras is greatly affected by the presence of American and European students and professionals. By contrast, parenthetically, when Iranians were faced with the need to learn Western music in the mid-nineteenth century, this might have been strange or difficult for them, but in the realm of possibility. Westerners made no bones about the ability of their music to speak to anyone. But for Westerners to have become Iranian musicians would have been, for social reasons such as the low status of musicianship, less acceptable. And by 1970 it was still problematic.

Not so in Madras. In the winter of 1981, I was able to identify at least twenty Western students of Carnatic music, in addition to a good many who were studying *Bharat Natyam,* the closely related form of classical dance. At least five of the musicians gave public concerts. On the whole, in dress, behavior, and approach to performance, they tried to be as traditional as they could, feeling perhaps more than the average Indian musician that this quality would be important. They adhered closely to the teachings of their masters, trying to show how well they controlled a music that was outside their personal tradition. Although their Western background was evident in their performance, they certainly did not intentionally introduce Western sounds into their music. When such "Westernisms" were mentioned among Indian musicians, they were regarded more as a matter of personal background, something that each musician may claim, rather than the result of a fundamental cultural difference. The Westerners entered the conservative side of the Carnatic tradition, did not themselves carry out innovation such as the use of guitar and mandolin (which some of them knew how to play), something that was being done at the same time by young Indian musicians. The presence of these Westerners among the Carnatic musicians and in large numbers in the audiences was taken for granted by the musicians and music-lovers of Madras, and commented upon in favorable and optimistic terms.

How, aside from their identity, have these American, French, German students been an influence of the West? First, they underscore the Carnatic musicians' essentially technical approach to music, testifying to an attitude that has come to approximate closely the Western. Further, they assure the Carnatic system the status of an internationally valid music. There are further parallel developments. Musicians in the Western classical tradition appear to feel that it would be highly beneficial to Third World cultures if they were to adopt and become proficient in Western music. In some non-Western societies, the converse is not true. Iranian musicians may believe that it would be important for the understanding of Iranian culture if their music became known in the West, but they stop short of claiming that it would actually benefit the West. Some Carnatic musicians, however, take the attitude that the introduction of Carnatic music to Europe and America, and its adoption, aided by such devices as English texts, would be valuable in bringing international understanding, a truly universal religious feeling, and even world peace.

It is important to the Carnatic musicians of Madras as individuals to have foreign students, and they do not fear the competition. There is not much to fear, as few Westerners reach the necessary levels of excellence in this extremely complex music; they begin their studies too late in life. One major exception for some years has been Jon Higgins, a professor at Wesleyan University, who was given the Carnatic title of "Bhagvatar," is consistently regarded in Madras as the prototype of the successful Western Carnatic musician, and often is cited as a counterpart of Zubin Mehta. He is judged by the same standards as Indian musicians, who attend his performances in large numbers, listening with curiosity and respect. Unlike other Westerners who are less advanced, he is not treated patronizingly by newspaper critics. While he is considered mainly as an outsider who has legitimately entered the system, there are also attempts to integrate him into it by suggesting that he is a reincarnation of a great musician of the past. His role in Madras seems to be one of showing the worldwide validity of Carnatic music, proving that it need not be changed in order to compete with Western music.

Broadly viewed, the entry of Westerners is, then, a strategy for the survival of Carnatic music as a system of sounds. The entry would probably not have been as easy several decades ago, when caste and class roles and the close association of the music with Hindu rituals provided greater strictures. The change in the social context of music to a Western-style form of intellectual and artistic entertainment facilitated the survival of the Carnatic system at one stage; the internationalization of the system through the integration of European and American musicians is a further safeguard against decline.

It seems likely that the case of Madras is unique, or at least most extreme. Other musics have become accepted and performed by an international community of musicians. West African ensembles exist in Europe and North America, and North American gamelans have developed a tradition of their own. But these foreigners do not meet musicians and audiences on their music's home ground. In Tehran of the 1960s, an American wishing to learn Persian classical music was told in no uncertain terms that the proper way to do this was to study the *radif* with a master; but as a public performer he would be an oddity, praised for proficiency despite being a foreigner. If Iranians wondered why in heaven's name he was trying to play their music, this may relate to the Iranians' regard of their music as something not capable of becoming universal, and of Western music as what they called, in the 1960s, "international music." The relationship was unequal; Iranians thought they could easily enter the Western system, but not the opposite.

The West has transmitted the concept of an internationally valid music to other cultures, which have varied in their acceptance of it. In the long run, however, such a concept may turn out to be essential for musical survival in the modern global village.

# REFERENCES

**Mantle Hood,** *The Ethnomusicologist* (New York: McGraw-Hill, 1971), especially pp. 230–42. **David P. McAllester,** "The Astonished Ethno-Muse," *EM* 23:179–90, 1979. **John M. Chernoff,** *African Rhythm and African Sensibility* (Chicago: University of Chicago Press, 1979), pp. 1–23. **T. Viswanathan,** "Karnatak Music and Foreign Students," Souvenir of the Indian Fine Arts Society (Madras, 1966–67), 103–7. **Jon B. Higgins,** "From Prince to Populace: Patronage as a Determinant of Change in South Indian (Karnatak) Music," *Asian Music* 7(2):20–26, 1976.

# 30
# Ethnomusicologists

The old joke says that the typical North American Indian family consists of father, mother, three children, and an anthropologist. By the same token it would seem since 1960 that many a non-Western community of musicians such as a Javanese gamelan or a group of West African drummers is constantly under the watchful eye of a music scholar waiting to record and ask questions. And as a result, many who work in ethnomusicology have been told by their informants: "If it had not been for you or people like you, who value our traditional music, we would have given it up because it seemed to have so little value in the modern world." To what degree such an assessment is realistic everywhere we may never know; but there are surely instances that could be cited. Ethnomusicologists may not have played the grand role implied, but they have had many bit parts. They have brought about both stability and change.

In the 1960s, Iranian music was undergoing a certain amount of revival in Tehran. Ma'roufi's *radif* was published, radio programs and concerts were beginning to be established. Even so, the University of Tehran did not take Persian music seriously, particularly its practical study, and its officials declined to establish a full program. Gen'ichi Tsuge, a Japanese student of ethnomusicology and recipient of a scholarship for Middle Eastern studies from Iran turned out to be interested mainly in Persian music and it was largely as a result of his need that courses in the *radif* were introduced and the authoritative musician Nour-Ali Boroumand was persuaded to come out from a kind of retirement to teach them. Through Dr. Tsuge, who evidently came at just the right moment, the revival of Persian music was given a shot in the arm, but it was also placed into a modern academic context. As a result, Persian music and its study were oriented more to Western teaching approaches. But more important, because of the special interest of Boroumand, a conservative musician, and his chairman, M. Barkechli, and because universities take a more humanistic approach than the practically oriented conservatories, it also retained stylistic traits of earlier times more than might have been the case without the involvement of the university.

In his student days, Professor Tsuge thus contributed significantly to a trend then already in progress, helping to redirect the salvaging of the repertory toward conservatism and stability. We see here in microcosm the kind of effect that Western and later also non-Western ethnomusicologists have typically had. Their view of music as something essentially and ideally unchanging, and their abhorrence, in their earlier history, of hybrid musical styles and the pollution of non-Western traditions by Western music, the mass media, and such concepts as popularization, surely had something to do with the revival of older traditions in many cultures. The interest of typical ethnomusicologists of earlier times in the musical sound, in contrast to the traditional social and intellectual practices of music, may have played a role in the development of techniques for the survival of the music per se, even if this had to take place outside the aboriginal venues and contexts. For the Westerner, the music "itself" was the issue; the cultural context was important, but could not be transferred to the West. The music itself could, and it was therefore what had to be preserved. Of course the interest of ethnomusicologists in bringing their teachers and consultants to the West as artists and professors also had an effect at home. The concept of music as culture-specific was attacked, as were the need to perform music exclusively in a prescribed social context, the norms for stability and change, the methods of teaching, and the relationship between teacher and student.

And on the home ground, there are many instances in which the efforts of ethnomusicologists are widely believed literally to have prevented the disappearances of styles and repertories, as, for example, the work of Catherine Ellis in Australia, Hugh Tracey in South Africa, Edith Gerson-Kiwi in Israel. But the ethnomusicological outsiders usually had only incidental effects, particularly by comparison with such Western-trained but native scholars as J.H. Nketia in Ghana, who tended to come a bit later but had more specific aims, strategies, and rapport, and played major roles in recent music history.

Even so, what is incidental to a society as a whole can be a matter of major impact to a small group of its people. I'll permit myself a personal anecdote. An important traditional venue for the performance of Persian classical music was an institution known as *dowreh,* a kind of club that meets regularly for some particular activity: weekly reading of the Qur'an, reading of poetry, discussion of religious or social issues. Some of them are devoted to music. They are very stable social units, consisting of perhaps six to eight men, who may be distantly related, and they do not easily admit new members or welcome guests. Wives, if in evidence at all, may listen to the proceedings in another room. While working in Tehran, I was aware of the music-making *dowreh* of my teacher and its sessions, known as *majles,* colloquially translated as "sitting," or "sitting around," which took place perhaps biweekly. Realizing that this kind of event represented one of the more typical venues for the performance of traditional classical music, I asked to be invited. It was not easy; the members were jealous of the ambience they had developed over a long period, a relaxed atmosphere among friends who, while formal in behavior, nevertheless felt very much at home with each other. After several tries, I succeeded in being invited.

The members, doctors, bureaucrats, two musicians, all quite Westernized in behavior, arrived, sat down to chat; some changed into a loose pajama-like garment. They dined sitting on the floor, had a few drinks, and smoked a few pipes of opium, then heard one of the members, a famous musician, improvise at length. Later my teacher was also prevailed on to play briefly. The music lasted about one and a half hours, and the entire gathering, four hours.

I had some difficulty reconciling what was clearly a rather ordinary and even modernized party atmosphere with the claims of a special ambience. Yet, though I attended several times, I was not permitted to record the music precisely because of fear that this would disturb the mood. Indeed, the whole matter of mood seemed to be of great importance. Who was or was not there seemed to make a great difference. My teacher felt that the style of the music would be affected if the social practices were disturbed. No women were present; if any were in the house, they would have to listen to the music while sitting in the kitchen. Only at the end did the host's wife appear to help him bid farewell to the guests.

The academic year was drawing to a close. I asked my teacher whether, as a special concession, he would permit me to bring my wife to a *majles*, particularly as he had explained that such events were really the heart of traditional Persian culture. He at first demurred, then said that he would speak to the host, and eventually relayed an invitation to my wife and me, pointing out that the host had asked him, my teacher, also to bring his wife so that one lone lady would not be embarrassed. Enjoyable but uneventful, the evening came and went.

Two years later, I returned to Tehran, and by chance was invited to a meeting of the same *dowreh*. To my great surprise, all of the members were now bringing their wives. As far as I could tell, the musical style had not changed. Later, I asked my teacher. He wasn't sure about changes in the music, but, he thought, one did have to keep up with the times.

# REFERENCES

**Mehdi Barkechli,** La musique traditionelle de l'Iran (Tehran: Secrétariat d'État des Beaux-arts, 1963).    **Bruno Nettl,** "Nour-Ali Boroumand, a Twentieth-Century Master of Persian Music," Studia Instrumentorum Musicae Popularis 3:167–71, 1974.    **Alain Daniélou,** Die Musik Asiens zwischen Missachtung und Wertschätzung (Wilhelmshaven: Heinrichschofen, 1973), 25–38.    **Marcia Herndon and Norma McLeod,** Music as Culture (Darby, Pa.: Norwood, 1980), 137–44.    **Hugh Tracey,** Chopi Musicians: Their Music, Poetry, and Instruments (London: Oxford University Press, 1948).    **Catherine J. Ellis,** "The Role of the Ethnomusicologist in the Study of Andagarinja Women's Ceremonies," Miscellanea Musicologica (Adelaide) 5:76–208, 1970.

# 31
# Opinions

A good many musicians in the Iranian classical tradition in the 1960s and 1970s began their musical training with Western music. Later, stimulated by nationalism, nostalgia, or a desire for something new, they moved into the Persian tradition, but while doing so, they continued to treat Western music as a kind of norm. Many knew Western music well, but their perception of it was colored by the fact that it is not, in the end, the music of their own culture. They looked at Iranian and Western music as parts of a hierarchy, making what may seem to be unfair comparisons. Some thought of Western music as a great international system to which Persian music can hardly be compared, but they were not happy with this situation, and thus tended to be defensive about Persian music and about their own relationship to Western music. On the other hand, a distinguished master maintained that the twelve modes of Persian music provided access to the entire universe of possible musical experience, while Western music, having merely two modes, major and minor, was much more limited.

If Iranian musicians were quite knowledgeable about Western classical music and its theory, in Madras musicians may be less well informed. Living in an extremely vital musical culture of their own tradition, they reach out to Western music as a kind of equal, a counterpart or complement to theirs, compared to which all other non-Western musics are less worthy of respect. If they are less knowledgeable, they are also less ambivalent than the Iranians about Western music.

In the view of the Carnatic musicians, the most important thing about Western music is its "harmonic" character, while Indian music is "melodic." Indian musicians have eschewed harmony in favor of a style of melodic development that far exceeds what may have ever been done in Europe, they say. The rise of large ensembles in the West is a direct result of the harmonic orientation of the music. By contrast, a major result of the melodic orientation of India is the prominence of ornamentation, recognized in its occasional presence in Western music but not regarded as comparable to the sophistication of Indian gamakas and their potential for emotional expression.

In Madras Indian and Western art musics are often said to be the only properly classical music systems in the world. Usually one speaks only of the Carnatic music, but the affinity of the two Indian systems is usually (if grudgingly) recognized, and sometimes they are together juxtaposed to the Western. The reason for singling out these two as the true classical musics must surely have something to do with the importance of Western culture in the development of modern India, and with the fact that it is by far the most accessible foreign music. But the suggestion that the musics of China, Japan, Indonesia, and the Middle East might also be "classical" is rejected for other reasons as well. One is the existence, in both India and the West, of essentially diatonic tone systems with seven scale degrees that have names, and the associated solmization. That other musics also have names for scale degrees is ignored. But the importance of these criteria tells us much of interest about Indian musical values and indicates that in order for a foreign music to be accepted as classical, it must contain something that is also important in South Indian music. Equality may also result from contrast. Indians may admire the sound of Western music but make little direct use of it. Take the matter of ideals in timbre and general character of sound. Indians value the great variety of tone colors available in the orchestra, but experimental orchestras in Indian music are exceptional at best, and diversity of timbre is not one of their features. In the central Carnatic classical tradition, some instruments (including the violin) are used in such a way as to approximate vocal music. Some Western instruments, such as saxophone and clarinet, imitate the traditional *nagaswaram,* while electric guitar imitates the traditional *vina.*

Among the other reasons given by Carnatic musicians for singling out Indian and Western music as the true classical systems is the emphasis on the fifth degree of the scale which, unlike other scale degrees, is not variable but always a perfect fifth. And the Carnatic musical culture, like the Western, characteristically pays much attention to great composers of the past, popular Western conceptions of Indian music as purely improvisational notwithstanding. In Madras much emphasis is placed on a central classical song repertory by a group of classical composers, and particularly by the so-called "trinity" who lived in Tanjore in the first decades of the nineteenth century.

The Indian musicians seek ways of associating Western music with their own, and they do this in part by identifying (sometimes spurious) common features, and (sometimes incorrectly) showing that they are absent in other musics. On the other hand, they also stress the differences between the two systems, showing that they are complementary and they together account for all that may be truly significant in world music. The confrontation of Indian and Western musics has had some minor effects on Indian music as sound, but the opinions that Indian musicians have of Western music help to tell us how they have come to terms with its existence. Indian musicians tend to think of the world of music as a set of discrete musical systems, and recent music history is indeed seen by them, as it has been seen by us in this way, as a series of confrontations. The approaches taken in these pages would be rather familiar to them.

The South Indian view of Western music is essentially one of admiration, tempered by a firm belief that their own music is at least as "good," both similar and different. An earlier Middle Eastern view expressed in the generally sympathetic writings of a nineteenth-century Arabic traveler in Europe, Faris al-Shidyaq, is not unlike that of present-day Madras. Faris says that the music of the "Franks" (i.e., Europeans) "can move one not only to tenderness, passion, or zest for dancing, but also to zeal and enthusiasm," but notes, rather like a modern ethnomusicologist, that "Frankish melodies . . . move only such among us as have become accustomed to them," that is, one must learn a music before appreciating it. He points out that harmony is a major characteristic of Western music, and he understands but criticizes the importance of notation: "The Franks have no 'free' music unbound by those graphic signs of theirs to which any verse may be sung, so that if you suggest to one of them that he should sing a couple of lines extempore . . . he cannot do so. This is strange considering their excellence in this art, for singing in this fashion is natural and was in use among them before these graphic signs and symbols came into being. I wonder how they sang before Guido d'Arezzo rose to prominence in Italy."

This Middle Easterner wrote at a time in which pressures from the West had not risen to the levels they were to reach in the twentieth century. In the early 1970s, by contrast, Iranian attitudes were on the one hand much more defensive, and on the other, much more directed towards adopting Western music as the dominant one of the culture, and introducing central characteristics of Western music into the Persian tradition. Thus, in modern Tehran, if one expressed an interest in "music," this was assumed by most persons to be Western music, and interest in Iranian music had to be specified. At the same time, in contrast to musical thought in Madras the concept of separate musical systems did not appear very much in discussion or conversation. People were less analytical and more critical; they took cultural and stylistic mixtures for granted. There was, interestingly, a widespread negative attitude towards Iranian classical music. Many people who knew of its existence (there were also many who were hardly aware of it) were incredulous that anyone should be interested in it or prefer it to Western music, and many thought it should be allowed to die out as something incompatible with modern life. Of course there were devout Muslims who thought badly of all secular music, and the average Tehrani might well have regarded Persian music as essentially boring and sad. Those Iranians who did like their classical music, as well as some musicians, tended to stress those of its aspects that were compatible with the Western. "We do have orchestras"; "We now happily perform our music on the piano"; and "We also have an Iranian piano, the santour"; these were typical statements.

Attitudes towards Western music are an interesting index of Western influence. In Madras about 1980, this music was imperfectly known, but it was respected as a sibling system to the Carnatic, portrayed as its complement in the world of music. The nineteenth-century Arabic traveler presents a sophisticated and balanced view. In Tehran about 1970, Western music dominated and musicians tried in various ways to work its major elements into the framework of their own music, taking its hegemony for granted. But as post-revolutionary Iran drove all music underground, Persian classical music became a rallying point for exiled opponents of the regime. Music took up its time-honored role of defending the identity of a people, as Westernized middle-class professionals who once identified themselves with Western music now turned back to a modernized form of their own cultural tradition.

## REFERENCES

**Pierre Cachia,** "A 19th Century Arab's Observations on European Music," *EM* 17:41–51, 1973.    **Swami Prajnanananda,** *Historical Development of Indian Music, a Critical Study* (Calcutta: K.L. Mukhopadhyay, 1973), 220–37, 420–22, 472–73; and *Music of the Nations, a Comparative Study* (Delhi: Munshiram Manoharlal, 1973).    **R. Rangaramanujam Ayyangar,** *History of South Indian (Carnatic) Music* (Madras: author, 1972), 338–49.    **S. Seetha,** *Tanjore as a Seat of Music* (Madras: University of Madras, 1981), 200–14.    **P. Sambamoorthy,** *South Indias Music,* book VI (Madras: Indian Music Publishing House, 1969), 120–27.    **B. Nettl,** ed., *Eight Urban Musical Cultures* (Urbana: University of Illinois Press, 1978), 151–67; and "Attitudes Towards Persian Music in Tehran, 1969," *Musical Quarterly* 56:183–87, 1970.

# 32
# Treasures

In Japan, David W. Hughes tells us, there are societies called *hozonkai* which strive to preserve traditional or folk songs. Such a description fits folklore societies in many nations, particularly of Europe, some of them founded in the nineteenth century. But these societies in Japan are different, for any one may be devoted to the preservation of only a single song. The movement began about 1911, and today there appear to be perhaps dozens of such societies, some strictly organized with membership rolls and dues, some constituted more informally. Membership involves singing the society's own song at meetings, making sure that authenticity is preserved in musical and textual content and in performance practice, and also seeking national recognition for what is perceived as a local product. Originally the idea was to "rescue" songs from performance in teahouses and similarly shabby contexts and to "recirculate the 'correct' version" (Hughes, p. 35). While these single-minded organizations actually differ greatly, Hughes says that they tend to have in common certain traits: they are strictly local organizations, have from fifteen to sixty members, are not professional or profit-minded, are rather conservative in general attitude, and are comprised largely of older people.

Everywhere one hears that older traditions are being destroyed by modern culture and that special efforts must be made to preserve them, lest the musical world be totally homogenized. Even so, the special approach of the *hozonkai* is related to some other characteristics of Japanese civilization and also is a good illustration of one type of response to Western-inspired musical change. Traditionally, Japanese classical and theater music is described as having derived from repertories that originated elsewhere: India, China, Korea, et cetera. Conceptually, these repertories have been kept separate and centuries later still continue to be regarded as distinct units within the contemporary repertory. The idea of a musical culture as a group of very discrete classes of music is important for understanding the Japanese system in other ways as well, as various genres of theater, chamber, and court music have substantially different styles, ideals of sound, even modes and instruments. Schools of musicians maintain distinct repertories, notation systems, and secrets of performance practice. To a significant extent, musical culture is compartmentalized, and music history is seen not as a series of mergers of styles but as the addition of new materials which take their place alongside older ones that also stay on, presumably unchanged by the experience.

The concept of preservation is thus important in a variety of Japanese music contexts, and to respond to the coming of Western music by separating the older music, including folk and local songs, and keeping it intact without change, is a method corresponding to earlier Japanese practices. But this consciously expressed need for preservation, with the implication that one should not only preserve traditions but actually see to the continued unchanged existence of specific artifacts, seems in its intensity to be more recent and may be related to the overpowering nature of Western music and the wide acceptance of many of its forms into Japanese musical culture. Two kinds of government action are interesting in this context.

The Tokyo National Research Institute of Cultural Properties (which was preceded by an organization perhaps more appropriately titled Cultural Properties Preservation Commission) includes music among its areas of activity, although it is more concerned with physical artifacts such as art works, manuscripts, and architecture. In 1980 it sponsored an International Symposium on the Conservation and Restoration of Cultural Property, devoted to the performing arts. Some attention was given to non-Japanese cultures, particularly Indonesian. But the bulk of the contributions in the published proceedings of this symposium concerns Japan, and this group of interesting and learned studies shows a noteworthy emphasis on music as a group of pieces or artifacts. These must be preserved in authentic form, one reads over and over. There is less interest in social contexts, processes, ideas about music. This concept of the piece as a discrete entity, unchanged and unchanging, is in line with the idea of traditional music as a group of discrete repertories, and also conforms substantially to Western ideas about music. The belief that what is interesting and important in traditional music is the maintenance of authoritative versions indicates that existence in preserved form is different from the kind of existence that the music must have enjoyed earlier. One imposes on it an unchanging, artifically stable format. Incidentally, this is not very different from Western academic attempts since the late nineteenth century to produce single, truly definitive versions of their classics in complete works editions of musical masters, or in *Denkmäler* editions.

The idea of preservation through imposition of an artificially static form is also evident in the designation of individual musicians as "national treasures" or, as stated in a similar Korean program, "intangible national treasures" (who, incidentally, are given permanent numbers). Performers, choreographers, drama directors, instrument-makers may all be included. They are outstanding individuals who richly deserve to be honored, but what most of them are expected to do—at least this is the public conception of their role—is to keep their art intact, to avoid contaminating it through hybridization with the Western art. For this they are supported by the government, giving occasional public performances, demonstrations, perhaps lectures and workshops, touring abroad, in what is otherwise a cultural environment that is only with difficulty distinguishable from that of Europe or North America.

Middle-class music lovers of Tokyo and Seoul indeed seem widely to regard the traditional heritage as something that was once unchanging, and that is now mainly a relic of the past. In 1981 a major festival of traditional music was held in Seoul. Performing groups from institutions devoted to music preservation, ensembles from university music departments, and "intangible national treasures" performed for audiences most of whose members were obviously quite unacquainted with these repertories, for their musical life was otherwise devoted to musics in Western style, and some of them were making significant contributions to it. A gap had evidently developed between two cultures of Korea, and to bridge it was the job of the government-supported performers. It's all not too different from the presentation of a Western nation's folk heritage at festivals and conferences, or from the performance of "early music" in authentic forms by costumed collegia musica. But while these are considered to be older forms of the contemporary musical culture, two distinct cultures were being juxtaposed in Korea. Or is it perhaps that the older tradition has begun to be regarded as completed history, much as have the Child ballads and Renaissance music in American academia?

# REFERENCES

**David W. Hughes,** "Japanese Folk Song Preservation Societies: Their History and Nature," in *International Symposium on the Conservation and Restoration of Cultural Properties* (Tokyo: National Research Institute of Cultural Properties, 1981), 29–46. **Eta Harich-Schneider,** A

*History of Japanese Music* (London: Oxford University Press, 1973), chapters 16 and 17. **William P. Malm,** *Japanese Music and Musical Instruments* (Tokyo and Rutland, Vt.: C.E. Tuttle, 1959) 23–24. **Fumio Koizumi and others,** eds., *Asian Music in an Asian Perspective* (Tokyo: The Japan Foundation, 1977). **Kang-Sook Lee,** "Korean Music Culture: Genuine and Quasi-Korean Music," *Korea Journal* 17(8):70–77, 1977. **Kyung Auh Sook,** "The Education of Musicians in the Republic of Korea," *ISME Yearbook* 2:21–28, 1974.

# 33
# Conferences

A conference of musicologists in Western Europe or North America may sometimes seem to have little to do with music. It is dominated by papers read in a more or less dry fashion by scholars who here and there also play musical illustrations, usually on the tape recorder, or perhaps vicariously through a colleague on the piano. Musical performances have not been the principal activity. By the same token, a festival of concerts or operas is rarely accompanied by presentations of learned papers.

In India a music conference is a kind of combination of the two, stemming from both the intellectual tradition of musicianship long extant in India, and Western ideas of scholarship. Large-scale musical events of the past brought a few musicians together for performance at court or temple. In certain respects these musicians were scholars; but their scholarship focused on the learning of songs and ragas, their meanings, symbolism, and proper performance. Early in the twentieth century, the idea of festivals began to develop in South India, and musicians performed, heard each other, and shared in concert series. Since the knowledge of materials—repertory, ragas, *talas*, techniques—was an important component of musicianship, conferences by the 1920s began also to include talks, demonstrations, and the reading of papers, something to which the Indian knowledge of British academic practice surely contributed.

A characteristic South Indian conference may last a week. Each day begins at around 8:30, with the singing of Hindu devotional songs. From 9:00 until noon there are papers and talks, and after a lunch break, the concerts begin. Young and lesser-known performers appear in the early afternoon, a featured performance by a famous singer may be heard at 6:30, and another, perhaps slightly less prestigious, at 9:00. Such conferences are ceremonial events, with opening and closing rituals on the first and last day, an opening speech by a political figure, and the election of a distinguished musician as presiding officer. Though they function as entertainment and provide a ground for competition, these events also symbolize the grandeur of the South Indian musical tradition, and when they occur, they briefly hold a central spot in the life of even a large, modern city such as Madras or Bangalore. But in this vignette the spot will shine on those morning paper sessions.

In 1981 the conference of the Madras Music Academy, perhaps the model for all South Indian music conferences, included a variety of presentations. A number of talks dealt with unknown compositions by nineteenth-century composers, coupling performance by the speaker with a plea for revival. One paper surveyed pictorial representations of ragas, *talas*, and tones of the scale in nineteenth-century art works in the state of Karnataka. Some papers presented older styles of performance practice, discovered by the speaker through oral tradition. Others tried to demonstrate that unusual instruments such as the guitar could be adapted to Carnatic music; or that traditional but less-known instruments such as the *ghatam*, the clay pot percussion instrument, properly fit into the framework of the Carnatic system. There were, too, some attempts at analysis of Indian music using Western approaches. All these sessions had a good deal in common with Western musicological meetings, and participants maintained that they would probably not have taken place in their particular form without the supporting influx of Western musical thought, particularly its interest in preserving the past, in authentic performance of earlier music, in the honoring of great masters of the past.

But the paper sessions in Madras had some features not characteristic of Western musicological meetings. They were in a minor if significant sense religious events, always begun with devotional music, the stage decorated with oil lamp, incense, and a small altar to Saraswati, goddess of knowledge, holding an instrument. There was always a clear relationship to the practice of music; the papers were intended to help musicians in performance, to expand their repertory, to instruct them in authenticity. All papers were illustrated competently and at length by the speakers, and some actually consisted of five minutes of talk followed by fifteen of singing or playing.

Technically, the papers were presented to a "committee of experts" appointed by the Music Academy, a group of older musicians and scholars who sat on the stage, spoke softly to each other, sometimes preened themselves in formal finery, walked on and off the stage, and generally drew some of the audience's attention to themselves. In a sense, these sessions were an opportunity for the experts to show themselves in public and the papers a way of honoring them, in order to emphasize the importance of the intellectual component of the Carnatic system. Most important, the speakers were almost exclusively musicians who might perform later in the day, and most of those performing in the conference also read papers. The presiding officer, a famous singer, was present for all papers and commented upon each, after which members of the experts committee might also speak.

Musicology is usually considered a phenomenon of Western culture, and in some respects it may well be. The kind of musicology practiced in German, Austrian, later other European and eventually American schools is surely characteristic of Western culture, comes out of its traditions of scholarship and musicianship as well as the general values of Western society. Ethnomusicology, however one defines it—the study of "foreign" musics, the comparative study of muscial systems, the study of music in oral tradition (a particularly strange concept to notation-steeped Western musicians), the study of music within the context of anthropology—is surely something that could come about only in a Western or Western-derived context.

But of course, if one defines musicology simply as scholarship about music, other cultures have their own traditions of it. The scholars of China, India, and the Middle East have been trying to explain music for centuries and have produced important treatises. We know that African and American Indian cultures have always had individuals who knew a lot *about* music—they might be performers as well, but this knowledge was also a specialty. But in some societies there has developed a kind of musicology which, while indigenous, has also been thoroughly influenced by styles of Western thought about music. One can sometimes distinguish between an old tradition of musicology—a musicological practice which is carried on by individuals who have studied at Western institutions and become, in essence, Western ethnomusicologists; and then, as in Madras, developments in which these two traditions are combined.

Indian musical scholarship has had a great deal of contact with that of the West. The research of Western scholars on Indian music is known and respected—in earlier times, that of A.H. Fox Strangways and the Reverend Herbert Popley; more recently, that of Walter Kaufmann, Harold Powers, Alain Daniélou, and many others. The publications of these scholars are available in bookstores and libraries, and tend to be valued equally with those of Indian scholars such as V.N. Bhatkande and P. Sambamoorthy. Much of this Western work fits readily into Indian conceptions of music scholarship, since it involves such problems as the history of treatises and the nature and classification of ragas, with which Indians themselves are concerned. By contrast, the research of certain other Western scholars—those working, say, in anthropology of music, folk and tribal music, semiotics, experimental analytical procedures—is less well known or understood, and is less congruent with typical research of Indian academics. This fits older traditions of Western scholarship and at the same time supports the traditional values of the musical system as a whole. It may be significant that Indian musicologists, while influenced by their Western colleagues, have not frequently studied in the West.

Again, it is instructive to compare India with Iran. There, too, musical scholarship has grown under Western influence, but, as is the case with the music itself, traditional models have been much less powerful. Modern musical scholarship in Iran derives more from direct Western training than from the long tradition of the music theory usually calleds "Arabic" (but carried on as much by Persians as Arabs), whose realm was often remote from musical practice. Take, for example, the controversy about the size of intervals. In the 1930s, a theory using quarter-tones as the basis for measurement was promulgated by A.N. Vaziri, while Mehdi Barkechli, beginning before 1960, preferred a system using elements of just intonation and various sizes of minor seconds. Neither relates closely to nor seems even to care about the performance practice of contemporary musicians, nor does it propose to affect it. The problem is a traditional one, going back to medieval theory, but both solutions are Western-derived. In other respects as well, Iranian music scholarship follows the lead of Western ethnomusicology, concentrating for example on transcription of music into Western notation, whereas Indians for both research and performance use an indigenous system with some Western elements. The idea of making sound recordings of authentic performances of the *radif* has played a great role in Iran; in India, memorization is still more respected.

Western influence has also developed a new body of scholarship in some American Indian cultures. Of course, formal scholarship with its professors and its journals did not exist in traditional American Indian societies, and, indeed, only a few Indians have taken to modern American ethnomusicology. But scholarship in the sense of learning and the accumulation of knowledge was important in Indian societies, as singers might be judged in large part by their knowledge of repertory and ceremonialism. When Indian musical cultures were endangered by Western domination, the appearance of persons recognized for their special knowledge of the old tradition was perhaps inevitable. Among some Northern Plains cultures in the 1960s, some individuals became known as singers who performed for social dances, but in the view of the society they contrasted with others who might not be active singers but who knew older traditions, including songs, and served as tribal consultants and authorities. In some other Indian societies these individuals took to Western approaches to learning, using anthropological literature, visiting libraries, and establishing archives. They worked actively towards preservation of older materials, trying to reconcile what had been learned by white scholars with their own personal traditions.

The history of ethnomusicology is full of incidents illustrating interaction in the realm of scholarship. The desire on the part of Arabic musicians and scholars to use techniques of Western musical thought in standardizing their theoretical system led to the famous Cairo congress of 1932, in which European scholars participated. After 1950, African scholars trained in Western schools of ethnomusicology, such as J.H. Nketia, fomented revivals of traditional music in the framework of modern nation-states, making the heritages of once separate smaller peoples common to the entire nation. In looking at the influences of the Western on other musical cultures, it is important to include the effects of European scholarship where its approaches have been combined with those of the non-Western intellectual traditions.

## REFERENCES

*Journal of the Music Academy Madras,* vols. 1–52, 1930–81; and the programs of the conferences of the Music Academy, especially that of the 55th conference, 1981. **R. Rangaramanuja Ayyangar,** *Musings of a Musician* (Bombay: Wilco Publishing House, 1977). *Who's Who of Indian Musicians* (New Delhi: Sangeet Natak Akademi, 1968). *Recueil des Travaux du Congrès de Musique Arabe, Caire 1932* (Cairo, 1932). **Erich M. von Hornbostel,** "Zum Kongress für arabische Musik Kairo 1932," *Zeitschrift für vergleichende Musikwissenschaft* 1:16–17, 1933. **Fumio Koizumi and others,** *Musical Voices of Asia* (Tokyo: The Japan Foundation, 1980).

# 34
# Macuma
## by William Belzner

Entering for the first time the Evangelical mission settlement of Macuma, deep in Amazonian Ecuador, can be disconcerting for the unprepared outsider. From the air, the Shuar community of Macuma looks like any other village in the jungle, except that it lacks the ever-present central plaza. But it's different on the ground. Remembering that I was in the deepest, most isolated part of the Ecuadoran jungle, I was surprised at once when I was met at the docking area by a large flatbed truck, followed by a jeep, which in turn was followed by twenty or so Shuar people on foot, a few guitars slung over their shoulders.

I was there to discuss my proposed field work with leaders of the Shuar people, also called Jivaro (and once famed for head-shrinking), a large but isolated Indian society. Since I arrived in the middle of a large conference of

the local Shuar Association, then in session in the church, I was escorted into
the home of one of the missionaries (all of whom are North American). Waiting in the kitchen for the head of the house to appear, I was taken aback by
the palatial surroundings, complete with modern stove and oven, waffle-iron,
blender; but then a pleasant youngish man appeared and escorted me up-
stairs to the main living room. Noting that he had studied some ethnomusicology in college, he spoke of my project with interest and proceeded
to play some Rachmaninoff on his very fine stereo.

Such incongruities continued throughout the day as I was told of the new
hydroelectric plant just built, saw more lovely houses occupied by missionary
families, toured the well-equipped radio station and equally impressive
machine shop, and traversed the well-tended grounds surrounding the community. Quite different from the life-style of the Shuar. I was soon introduced
to the young vice-president of the Shuar Association who was to act as my
guide for the remainder of my stay, and almost at once heard of both the gen-
erosity of missionaries and the need to regain Shuar autonomy and Shuar
identity. Thus this intelligent and articulate man almost immediately provided
me with a key to understanding the fundamental contradictions inherent in
the Shuar musical system as I was to observe and record it in the coming
days. Many of the types of musical change and responses to outside intrusions noted by ethnomusicologists were represented here, from abandonment of traditional music to reduction of repertory and on to artificial preservation, diversification of contexts, exaggeration of indigenous musical traits,
and reintroduction of older materials in changed form. Each of these processes affected certain groups of Shuar at certain stages of their lives, each for different reasons. On the whole, the Shuar of Macuma are not highly Westernized, but they have learned to interact in and with the modern world. The
types of change in their music are reflections of the pressures they have experienced. They have learned to use bits and pieces of the modern world in
order to forge new identities in situations where traditional values cannot suf-
fice, and they often walk a fence between their two worlds. Yet to them, their
identities and their responses to the modern world remain Shuar.

Let me illustrate briefly the range of musical phenomena that characterize
the interaction of the two worlds. My first visit to the radio station archives
with my young friend allowed me the chance to question him intensively
about the different genres of Shuar music. We listened for several hours to a
variety of songs and pieces, but he identified only three genres: *nampet,*
social dance songs; *anent,* hunting (magic) songs; and *cantos de cultivar,*
women's gardening songs. This contrasted markedly with what was known of
traditional Shuar classes of music in other areas of the jungle, where the
genres include many other sorts, including songs sung during the head-
shrinking feast. My informant admitted that many of these had now disappeared, mainly because they violated Christian teachings or occurred during
ritual activity prohibited by the missionaries. He countered this bleak vision of

cultural loss by pointing to the massive archive of this "forbidden" music, all recorded in the past few years by the Education Committee of the Shuar Association on equipment and tapes provided for the purpose by the missionaries!

The director of the radio station, a native Ecuadoran missionary from Quito, later expressed to me his fervent hope that someone would use these tapes soon to teach some of the traditional Shuar songs in the local school. As a former teacher himself, he recognized the importance of establishing a dual identity among the schoolchildren; they should be good Ecuadorans *and* good Shuar. He saw music as one important means to this end and urged me to transcribe Shuar music into Western notation and teach it to the children.

I mentioned earlier some young men who always seemed to carry guitars around. I never saw them play, except to strum a chord now and then, but they carried the instruments around wherever they went. The Rachmaninoff-playing missionary one day explained to me that he had recently begun giving guitar lessons to a group of these young men, at their request. They were mission-educated youngsters and were quite taken with some of the popular national Ecuadoran styles such as *cumbia* and *san juanito*. All of them had visited the small urban center of Puyo, had heard the music and seen the dancing in local dance halls, and now wished to emulate some of this urbanity. Radios were common in Macuma, and this music could often be heard even on the local radio station. But to these young men, mastery of the national styles would indicate mastery of the patterns of behavior and identity as Ecuadorans, and symbolize their rejection of their "primitive" Shuar identity. None of these young men admitted the slightest knowledge of traditional Shuar music, despite the fact that their parents had sung or played some of this music to me in their presence.

One Sunday I was privileged to be invited to a church service in a nearby hamlet. Led by a young Shuar man assisted by the musical missionary, the service consisted of Bible readings (in Shuar), the bearing of testimony by two people, the singing of hymns accompanied by guitar. It was attended by a few young men and some twenty mostly elderly women. They sang in unison while the missionary, with his family, provided harmony—and later expressed disappointment that the Shuar had not also harmonized as he had spent much time trying to teach them. But in fact, these hymns violate every element of traditional Shuar music and were openly satirized by most of the Shuar I met, when missionaries were not present. Even so, they were played on the radio each night immediately before any message of religious content, and they were praised by older widows who were dependent on the mission for their sustenance.

The musical missionary seemed to recognize the lack of interest in these hymns and admitted that he too found them uninteresting. He hoped instead to develop a truly indigenous hymnal using Christian texts in the Shuar language.

Early one morning an older Shuar man knocked on my door and invited me to visit him, take pictures, and record him and his wife singing and performing indigenous dances. As he lived about an hour away, he set the meeting time for noon. I had seen him several times in the village, always nattily dressed in Western-style clothes, and had heard that he had only recently returned from working in the highlands. The missionaries claimed that he was not a "good" Shuar and warned me not to take what he said too seriously.

I arrived at his house at the appointed time, noting that he had a small traditional roundhouse next to a new (and seemingly abandoned) square woodplank house. When he heard me call, he rushed out of the roundhouse and on to the balcony of the other, and invited me up. Gruffly urging his wife to feed me the traditional manioc beer, he disappeared into one of the rooms of the newer house, to emerge minutes later dressed in the traditional Shuar men's skirt, his hair slicked back and covered by a bird feather crown, and carrying his shotgun, a flute, and a musical bow. He brought out a carved stool, sat down, placed the gun across his lap, gestured angrily at his wife to serve him his *chicha,* smiled, and urged me to take pictures. This done, he proceeded to pluck unrhythmically on the musical bow and later to play, poorly by Shuar standards, his two-holed flute. Thoroughly embarrassed, I thanked him and bade him goodbye.

# REFERENCES

**William Belzner,** "Music, Modernization, and Westernization Among the Macuma Shuar," in *Cultural Transformations and Ethnicity in Modern Ecuador,* edited by Norman Whitten (Urbana: University of Illinois Press, 1981), 731–48. **Michael J. Harner,** *The Jivaro: People of the Sacred Waterfalls* (Garden City, N.Y.: Natural History Press, 1972).

# 35
# Māhour

Beginning shortly after 1900 and going on to the 1930s, small issues of several hundred records of Persian classical music were produced by British, French, German, and American companies to be purchased largely by Iranians. Today, much of this music would be considered light classical or even popular in style, as the records contained performances devoted almost exclusively to composed genres, virtually omitting the characteristic improvisations since these could not be adequately performed in the available time and at any rate might appeal only to a small segment of the potential market. Out of this kind of record grew a substantial industry of popular 45-rpm discs, produced by a few large and many small businesses in Tehran that flourished in the 1960s and 1970s. While these short-playing records helped to establish genres mixing popular and classical elements, the history of recorded classical music took an independent turn in the 1960s. One important development was the production of a number of records made for scholarly and educational use, at first edited mostly by foreign scholars and made predominantly for European and American markets. Then around 1968, LP records began to appear that were produced in Iran for a clientele of music-lovers beginning to revive Persian classical music as fashionable listening. They were different from the early 78s, and also from the records of scholarly and educational interest, being comprised of long, full-blown performances rather than excerpts or short individual pieces.

Most prominent was a series of about thirty discs with labels in Persian and English, entitled *Master Performers of Persian Traditional Music.* Contrary to concert practice as it had developed by about 1970, these records do not include performances by small ensembles, but, following the more traditional practice used in private concerts at small social gatherings, they consist of solo performances accompanied at most by a drum. But contrary to older tradition, and following trends developed in the course of the twentieth century, the series includes only instrumental music, avoiding the vocal performance once central. It is difficult to know with what accuracy these records reflect the tastes and values of their time, and how widely they were distributed, but most prominent instrumentalists of 1970 are represented in this series.

About two-thirds of the records in *Master Performers . . .* manifest some Western influence. Intonation of three-quarter-tones is often adjusted to make these intervals closer to the semitone. Hints of Western harmony appear in isolated spots, particularly at endings of pieces and sections. But altogether, this is traditional Persian classical music, modernized a bit here and there to add some spice and a touch of the contemporary. A good proportion are performed on violin and piano. Other Western instruments are used, but their presence seems almost to have the purpose of showing that one can actually play Persian music on them. A drum solo record includes sound effects produced on the traditional goblet-shaped *zarb* and a tone-poem-like piece imitating a train.

In contrast to many records in this series, one in particular clearly contains materials that are specifically Western in total sound and structure and might therefore be labeled as Westernized. Performed by the santour virtuoso F. Payvar, it contains, like the others, full-blown performances of *dastgāhs,* each lasting from twenty-five to thirty minutes and, according to the tradition, consisting of several sections, composed and improvised. The performance at hand is of *Dastgāh-e Māhour,* the Persian mode most like the Western major, although it normally includes a descending lower seventh. There are also sections departing altogether from the principal scale, comprising, as Iranian theorists put it, modulations, or, if you will, sustained use of accidentals, while the fundamental tonic remains undisturbed. Now, confronted with the concept of a Westernized piece, we might expect prominent features from Western music to be evident throughout: for example, composed music performed by a large ensemble, in the major mode, and most characteristically of all, harmonized with triads and seventh chords. But while these are present in this performance, they appear only occasionally. The performance is comprised of the following sections, some of which could be regarded as essentially Western music adapted to a Persian musical environment, while others exhibit no special evidence of Western influence; and others again are intermediate.

We first hear an introductory metric piece. A traditional performance would begin with the stately, metric *pishdarāmad,* a genre that came into existence, so Iranian tradition has it, in order to be played by an ensemble in a Western-style public concert context. In this case, the piece, performed of course solo, is labeled as a *Tarāneh,* a popular song genre. It is in fact a definitely Western tune with Alpine flavor, related perhaps to "Trumpet Holiday" by Leroy Anderson, dominated by arpeggiated melodies with alternation of tonic and dominant, yet performed monophonically. The underlying harmony is obvious.

After the first strain, the music moves into secondary themes which include some modulations to other modes on the same tonic, just as the dastgāh of *Māhour* would, in the course of a traditional performance, introduce *gushehs* with different scalar configurations. Although the melodic material itself is now still in the Western style of the first strain, the arrangement of lines and sections here is very much like that of the most classical kind of *pishdarāmad,* a form that follows the *radif* from the initial *darāmad* through several *gushehs* and finally returns to the beginning. As expected, the first strain reappears at the end. In keeping with older practice, intervening secondary modes appear, based on scales derived from the *gushehs* of *Māhour*, but so does Western harmonic minor.

There now follows, very briefly, some much more strictly Persian material, the *darāmad* of the *dastgāh*, in the non-metric, improvisatory style of *āvāz*. But the endings of subdivisions have Western cadences, outlining tonic, dominant, and tonic triads respectively.

An extensive *chahār mezrāb* in traditional style is next. This type of piece is fast, metric, with a rhythmic ostinato, intended to show off the performer's virtuosity. For this one, the melodic material is not incompatible with Persian melodic practice, but seems definitely to have been conceived with a view to approximating Western music. The implication of two voices, produced through alternation between melody and bass in a monophonic texture, is a traditional feature of this type of music. But then there is the definitely Western tendency to alternate tonic and dominant. Occasionally, other chords indicating functional harmonic movement are also implied. Yet certain melodic turns characteristic of *Māhour* as well as modulations to the tonalities of others *gushehs* also appear.

We now hear a long *āvāz*, the non-metric improvisation once central in a performance, which in traditional style moves through several *gushehs*—Goshayesh, Delkash, Shekasteh, Khosravani, Feili—and returns to the main tonality of the *darāmad* of *Māhour*. This part of the performance gives little if any evidence of Western influence through its course of seventeen minutes, but at the very end, a melodic triad cadence takes you by surprise.

The performance ends with a quick, metric piece in six-eighth meter, its theme centering on the major triad. Occasionally, there are double stops at cadences, the last of them preceded by a Western cadential figure with implied parallel sixths. Traditionally at this point would come a *reng*, a kind of dance piece, but what we have is definitely more in the virtuosic style of the *chahār mezrāb*.

It is difficult to describe verbally the course of such a recording, and the reader may now have only a vague idea of the sound of this music. But it is clear that if we are to assess the amount and kinds of Western influence in an Iranian performance, we may find it in varying kinds and degrees at different points of the work. How much is there, and where is it? There is no doubt that in the hybridized musical culture of Tehran, this entire performance would have to be classed as Iranian music. One could well designate the first strain of the piece as definitely Western, for it would be absolutely acceptable as such to Western listeners. The rest of the performance would have to be regarded as in essence Iranian, if one viewed it in terms of its larger sections or movements. But if we assess the degree of "Westernness" in shorter subdivisions of the music, we can again find several that completely fit a Western musical context. Most of them appear at cadential points; and at least one, the theme of the final *reng,* at the beginning. It would seem that the performer is limiting the amount of Western material, but placing it strategically at points important to a listener oriented to Western music. And again, considering the interrelationship of the movements, the introductory piece is substantially Western, the final one almost so, while the interior *chahār mezrāb* and *āvāz* have fewer Western components. The unusually large amount of virtuosic material—rapid introductory and final pieces in addition to the *chahār mezrāb*—is perhaps also an imitation of a feature of Western music seen by Iranians as significant.

But if this performance features some central elements of Western music, the musician also makes sure that important practices of the Iranian tradition are preserved. The initial piece, with its modulations to distant *gushehs,* follows a definite classical practice; the *chahār mezrāb* has a similar structure. All of the major components of a full-blown performance are there, excepting only the optional *tasnif.* It is as if the performer were saying to his listeners, "You see, our Iranian system can be expanded to accommodate even pieces with totally Western content, and still remain intact." He does not use the technological tools of Western-directed modernization—a Western instrument, a largely composed structure, an ensemble, but plays alone, in the most traditional manner of performance. And yet he seems to espouse Western values, taking harmony, an essential musical feature of the West, and inserting it at strategic points. His photograph on the record jacket, showing him dressed in Western suit and tie with cuff links, seems also to symbolize the modern social context of this music, a music Western tourists were more likely to encounter in hotel lounges played by musicians in seventeenth-century costumes. It is as if Payvar were saying: "For you tourists, this may be exotic music, but for us it is the lifeblood of cultural expression; we want to make it part of our life in the modern world."

## REFERENCES

Ella Zonis, *Persian Classical Music: An Introduction* (Cambridge: Harvard University Press, 1973), 82–85, 137–48. **Erich M. von Hornbostel and Otto Abraham.** "Über die Harmonisierbarkeit exotischer Melodien," *Sammelbände der internationalen Musikgesellschaft* 7:138–41, 1905–6. **Record:** The performance discussed above appears on *Master Performers of Persian Traditional Music (Taknavazan musiqi-ye Iran),* ARTMS-11, side 1.

# 36
# Duck Dance
## by Victoria J. Lindsay-Levine

What happened to the music of those American Indian tribes which were divided in the course of U.S. history, each faction continuing to exist independently in its own location for more than a century? The Choctaw people, originally dwelling in the lower Mississippi basin, became separated during the nineteenth century into three bands whose descendants now reside primarily in Mississippi, Louisiana, and Oklahoma. Even before this separation, they had embraced Christianity along with various other Anglo-American institutions. Thus began the gradual disappearance of the contexts that had been used in the performance of native Choctaw music.

Only the social dance repertory has endured into the 1980s, and not without considerable change. A comparison of three versions of the Duck Dance illustrates. This dance has cognates among several Southeastern tribes, is performed by couples, and features maneuvers that imitate the movement of ducks. Its song is generally typical in composition of Choctaw social dances bearing animal names.

In Mississippi and Oklahoma the basic musical elements that comprise the Duck Dance song are virtually identical. They share the same kind of pentatonic scale, a strophic form that repeats the refrain several times before the verse returns, a characteristic grouping of four and five beats, an overall descending contour. The vocables that comprise the song text are alike in the two renditions, and both song leaders begin the dance with a unique repeated introductory phrase and conclude the number with a shout characteristic of Choctaw songs. The song leader often performs the Duck Dance as a solo, but the dancers have the option of singing along. But the Louisiana version of this song in most respects bears only minimal resemblance to the other two performances. It consists of two contrasting parts with varied repeats, and the melodies and vocables are entirely unlike those of the Oklahoma and Mississippi version.

We might be tempted to conclude that the Duck Dance has remained fairly stable in Mississippi and Oklahoma, and was modified in Louisiana. But in the realms of singing style, performance practice, and performance context, striking differences appear among all three versions. In Louisiana and Mississippi, vocal production is relatively relaxed and intonation seems basically compatible with that of the West. In contrast, the Oklahoma singers cultivate a relatively tense singing style that produces slight rhythmic pulsations and a wavering intonation unfamiliar to Western ears.

Song leaders in Mississippi accompany the Duck Dance with striking sticks; in Oklahoma it is a native-made double-headed drum exhibiting Southern Plains powwow influence in its construction, but not in its use. The Louisiana singer performs unaccompanied. At certain points in the dance, the Mississippi dancers and the one Louisiana singer recorded say "quack, quack," clearly an English word for duck sounds. The Oklahoma dancers use a duck call whistle at this point. Mississippi Choctaws perform the Duck Dance at generally Indian-oriented events such as the annual Choctaw Fair held in Philadelphia, Mississippi; in Oklahoma, the Choctaw–Chickasaw Heritage Committee performs at Indian-oriented events as well as for white audiences. But the Louisiana Choctaws no longer perform social dances, at least not in public.

The three versions of the Duck Dance exhibit both direct and indirect influences from Anglo-American culture. The loss of most Choctaw song genres, the various degrees of impoverishment within the surviving repertory of each region, are two of the most obvious and general effects. Of course, general Westernization includes the use by Choctaws of Western musical technology to document and preserve Choctaw native songs for dissemination to white as well as Choctaw listeners, and the belief that Choctaw songs must be recorded by some tangible, permanent device probably also derives from Western musical values.

The marked differences in style, performance practice, and performance context of the Duck Dance in each region illustrate more subtle responses to Anglo-American culture. The intonation and singing style practiced in Mississippi and Louisiana may perhaps be the products of long contact with Western musical values as learned from missionaries and educators. The Heritage Committee singers, on the other hand, evince a different reaction to white musical culture in their vividly antithetical style of vocal production and intonation, sharply distinguishing the Indian style from that of the whites. With regard to percussive accompaniment, the Mississippi Choctaws consider striking sticks as the more authentic choice, yet evidence suggests that the drum has historical precedence; it has been proposed that striking sticks came into general use among the Mississippi and Louisiana Choctaws in response to ante-bellum prohibitions against the use of native-made drums by non-whites. In this light, the Oklahoma Heritage Committee's use of a hand drum implies the dual objectives of restoring an earlier practice and heightening the distinction between Indian- and white-derived performance practice. If saying "quack, quack" is an obvious intrusion of white culture, the Oklahoma use of a mechanical duck call reflects a different sort of white influence, enhancing the entertainment value of the dance for a predominantly Anglo audience.

We return to the opening question with the following answer: what seems to have changed most in the native music of the three Choctaw bands is details of style, performance practice, and performance context, which insinuate transformed musical concepts and values. These changes, in turn, reflect divergent patterns of acculturation, which probably derive from three quite dissimilar socio-cultural environments and unequal opportunites for successful economic assimilation.

The Louisiana Choctaw, presumably a group small in number, were separated from the main tribe early in the nineteenth century; their ensuing history is relatively obscure, but they are known to have sung and danced with neighboring remnant tribes before discontinuing social dances early in this century. Perhaps early isolation, prolonged contact with other tribes, and substantial cultural (if not economic and social) assimilation account in general for the conspicuous alterations in the Louisiana repertory.

The Mississippi Choctaws have preserved a continual, but not unchanged, tradition of social dance performances. Theirs was historically a hostile environment, and they found themselves engulfed in racist attitudes, hemmed in by white culture but denied access to the social and economic incentives necessary to assimilation. Hence they retained native culture traits, including social dance performances, as a means of reaffirming Choctaw identity and group cohesion. It was a matter of cultural survival.

In contrast, the Oklahoma Choctaw long practiced intermarriage with whites and, following their removal west of the Mississippi River, plunged wholeheartedly into white culture. By the middle of the nineteenth century, they had established a public school system, businesses, and plantations co-owned by whites, and a government modeled after that of the U.S. When Oklahoma achieved statehood, the Choctaw consciously decided to abandon what remained of their indigenous culture; by the late 1930s, public social dancing had ceased, to be revived only in the last decade along with other native traditions. Yet the desire to revive the repertory seems to have been ever-present among some Oklahoma Choctaws. In spite of fairly successful economic assimilation, they retained a vital and distinct sense of Choctaw identity.

For each band, then, Choctaw social dances and songs convey discrete concepts of ethnicity. For the Louisiana Choctaws, the songs signify a cultural heritage that is remote, fragile, and in danger of slipping into oblivion; for the Mississippi Choctaws, the songs embody continuity with the past and cultural survival. But in Oklahoma, the Choctaw social dance traditions denotes a rediscovered pride in native American ancestry as well as a reinterpretation of what it means to be Choctaw.

# REFERENCES

**David I. Bushnell,** *The Choctaw of Bayou Lacomb, St. Tammany Parish, Louisiana,* Bulletin no. 48 of the Bureau of American Ethnology (Washington, 1909).   **H.B. Cushman,** *History of the Choctaw, Chickasaw, and Natchez Indians* (Stillwater, Okla.: Oklahoma State University Press, 1962).   **Frances Densmore,** *Choctaw Music,* Bulletin no. 136 of the Bureau of American Ethnology (Washington, 1943)   **James Howard,** *Choctaw Social Dances* (unpublished manuscript, in press, Stillwater, Okla.).

# 37
# Concertos

Three concertos. Are they Western music, or Chinese, Indian, Japanese? Hard to be sure. They raise questions about our conception of boundaries between musics. Most of our illustrations so far have presented music that is rather clearly non-Western in sound if not conception. Here we move to the other side of the broad band of demarcation which we have been trying to characterize.

The Chinese work is entitled "Liang San Po and Choj Yin Tai," but colloquially it is known as the "Butterfly Concerto." Composed in the 1950s for *erh-hu* (spiked fiddle) and orchestra, it has also been arranged for other media, including a kind of sonata-like violin and piano duet. Following one strand of the Chinese classical tradition, it is a piece of program music with a story reminiscent of "Romeo and Juliet" in which two lovers meet a tragic end and then turn into butterflies, living happily on in that form. The three movements are entitled "In Love," "Resisting Marriage," and "The Butterflies." In one recording the accompanying orchestra has seventeen performers of Western instruments and nine of traditional Chinese *p'ip'a* (short-neck lute), flutes, *cheng* (zither), *yang ch'in* (hammered dulcimer), and spike fiddles. The overall sound, however, is that of a Western orchestra concentrating on pentatonic melodic material with simple though competently wrought harmonic accompaniment. The soloist, a formidable virtuoso, makes his fiddle sound very much like a Western violin, and so it is rather unlike the sound of an *erh-hu* when it is playing traditional Chinese solo or chamber music.

Basically, to Westerners, the work sounds like Western music. It is dominated by functional harmony. The pentatonic themes are reminiscent of more traditional Chinese melodies, but they are also compatible with Western works that imitate (or pretend to imitate) Chinese melody. Within the context of Western composition of the mid-twentieth century, it would be extremely conservative and very likely labeled as light or semiclassical.

But in the Chinese view, it is Chinese music. The stylistic similarity to Western music is not an issue. In the socialist philosophy of music, it is in a style thought to be accessible to the whole Chinese people. The view of Chinese musicians and cultural authorities seems to be that if this music was composed by Chinese in China and is performed there, it is properly Chinese, the stylistic relationships to older Chinese music and to Western music notwithstanding.

In the period 1920–50, a good deal of music exhibiting the style of this concerto, especially a body of art song with Chinese-derived melodies accompanied by piano and in the spirit of German *lieder,* was composed explicitly for the purpose of creating a kind of Chinese music compatible with the modern world. And despite the anti-Western attitudes of the Chinese government at various times since 1950, many Western elements of style and social context, particularly using Soviet models, have been introduced. In China, the boundary between Western and native music appears to concern less the style than the identity of musicians and the venue of creation.

Another concerto is by the great sitar virtuoso Ravi Shankar, his second for sitar and orchestra, called *Raga-Mala* and composed in 1980. It was written mainly for Western musicians and audiences and thus might well be called Western music with Indian influences. But of course it is by the man who epitomizes the concept of Indian music in the West. At first hearing, its four movements surely sound like Western music, a massive symphony orchestra occasionally becoming the background for the very specifically Indian sounds of the *sitar.* Its name is that of a traditional Indian genre in which a musician, instead of playing or singing a piece in one raga (as is usual), modulates rapidly from one to several others, finally returning to the original. The concerto makes use of Indian ragas as well as various rhythmic and melodic devices from Indian music. But to Americans and Europeans, its overall sound is not really Indian.

And yet, when subjected to a kind of quantitative analysis, Ravi Shankar's concerto gives us more traits of Indian music than of Western. Take harmony and counterpoint, for example. There are no chords, only a bit of occasional catch-as-catch-can counterpoint; it is the great contrast of timbres and of range among the various instrument groups that gives the impression of Western orchestral texture. One has the feeling that there is a lot going on at one time, but this is a result more of the rhythmic complexity of Indian music transferred to the Western medium than of the kind of rhythmic complexity produced by a Charles Ives or Elliott Carter. Although the composer writes that this music is really more Indian than Western, as it is based on the raga principle, one Indian music critic considered the *Raga-Mala* concerto "a lot of noise," evidently relegating it to the Western sphere on the basis of its sound.

Ravi Shankar became acquainted with Western music early in his life, and learned the benefits and dangers of stylistic hybridization through the work of his brother, the famous dancer Uday Shankar. In this work, in his *sitar* performances, and in his several recordings with Yehudi Menuhin entitled "East Meets West," he shows the importance that he attaches to maintaining some kind of conceptual boundary between Indian and Western music, evidently regarding the world of music, as do Indian musicians at large, as comprised of a series of discrete musics definable by style. Quite a different approach from that of the Chinese, for it is not provenance but basic principles of structure that determine this music to be, at least for the composer, essentially Indian.

A third concerto. When I first heard it, I couldn't quite decide why it sounded so strange. Was it a familar Baroque concerto reproduced on a syn-

thesizer that didn't execute the ornaments properly? Played on a large harp
with something that made it sound a bit like a harpsichord? Or string orchestra
pizzicato curiously amplified? The radio announcement made it clear but also
raised questions. It was Vivaldi's familiar "The Seasons," played by the Koto
Ensemble of Tokyo, six traditional *kotos*. Clearly Vivaldi, but done in such a
way as not to be really acceptable to Vivaldi aficionados in Europe and
America, even perhaps Japan. Was it really just the ornamentation? But then,
it was an arrangement, hardly farther from authenticity than Stokowski's version of Bach organ fugues played by the Philadelphia Orchestra to popularize
Bach in the 1940s. Ah yes, but in our culture the symphony orchestra is a
symbol of quite a different sort from the *koto* in Japanese culture. But was this
in any way Japanese music?

Another record. The first time I heard this kind of music, it seemed the
strangest sound I had ever heard. Interminable notes by shrill, high winds;
endless glissandos; sudden dissonant chords as if made by sirens; occasional
plucked strings. All incredibly slow, yet the sudden drumbeats, accelerating
drum rolls, strokes of gongs gave it action. *Gagaku,* music of the Japanese
court orchestra, and it too had its *koto.* Of course there is much more music in
Japan, an incredible variety of sounds if you count folk music, the classical
solo and chamber music, kabuki and noh drama, popular music in Western
styles, Buddhist chant, Western classical music, the Western-oriented avant-
garde. There is almost everything we have in Europe and America, and also
almost everything they have had in Japan. It would seem that Japan has always had a lot of kinds of music. At least the Japanese think so, with their
conception of musics as separate categories, the importance of boundaries
between kabuki, noh, *gagaku,* even the separation of *gagaku* into music of
the "right" and "left," each category comprising music of different age or national origin. In a way, as we have already observed, Western music was simply added to the others already there, a large category, but simply another
category.

But the conception of Western music as a grand system encompassing
many interlocking and mutually influential types has also affected the recent
development of Japanese traditional music. There are at least a few works,
such as those of Shinichi Yuize, a *koto* virtuoso, in mixed style with such
Western elements as functional harmony and larger ensembles. And there is
the example of the *koto* itself, which plays *gagaku* and Vivaldi and has
become socially and musically a kind of national instrument capable of span-
ning the many styles and genres and movements. The *koto* ensemble somehow underscores the claim that Japan makes on all of the musics that can
now be heard in its cities and villages.

We are left with questions: Why does the *koto* find a place in Western
music in Japan, when there are no violins in *gagaku?* And how is it that a
Western symphony orchestra can play a work whose structure is fundamentally Indian, while one of the most popular instruments for Indian music is the

violin? And how can music regarded as a model for specifically Chinese composition, in a society determined to find its own way without association with extant cultural systems, sound so quintessentially Western? It must all have to do with the attitudes of these societies towards their own traditions, towards the international culture derived from Europe, towards culture change, and towards the role of music in society. But surely, the degree to which a style is claimed by a society as its own depends only in part on the extent of its compatibility with the culture's traditional sound.

# REFERENCES

**Kuo-Huang Han and Lindy Lee Mark,** "Evolution and Revolution in Chinese Music," in *Musics of Many Cultures,* edited by E. May (Berkeley: University of California Press, 1980), 10–31. **Ravi Shankar,** *My Music, My Life* (New York: Simon and Schuster, 1968). **Records:** Lian San Po and Chok Yin Tai (A Violin Concerto) on *The Chinese Violin,* Candide CE 31037. Ravi Shankar, *Raga-Mala—Garland of Ragas—Sitar Concerto No, 2,* EMI Angel DS-37935, 1982. *Koto Vivaldi: Antonio Vivaldi, The Four Seasons, Angel Records* S-37450. See notes on liners of these three records as well. *The Japanese Koto,* Cook 1132, 1955.

# REGULARITIES

# 38
# Correspondences?

The illustrations have shown a world of great musical diversity. In linking the cases described here to the last thoughts of the opening section ("Approaches"), the difficulty of fitting a given piece of music, a person, event, or institution into any single one of the proposed response categories immediately becomes obvious. Most can be analyzed as partaking of two or several processes, showing a mixture of motivations, choices, directions. Even though restricted by a body of descriptive literature as yet small (and by the limits of my field experience), the illustrations nevertheless provide a bewildering variety.

But if the next task is to match up cases and categories, and then to identify general characteristics of the results of musical interaction—in the whole world and in its several major culture areas—a summary of what it is that has been illustrated may be in order. Several of the vignettes deal with institutions and events. "Powwow" shows how an institution changed in social context, personnel, and to some extent musical style, but still maintained its identity. "Concerts" illustrates the way in which a traditional music repertory is kept intact in the face of almost complete change of its performance context to Western-style concert life. "Music School" explores Western teaching methods, institutions, and curricula, introduced and used for the sake of changing but also saving traditional art music repertories in Asia. "Conferences" concerns the imposition of Western-style conceptualizations, via scholarship and a compatible institution, into an Asian musical culture.

Although many of the illustrations involve conceptual and behavioral aspects of music, some concern primarily matters of sound and style. The tendency to establish large ensembles of traditional instruments, to play modernized versions of the old music with the exterior trappings of Western orchestras and bands, is the subject of "Orchestras." The use of Western functional harmony, to varying degrees and in ways more or less appropriate to standard Western music, is illustrated in "Harmony." "Notes" discusses the use of notation systems, some derived from the modern Western one and some indigenous, but even more, the concept of notation in a modern musical society, as applied to several Asian cultures. "Māhour" examines a long, multi-sectional performance to determine the points at which elements of the Western musical style are introduced in order to symbolize the interface of tradition and modernity. And a similar purpose is the comparison of three "Concertos" which, in contrast to the work discussed in "Māhour," are clearly dominated by Western style elements though regarded in their own cultures as related to the tradition to varying degrees.

149

There might have been no end to the number of illustrations that could have been given in the realm of instruments. "Violins" shows one major instrument to have been widely adopted but changed in shape and construction in one culture, introduced physically intact in another though adjusted in its playing technique to conform to traditional sound ideals, and used in a third culture with the characteristic Western violin sound which then itself became a component of the non-Western tradition. "Pianos" notes that these instruments were also brought to many parts of the world as major symbols of Western music and Westernization. In some societies they became associated with traditional instruments which then assumed the symbolic significance that the piano holds in Europe and the Americas. "Emblems" discusses national instruments, a concept related to the Western idea of nation-states. Some instruments assumed this essentially Western function, as did some musical styles, as suggested in "National Music." "Victrolas" indicates the importance of the technology of recording in producing changes in non-Western music that might not have brought about a Western sound, but did produce Western-like behavior of the musical tradition, along with important changes of transmission patterns in the aural tradition.

The thrust of this essay is to view musical systems and cultures as if they had lives of their own and were capable of acts and responses, but of course, these are really the result of decisions by individuals who may differ greatly despite sharing a culture. A group of the illustrations describes some of these individuals and their unique roles in the interface of Western and non-Western. "Americans" compares two singers of Plains Indian music and their attitudes towards maintaining their traditions. For one it is an emblem of modern Indian culture, and for the other, a relic to be treasured; and yet their musical styles are almost identical. "Innovators" describes various performers in one Asian art music tradition, indicating the attitude towards innovation and the musical results, and saying something about the evaluation of each by his peers. "A Champion" gives a short biography of a famous Iranian modernizer of music who worked hard but with varying success to bring changes of all sorts in his native tradition and its social contexts, specifically, so he said, in order to keep it alive. "Visitors" deals with the role of European and American students in non-Western societies and suggests that their eagerness to learn the musics as performers has actually effected adaptations and changes in attitude on the part of their teachers. In "Treasures" we see that some nations have dealt with the coming of Western music by establishing individuals as "national treasures" to maintain the older tradition—theoretically, at least, unchanged and unaffected. And "Ethnomusicologists" suggests that Western scholars too have played a substantial role in helping non-Western societies to keep their traditions, but have also affected the direction in which the tradition moves.

Of course most of these illustrations come from cities, but in some instances, the facts of urban life seem to be especially potent factors. "Streets" looks at a few institutions that function to draw together the many musics coming from a heterogeneous population. "Two Cities" compares the ways in which traditional classical music of a rather similar style has fared in two somewhat analogous instances. In one city, the music was kept alive through the sacrifice, as it were, of traditional religious and social institutions, and in the other, it saved itself by changing the style in a social context that remained relatively unchanged. "'Pop'" deals with the establishment, throughout the world's cities, of a Western-derived popular music dependent for dissemination on Western technology, with functions and uses very much like those of popular music in the West, but nevertheless maintaining some aspects of the older musical traditions. "Juju" moves to a more specific illustration in a West African city and is concerned with a music intermediate between Westernized and tradition-oriented popular styles. "Migrants" discusses three instances of traditional music as practiced by non-Western people who have migrated to cities from the countryside where they gained—in what was once their own country—the status of minorities.

If the scenes so far have been largely secular, the relationship of music for Christian worship to traditional music and the interaction of Christianity with older religious systems provide another focus of illustration. "Old-Time Religion" indicates the role of music in nativistic movements, comparing one that opposed accommodation with Western cultures to a later one that supported it. "Indigenizers" and "New-Time Religion" both deal with the use, on the part of church musicians in non-Western societies, of indigenous styles and repertories, and they illustrate several ways in which Western musical style elements are introduced.

The cases given here largely involve synchronic views of societies as they are caught in moments of change; but a few of them, at least by implication, also span longer periods and exhibit the multiplicity of directions in which our musical culture may move. "Duck Dance" explores three versions of a ceremony among three bands of an American Indian tribe that have been isolated from each other for a century, and suggests reasons for their varying degrees of accommodation with Western practices. "National Music" shows the competition between a Western-derived popular music and a classical tradition for a status resulting from Western conceptions of culture and politics, the principal musical expression or "Great Tradition" of a multi-cultural nation-state. In "Opinions," we see that the views of Western music held in various societies differ, and note that they determine in part the responses made by the traditional music system. "Macuma" shows the large variety of attitudes held towards traditional and Western music in a small South American Indian community. "Compatibles," finally, looks once more at the familiar concept of syncretism, giving some examples which indicate that stylistic compatibility is not the only factor dictating its presence or absence.

But now, how do these illustrations fit into the network of response categories? Let's look at a few from our list. The Australian aboriginal people who were lamenting the loss of their traditions in "Migrants" are examples of the category of "virtual abandonment." But usually it is more complicated. By my definitions violins as used in Iran ("Violins") were clearly agents of Westernization, and in South India, of modernization. But the music produced on each instrument would include several other response categories—exaggeration, co-existence of style elements, transfer of discrete style elements, several of the styles in Shiloah and Cohen's continuum. The piano in Iran ("Pianos") is also an instrument of Westernization, but its music involves the transfer of discrete musical traits from Western music to the Iranian tradition, and its repertory would have to be regarded as "ethnic fine" or perhaps "pseudoethnic" music in the taxonomy of Shiloah and Cohen (S & C). Ali Naqi Vaziri, the Iranian ("Champion"), himself stated his aim as being modernization, much as it has been defined here, but looking at it in greater detail we see that he did so by Westernizing the musical style, effecting the transfer of discrete traits from Western music to Iran, and modernizing social contexts of music such as teaching institutions.

The national instruments ("Emblems")—*valiha* in the Malagasy Republic, marimba in Guatemala—illustrate diversification of musical contexts into several styles, but again, the transfer of discrete musical traits. Almost by definition—they are "national" because of their stylistic diversity—their repertories illustrate a number of the musical types in the S & C continuum. A similar configuration of results is implied in the conceptually related idea of a "National Music." Attitudes toward Western music in Iran ("Opinions") signify Westernization, the desire of Iranians (then) to be included in the Western cultural system; and, in India, modernization, the desire to modify their musical culture (by accepting a sister-system into their purview) without abandoning its essentials.

"Powwow" presents a North American Indian ceremony in successive stages and with increased intensity of modernization. In S & C's terms, the music itself is "traditional" in recent performances of the Sun Dance, becomes "neo-traditional" in the North American Indian Days powwow, and perhaps "pseudoethnic" in its Michigan manifestation. In Michigan, as well, the high, tense, pulsating vocal sound intended to jar the ears of the white audience was a case of "exaggeration," and the use of this music in a context otherwise dominated by country-and-western could be termed "pluralistic coexistence." At the same time, the Indians who came to Michigan may well have virtually abandoned traditional Indian music, while those in Montana used some songs in the manner of nativistic revival. In any event, the standardization of forms, the small number of competent singers, and the abandonment of verbal texts in Indian languages signals reduction of the musical system.

In "Harmony," we see something of a spectrum, with varying degrees and uses of the functional harmony of Western music found not only in different cultures but also within one culture. Generally speaking, the pieces that have only small bits of harmony can be interpreted as illustrating modernization, and those with more, Westernization. But there are interesting examples of syncretism, using compatible traits: the drone under the parallel thirds of India; the movement from major to minor, based on pentatonic melodies, in the Andes; the single chord following the triadic scales in the Navajo song. Further, the use of harmony in world music is often an example of the transfer of a discrete musical trait.

"Americans" shows the confluence of several of the given responses in the lives of individuals. The Arapaho singer tried to practice isolated preservation of music, and in his singing of Peyote songs, he presented material resulting from nativistic revival with a combination of stylistic traits illustrating the tendency to consolidate material from a variety of non-Western cultures. The Blackfoot singer changed his attitude several times in his life, from virtual abandonment of his native music to the singing of a repertory with reduced traditional features and impoverishment of variety, but performed in an exaggerated singing style. Finally, he also participated in attempts to preserve, in museumized fashion, some of the oldest material.

The change of social context of a musical tradition is the most significant thing to note in "Migrants." The Australian response to the coming of Western music, we have noted, was virtual abandonment of the tradition, followed by desire for preservation of some kind. The American Indians in Chicago, with their rich pan-Indian culture, might give us singing in an exaggerated performance style, of songs combining style elements (consolidation) and involving transfer of discrete musical traits, and a diversification of social contexts for music once much more restricted. At urban Indian events, one may hear samples of humorous juxtaposition of traditional and "white" music. In partially similar circumstances, the people of suburban Johannesburg show diversification as well—music of one native people shared by several culture units—and also the syncretic results of stylistic compatibility and the transfer of discrete musical traits from Western to modernized African music.

There are also illustrations that show certain instances of musical life to be capable of analysis in terms of a single overriding response. Vaziri, in Iran, really applied all of his energies to modernization, changing concert life, giving instruments to women, altering instruments, notating, founding ensembles, but all for the purpose of keeping a discernibly Iranian musical tradition in existence. The individuals described as "national treasures" ("Treasures") are people whose role has become clearly the artificial preservation of tradition—artificial not in terms of their devotion to the art, but in terms of the role they play in the cultural life of their nations. Inquiries from outside the culture ("Ethnomusicologists"), whatever their purpose, tend to involve preservation (conserved or museumized, depending on the conditions) and also the compartmentalization of components of musical repertories.

But as said before, usually the situation is less one-sided. In "Macuma" the author encountered, within a short space of time, virtual abandonment, use of traditions as varying kinds of symbols, but most, a variety of approaches to conservation or museumizing; and also there is transfer of traits and stylistic coexistence. "Duck Dance" shows one ritual of Choctaw tradition to have survived by means of conservation in Mississippi, adaptation of discrete transferred musical traits in Louisiana, and nativistic revival in Oklahoma. "Juju" gives us a syncretic repertory resulting from stylistic mixes and consolidation which became in a way official ("National Music"). It also signals reintroduction of materials previously abandoned or de-emphasized, as does "Indigenizers," which shows us the difference between compatible musics ("Compatibles") and other sets of traits in terms of the combination of style traits and the tug-of-war between Westernization and modernization. "Old-Time Religion" describes nativistic revivals by means of stylistic consolidation and a certain kind of museumization.

The reader can easily supply further analysis of this sort. There is unexpected wealth and variety in music and musical life resulting from the interaction of musics and societies, and while sets of responses such as those proposed by Shiloah and Cohen, Kartomi, and myself may help in organizing them, they do not really do justice to the complexity of the situation, the interaction of musical elements, ideas, concepts, institutions, instruments, performers, and the rest. The illustrations give us a sense of a many-splendoured twentieth century, showing the inventiveness and genius of mankind as artist under a variety of pressures. And of course there is far more that might have been illustrated from many parts of the world: film, radio, television; the role of various modern political movements; instrument technology; effects on intonation; singing style . . . and for that matter, the English-uniformed wedding bands in Benares; the music of West African composers trained in England and France; the Russian-like harmony of supposedly indigenous songs among the Tlingit of Alaska; and much more. We have only scratched the surface.

# REFERENCES

**Margaret J. Kartomi,** "The Processes and Results of Musical Culture Contact: A Discussion of Terminology and Concepts," *EM* 25:227–50, 1981. **Amnon Shiloah and Erik Cohen,** "The Dynamics of Change in Jewish Oriental Ethnic Music in Israel," *EM* 27:227–52, 1983. **Bruno Nettl,** "Some Aspects of the History of World Music in the Twentieth Century...," *EM* 22:123–36, 1978.

# 39
# Regions

Examination of individual culture units, tribes, small nations, and cities, with the intent of proposing a scheme of responses to Western music, would surely show that a unique configuration operates in each instance. But if there is a group of factors that determine musical results, factors such as length of contact, relative complexity and similarity of culture and music, attitude of a society towards change and musical diversity, and the general valuation of music, some regularity within each culture region would surely be expected. Let's look at a sampling.

Sub-Saharan African societies seem to be characterized by the development of popular musical styles that bear close resemblance to those that were created in North America and, even more, in the Caribbean. It is partly a matter of the compatibility that favors syncretism. The various kinds of popular music—highlife, Congo jazz, *juju,* though differing in detail, all have elements in common: simplified Western harmony, percussion ensembles, emphasis on brass instruments, elements of improvisation, complex and Latin-sounding rhythms. Their counterparts in the Americas—jazz in general, but also various more specifically Afro-American derived genres such as R & B, reggae, Ska, rock-steady, Mexican *tropical,* and many more, have significant similarities. Here is an area in which cross-fertilization has worked to produce integrated, homogeneous—if regionally distinct—repertories. It is all a result of the export of African music to the Americas, its contact with Northern and Southern European styles, the development of syncretic forms in the New World, and their reintroduction to Africa by way of American and Caribbean bands and a few repatriates from slavery. The establishment of a large body of Protestant hymnody and of Catholic church music in partially African but largely Western styles follows similar principles. Western instruments have not been introduced to a very large extent, and the fundamental principles of African sound—antiphony, percussiveness, heterogeneity in timbre, variation—have remained the same.

Foreign influences other than Western have also played a role, particularly from the Middle East in the Islamic parts of the continent, and from India in what was formerly British-occupied East Africa. While there is a variety of responses to Western music, the introduction of aspects of Western musical life and sound do not seem to have disturbed fundamentally the maintenance of a distinctively African kind of musical culture.

In the Middle East the situation is different, with simultaneous or alternating experience of modernization and Westernization. The musical system, as it were, is trying to resolve the conflict. Potentials for syncretism seem unlikely, as the traditional musical styles and even the conception of music depend on aspects of culture quite different from those of the West. Traditional styles have emphasized soloistic improvisation and richly ornamented vocal performance, with the characteristic sounds and uses of the voice remote from those in the West. The traditional conception of music has permitted neither a concert culture nor a complex system of religious music. Even so, compatibilities are not totally absent, as for example a tradition of musical scholarship, separation of art and folk musics, patronage by royalty and aristocracy.

In general, the societies in the Middle East have responded to Western music in the following pattern. Significant parts of the society have adopted Western music outright; there are many composers and performers who simply participate in the European system of art and popular music, and do so effectively. Beyond this, however, the traditional musical system shows evidence of both modernization and Westernization. The social contexts of music, concepts and behavior patterns, while bending, have not broken. There are concerts but traditional performances in home or garden continue. The conception of music as in essence aurally conceived and vocal, with modal units as the bases of musical thought, has been modified by increased prestige of the composer and instrumentalist, by the tendency to use notation instead of memorizing and improvising, growing interest in interval measurement and lessening emphasis on motifs as central features of modes. But there has been no wholesale shift to a Western approach to music. Musicianship is no longer quite the downtrodden profession of the past, but it is hardly prestigious. The traditional approaches seem to have persisted more as one moves east from North Africa—more in Iran and Afghanistan than in Egypt and Turkey; and more in Shi'ite than in Sunni areas. The introduction of Western elements has been particularly notable in the musical sound; and it is again Western harmony, performance by large ensembles, and emphasis on technique that are most significant. Used as a symbol, even where it appears to have no proper musical function, harmony illustrates the desire of Middle Eastern musicians to associate themselves with the Western cultural system.

The issue of modernization versus Westernization is complicated by the need to determine the relative centrality of various components of the music system. In several illustrations, we have called the typical events in Tehran Westernization but the classification bears closer scrutiny. It is true that in the typical musicologist's understanding, it is the musical sound that is inevitably central, and if concept and behavior are altered to maintain that sound, this is modernization (or something of that sort), while the opposite—sacrificing the essence of this stylistic center—would quintessentially be Westernization. And yet, if a society insists on maintaining the stability of certain musical ideas and behavior patterns while permitting the sound to change, one might also argue that it had judged the sound to be dispensable and thus non-central. Such an argument could well be made for a society in which music is traditionally not

highly valued, and narrowly defined, and perhaps it fits the Middle Eastern situation.

Several of our illustrations have concentrated on comparison of the Middle East, and particularly of Iran, with India—particularly South India. There are important relationships between the two culture areas, among them the role of Islam, a characteristic political organization in the older tradition, economic structure, a complex of social and ethical values. Even more important for us are structural similarities of the musical systems. Both emphasize a contrast between Great and Little Traditions as described by Milton Singer, that is, unity of a classical system and diversity of folk and tribal traditions. In both areas there are important improvisatory genres in the classical music, an emphasis on lutes, monophonic texture, systems of melodic and rhythmic modes, and contrast between metric and non-metric. In a world context the South and West Asian musics belong to the same general musical area. It is interesting therefore that their responses to the coming of Western music have been substantially contrastive.

Speaking very broadly, we may say that the Middle East has accepted Western music itself in larger quantity and more readily than has India. The establishments of Western music such as concerts, symphony orchestras, opera, and chamber music societies are better developed, more numerous, of higher quality. But the traditional classical musics have been maintained differently; in the Middle East, with difficulty and through a revival involving a small number of musicians; in India, more intensively but in altered social contexts. In the Middle East, musical styles adapted Western elements more than in India. The different treatments of the violin in the two areas are indicative. Rural musical practices have been relatively unaffected by Western music in both areas; but in the Middle East, knowledge of outside musical forces and the tendency to develop interethnic practices seem somewhat more developed. In the realm of urban popular music, both areas maintain stylistically mixed repertories. Although it is admittedly difficult to apply any kind of measure, Indian film music has a closer relationship to Indian classical traditions than is the case, respectively, in Middle Eastern night-club and entertainment music. All in all, if the Middle Eastern response has tended towards Westernization of the whole system, the Indian one has been far more a matter of modernization.

Of the larger culture areas of the world, South Asia may be the one coming closest to practicing virtual rejection of the impinging music; and perhaps, along with Java and Bali, it comes closest to having a full-blown musical system in a modern urban context built almost entirely on a repertory of non-Western sound. But it is also noteworthy that Indian music has adapted and absorbed Western elements to a degree of total incorporation. Few Indians consider or even realize that violin and harmonium came from Europe, and some furiously deny it. Classical Indian musicians seem to perceive and to articulate carefully the distinction between central and peripheral aspects of the musical system. The violin, as an instrument, is peripheral in a vocally oriented culture, and its adaptation is not a disturbance. The sound of Western violin playing, however, is far more central to Western music, and thus its introduction would be more disturbing to the central features of Indian musical sound, vocal tone color and ornamentation. And so, those things that are central to the sound of Western music—harmony, lengthy pieces, ensembles with variety of tone colors, modulation, far-flung experimentation, primacy of instrumental music—have hardly intruded. The less central—instruments, the concept of music as entertainment on any occasion, without event-specific restrictions on performance, Western-style middle-class concert audiences and behavior—have in recent times become central also to Indian musical life. Much of this is the opposite of the Middle Eastern experience.

When one searches for reasons, the most obvious is the different value placed on music in the two societies. In the Middle East, the ambivalent view of music prompted an attempt at emancipation, as it were, by removing music from the traditional culture through style change in a Western direction in Hindu India, a culture in which Muslim musicians, interestingly, have played a major role, music has all along been a respected and essential part of the religious and social systems. The issue was not to remove it but to find ways of helping it to survive.

Another interpretation of the differences between the two areas involves the place of music in the cultural system. In the Middle East, those things that were accepted as specifically musical (not counting, of course, such phenomena as Qur'an-reading and prayer, structurally like music but not so classified) were not regarded as central. In earlier times, they were often relegated to persons who were themselves peripheral to the culture (Jews, Christians, ethnic Muslim minorities such as Kurds), and published inventories of the components of the culture in the 1960s by Middle Easterners would rarely include music along with religion, literature, social and political values. In preserving the culture holistically, it might not be necessary to include music, which thus could be Westernized. In India, the higher status of music placed it closer to the central values of culture. Performances of music are explicitly said to be essential in rites and ceremonies, they are considered important parts of everyday life, and it is probably fair to say that most Indians would not feel that they properly possessed their culture if they did not have its music. These comparisons apply most to urban populations in the areas discussed, but the conclusions are not contradicted by what is known about smaller towns and villages.

Characterization of the responses to Western music in the nations of the Far East would have to be made in terms radically different from those proposed for South and West Asia. In Japan and Korea, Western music has become so important a factor that musically these nations might well be regarded, at least in their urban centers, as members of the Western cultural system. Their contributions to Western musical culture since around 1960 match those of European and North American nations and their popular musics partake fully of the Western stylistic spectrum. Traditional music exists, but largely in preserved and museumized forms, and in some cases it is being reintroduced in processes like nativistic revivals—as in the introduction of Korean music through festivals, and in Japanese folk song preservation societies. The proportion of musical energy devoted to Western music is great, and to traditional music rather small, except in rural areas, compared with the Middle East, to say nothing of India. In China—the People's Republic of China, Taiwan, Hong Kong—Chinese traditional music was for a long time neglected and virtually abandoned. It was replaced by Western forms, Russian-derived in the People's Republic, Western European and American elsewhere. It goes without saying that Marxist–Leninist–Maoist theories about the role of the arts in socialist societies were major factors in determining the fate of Chinese traditional music in the twentieth century.

The total musical culture—concept, behavior, sound—of the Far East having become substantially Western, we could call this a case of Westernization. The traditional music has been preserved in a way similar to that used for preservation of folk musics in Western nations, through special institutions, designation of individuals as carriers of traditions, departments of traditional music in conservatories teaching a diversity of styles, all with an aura of exoticism and rediscovery.

Oceania and Southeast Asia exhibit a great diversity of intercultural musical relationships. The political and military experiences of the nations of Indochina make study of our subject difficult, but what is known of musical life indicates a situation not greatly different from the rest of the Far East. Indonesia has maintained a strong tradition built around certain principles widely held in several of its traditions—the chime orchestra and the kinds of relationships among instruments in an ensemble that characterize its most complex form, the gamelan; and it has done so while absorbing intrusions from such sources as Hinduism and Arabic-derived Islamic culture. Older traditions have been strongly maintained and expanded, in keeping with the needs of modern nationalism. As in India, the sound has changed less than contexts and ideas, which have become rather Westernized. Australia and the islands of Polynesia and Micronesia, with simpler musical styles and cultures more readily swept away by European values and Christianity, have exhibited a different reaction, dependent, interestingly, on the fundamental character of the musical style. The areas in which polyphony is traditional— parts of Micronesia and Polynesia—have developed Christian hymnody combining Western harmony with elements of the older harmonic tradition. In Australia, one finds virtual abandonment of the tradition in some cultures, conservation and museumization in others.

The North American Indian cultures, however small their populations, are particularly interesting in this discussion because of the extent to which their music has been studied and recorded. Their stylistic relationship to Western music is such that syncretic materials could not easily be developed and their use of music as a way of drawing cultural boundaries supported this attitude. On the other hand, Western music has had a multitude of indirect effects, particularly on ideas about music. While the tendency of North American Indians has been to Westernize their cultures, that is, to make them part of the general American social system—some Indian groups certainly notwithstanding—music in particular has been used as a shield to contradict this trend, as a symbol of traditional cultural identity. Thus it was often treated with the techniques and approaches of a culture wishing to modernize. Of course, these processes characterize music and its functions in many cultures, but perhaps nowhere so clearly as among North American Indian tribes. But if this generalization is defensible, our illustrations of Choctaw culture and of Peyote and Ghost Dance music also show considerable differences among North American Indian peoples in their attitudes towards cultural traditions, music, change, and white Americans.

In Latin America, the experience of many isolated tribal groups may be comparable to that of North Americans. But the amount of stylistic mix is greater in groups such as the Shuar of Ecuador. Surely the tendency in North America to place Indian peoples on reservations in isolated locations, while Latin American Indians were absorbed more easily into the general population, is responsible in part for the greater tendency among the latter to develop syncretic forms in culture, religion, music. Thus, the adoption and adaptation of the violin among the Shuar, and its use for a type of music previously produced only on traditional instruments, is quite different from the acceptance of the violin among the Northwest Coast Indians for the purpose of playing country-and-western music with Indian subject matter, or on the other hand, the development of the "Apache fiddle" from a confluence of musical bow and Western violin. Elsewhere in Latin American, the combination of Hispanic, Indian, and in many places also African cultures has fused a series of musical repertories with a basically Western character, with the central characteristics of European music, but with regionally distinct sounds.

With its multitude of divisions and regions, as an area whose aboriginal music has for centuries been affected by Western music, Latin America has been held up as an example of the most successful sort of Westernization, since the native tradition was usually incorporated into the Western musical system and resulted in styles with strongly regional character. But an alternate analysis may show otherwise. The largely non-Western population of the area long ago adopted Western musical principles as central and went on to build on these a regional non-Western culture; the question of responses in the twentieth century might therefore have to be directed towards the few remnants of isolated tribal music. Or, interaction between Latin American Western music and a kind of mainstream of the West, perhaps coming from North America, ought to be compared to the effect of Western avant-garde music on modern, Western-oriented Japanese composers. The question of intercultural musical relationships has highly diverse ramifications; the Western–non-Western paradigm, while helpful for certain kinds of study, is tenuous and often breaks down. Latin American may be its weakest link.

Given the tentative nature of our classifications and the internal diversity of each society, the major culture areas of the world do at least tentatively stand up, in degree and direction of response to Western music, to broadly general characterization.

# REFERENCES

**John Storm Roberts,** *Black Music in Two Worlds* (New York: Praeger, 1972); and *The Latin Tinge* (New York: Oxford University Press, 1979). **Daniel M. Neuman,** *The Life of Music in North India* (Detroit, Mich.: Wayne State University Press, 1980). **Bruno Nettl,** ed., *Eight Urban Musical Cultures* (Urbana: University of Illinois Press, 1978). **J.H. Kwabena Nketia,** *The Music of Africa* (New York: Norton, 1974). **William P. Malm,** *Music Cultures of the Pacific, the Near East, and Asia,* 2nd ed. (Englewood Cliffs, N·J.: Prentice-Hall, 1977); and *Japanese Music and Musical Instruments* (Tokyo and Rutland, Vt.: C.E. Tuttle, 1959). **Ronald Riddle,** *Flying Dragons, Flowing Streams: Music in the Life of San Francisco's Chinese* (Westport, Conn.: Greenwood Press, 1983). National Academy of Arts, *Survey of Korean Arts: Traditional Music* (Seoul, 1973). **Bang-Song Song,** *Source Readings in Korean Music* (Seoul: Korean National Commission for Unesco, 1980). **Eta Harich-Schneider,** *A History of Japanese Music* (London: Oxford University Press, 1973). **Dieter Christensen and Gerd Koch,** *Die Musik der Ellice-Inseln* (Berlin: Museum für Völkerkunde, 1964). **Gerard Béhague,** *Music in Latin America: An Introduction* (Englewood Cliffs, N.J.: Prentice-Hall, 1979); and "Latin American Folk Music," chapter 9 in Bruno Nettl, *Folk and Traditional Music of the Western Continents,* 2nd ed. (Englewood-Cliffs, N.J.: Prentice-Hall, 1973). **Elizabeth May,** ed. *Musics of Many Cultures* (Berkeley: University of California Press, 1980), especially chapter 9 on Australia. **David P. McAllester,** "An Apache Fiddle," *Ethnomusicology Newsletter,* no. 8 (September 1956), 1–5. **William Belzner,** "Music, Modernization, and Westernization Among the Macuma Shuar," in *Cultural Transformations and Ethnicity in Modern Ecuador,* edited by Norman Whitten (Urbana: University of Illinois Press, 1981). **Bruno Nettl,** "Some Influences of Western Civilization on North American Indian Music," in *New Voices in American Studies,* edited by Ray B. Browne (Lafayette, Ind.: Purdue University Press, 1966), 129–37. **Theodore C. Levin,** "Music in Modern Uzbekistan: The Convergence of Marxist Aesthetic and Central Asian Tradition," *Asian Music* 12(1):149–58, 1979.

# 40
# Tendencies

Having celebrated diversity, we return to the assertion that the coming of Western musical culture to the rest of the world may be viewed as a single complex event and now ask whether there are universally applicable regularities in the responses. What has happened most frequently, and what generally valid trends can be identified?

First and most obviously, Western music in some form was taken up by each society; and along with this, traditional music was maintained, never in its complete form and cultural context, but almost always to some degree. Abandonment was at most "virtual" but perhaps never absolute. Of course the traditional music was always substantially weakened or reduced in one way or another. In the twentieth century, on the other hand, a large proportion of the world's societies undertook some kind of revival of the native tradition. The revivals took many forms. In some instances, they have amounted to nothing more than ethnomusicological, historical, or archeological study. There might have been the collecting of material from a small number of elderly performers, or the establishment, as has been the case in some North American Indian tribes, of tribal archives. Revival has also involved the creation of national performing groups who produce music and dance outside the traditional context, on stage, in forms quite unlike the original. Elsewhere, nativistic movements such as the Ghost Dance in the North American Plains or the creation of preservation societies in Japanese villages have sparked musical revival. Nationalism in the modern states of the Third World has produced government sponsorship and patronage of nationally significant forms, while radio corporations, concert managements, and ministries of education and art have striven to reintroduce older traditions that had been losing ground. In some measure and a variety of ways, the old music has been brought back.

The phenomenal growth of cities in all parts of the world had a major impact on the interaction of musics. Secondary urbanization especially played a major role in music history, making a citadel of multi-cultural mosaic out of a center of population. During the twentieth century, the numbers in many cities increased tenfold, and some grew from village size to several million in a few decades. The increased population resulted to a large extent from the availability of Western technology, which drew together ethnic groups from the entire nation as well as immigrants and temporary laborers from abroad. The most Westernized sectors of any given citizenry also tended to settle in the largest cities. The interaction of musics from various parts of a modern nation-state, and of these musics with Western forms, is one of the most colorful chapters in this field of study. In Johannesburg, Lagos, Tehran, Bombay, Hong Kong, Tokyo—and also, to a smaller extent and quite differently, in Chicago, San Francisco, Adelaide—we see the creation of popular musics, all with essentially the same kind of performance venue, social contexts, audiences, but with many different kinds of style combinations. The older native tradition was normally used to modify what was essentially a Western structure. In all of these cities, we find multicultural and nationally oriented performances of the older music. And in all, there are institutions for teaching and preserving the native music on the assumption that it will find its way into a Western-derived social context.

And the twentieth century has also specialized in the creation of musics that are the result of voluntary or forced emigration. A field of great potential for insight into musical behavior under a variety of conditions, immigrant music includes such varied phenomena as the changing of a diversity of American Indian styles into a unified American Indian culture in Minneapolis, the establishment of Turkish and Greek night clubs in Frankfurt, the effects of German-Jewish immigrants and their European art music on immigrants from Middle Eastern nations to Israel, the assembling of Chinese from various parts of China in a music club in San Francisco. Music has had a recognized role in the communities of immigrant groups in the Americas and elsewhere for centuries, but the large numbers of foreigners and their tendency (in contrast to those of the nineteenth century) to avoid isolation, lamentable as the reasons for moving often are, have had a major impact on the world's musical culture.

If in most of the world's societies measures were taken to keep the old tradition intact in some way, only in rare cases were attempts made to place its sound into the framework of the Western musical system. Instead, all kinds of changes have been made in the social context, performance venues, the ways music is conceived. Music once ceremonial becomes entertainment but its sound has been substantially maintained. On the other hand, Western and traditional musics are rarely performed together in the same concert. Although there is hardly a proper way to measure these things, we could say in only rare cases that the sound has changed more than social context, behavior, or ideas. Normally it is the musical style itself that has in some fashion been maintained.

What has happened most is the modernization of the world's music, and much less, in the sense defined here, Westernization. But in order to bring this about, the world's societies have had to accept fundamental changes in their musical cultures. In India, performance times and seasons of ragas have been largely abandoned. Among the Blackfoot Indians, music for medicine bundles has been neglected in favor of songs for social dances. Traditional ways of teaching in Iran have been replaced by conservatory and notation. A block of houses in Madras may produce sounds of everything from Carnatic songs and Beethoven to film music and rock. The introduction of Western methods of transmitting music—everything from schools and notation to

records, radio, film—have been adopted everywhere. Of course they have ir-
revocably affected the sound, so say some teachers, depending on what, in
the view of the society, is required of a music to maintain its integrity. Radio
has kept the sound of Middle Eastern music intact but has reduced the role
and scope of improvisation. Notation may make it possible for people to learn
music efficiently, but they may no longer have the same regard for it.

The introduction of Western musical elements seems governed by two
main factors. The first is compatibility and the accompanying possibility of
producing syncretic products. One might have expected a large amount of
syncretism to have taken place in the musical world. There are, after all,
numerous points of similarity in musical style, idea, and instruments that
could be used as points of departure. But in fact, the most successful example
of musical syncretism continues to be the one that was first identified, the
combination of African and European elements into modern African and
Afro-American styles, almost as if the concept of syncretism had been derived
specifically to describe this relationship. One might have expected South Indian music to produce syncretic forms; after all, the similarities are not only evident to the outside (and presumably objective) observer, they are also recognized by Indian musicians—emphasis on tonic and dominant, the seven-tone
scale, importance of quadruple meter. One might also have expected the
traditions of large ensembles in Indonesia and in Europe to have produced
syncretic combinations. But evidently the relationship between the societies,
their attitudes toward change, and the general evaluation and function of
music are as important in determining syncretic possiblities as are the compatibilities of style elements.

On the other hand, the various social and political systems recently introduced throughout the world have all developed and imposed their special
views of the proper function of music in society and then produced policies to
put them into effect. And yet, the musical results have been surprisingly uniform. The establishment of orchestras of traditional instruments on similar
musical tracks in Iran, Soviet Central Asia, China, and India can hardly be the
result of different governmental approaches to the arts; nor can the composition of concertos, based on traditional melodic patterns, for *sitar, erh-hu,* and
*santour.*

The second factor governing the introduction of Western elements is their
relative centrality in Western music. The feature all along called the hallmark
of Western music, functional harmony from the period 1700–1900, often in
simplified versions, is the most essential. The introduction of the Western
sound into a non-Western system has almost always meant the use of this
particular harmonic scheme. If the uses vary in kind and degree, its introduction in itself is one of the most obvious regularities. A second such feature is
the use of large ensembles—orchestra, chorus, band. Notation, respect for
composer and for the stable, even static composed work, a high degree of
predictability in length of performance and its components, all these are also

widespread. And the adoption of particularly central Western instruments, violin, piano, guitar, also counts among the regularities.

It is difficult to know what the cultural functions of music may have been for any society in the distant past. Perhaps one of them has always been the reinforcing of cultural boundaries, the support of cultural integrity. Whether or not a true universal, this function of music has increased in significance as cultural boundaries become more blurred and in need of defense. The twentieth century may be special in many ways. There is increased possibility of communication among culture groups—the virtual enforcement of communication. The fact that most humans can no longer conveniently exhibit their cultural specialness by dress, social structure, material culture, or even by their location, language, or religion has given music an increased role as emblem of ethnicity. Culture units, nations, minorities, even age groups, social classes, educational strata all identify themselves by adherence to particular repertories and styles of music. As other means of identification become less effective, music is increasingly stressed. I would argue that this is why world music of the twentieth century has retained its diversity. If there is a general conclusion to be drawn from the ways in which the world's societies have responded to the coming of Western music, it is that each has tried, sometimes at great cost, to retain some significant degree of musical identity; and that each has found ways to symbolize, in its music, the positive, negative, and ambiguous aspects of its relationship to European-derived lifeways and values.

---

*Browning, Montana, 1983.* Again it was time for North American Indian Days on the Blackfeet reservation. The community looked more than before like a small town of the West, businesses and housing had developed, there was more industry. Few residents had the down-and-out look of impoverished reservation folk of the 1950s. Would the North American Indian Days ceremony now also look and sound more like a phenomenon of the white American West?

The answer was mixed. The dance ground had been enclosed in a small stadium-like structure. There were many dancers, far more, indeed, than in 1966, and all wore elaborate costumes to which were pinned numbers for use by judges in contests. The costumes were much more colorful and less traditional than in 1966; and the entrances of the lines of dancers were carefully prepared and coached by someone with an eye for the dramatic. Instead of just two or three singing groups as in earlier years, there were eleven, from various parts of the reservation and elsewhere, and instead of singing for an hour or two each would sing one song at a time in alternation with the others. A few women had joined the singing groups. The master of ceremonies,

Chairman of the Tribal Council, carefully maintained order. The audience consisted of Indians and whites; there were lots of cameras and cassette recorders. Many singers were young and children danced alongside their parents and grandparents. It was all much more thoroughly organized than two decades before, so that one might almost have thought that it was a show put on for tourists.

And yet, it was clearly also a ceremony of the Blackfoot people. There were only a few members of other tribes, far fewer white hobbyists dancing than before, speeches explicitly in the Blackfoot language. The Browning folk were now living rather like others in Montana; but it was here, at North American Indian Days, that they could show the world through their dances and songs that they were indeed still the Blackfoot people. And if their uses of songs and their ideas about them had changed, the special sound of their music showed no sign of abating.

# Bibliography

## GENERAL AND THEORETICAL

Archer, William Kay. "On the Ecology of Music." *EM* 8:28–33, 1964.

———, ed. *The Preservation of Traditional Forms of the Learned and Popular Music of the Orient and the Occident.* Urbana: University of Illinois Institute of Communications Research, 1964.

Barnett, H. G. *Innovation: The Basis of Cultural Change.* New York: McGraw-Hill, 1953.

Bascom, William. "The Main Problems of Stability and Change in Tradition." *JIFMC* 11:7–12, 1959.

Baumann, Max Peter. *Musikfolklore und Musikfolklorismus.* Winterthur: Amadeus, 1976.

Bezić, Jerko. "Die Akkulturation als Fortbestandsmöglichkeit der Volkmusik." *International Review of the Aesthetics and Sociology of Music* 5:209–15, 1974.

Blacking, John. "Some Problems of Theory and Method in the Study of Musical Change." *YIFMC* 9:1–26, 1978.

Blaukopf, Kurt. "The Sociography of Musical Life in Industrialised Countries—a Research Task." *World of Music* 21(3):78–81, 1979.

Boilès, Charles L. "A Paradigmatic Test of Acculturation." In *Cross-Cultural Perspectives on Music,* edited by Robert Falck and Timothy Rice, 53–78. Toronto: University of Toronto Press, 1982.

Bose, Fritz. "Musikgeschichtliche Aspekte der Musikethnologie." *Archiv für Musikwissenschaft* 24:239–51, 1966.

———. "Volkslied—Schlager—Folklore." *Zeitschrift für Volkskunde* 63:40–49, 1967.

Daniélou, Alain. "Cooperation and Exchanges in the Field of Music Between Countries of Different Cultures." *ISME Yearbook* 3:40–45, 1975–76.

———. "Plurality of Cultures or Synthesis." *Asian Music* 2(2):1–6, 1969.

———. "Popular Religious Music in the Twentieth Century." *Cultures* 1(3):227–36, 1974.

de Leeuw, Ton. "Interaction of Cultures in Contemporary Music." *Cultures* 1(3):13–32, 1974.

Elbourne, Roger. "The Study of Change in Traditional Music." *Folklore* (London) 86:181–89, 1975.

Gilbert, Henry. "The Survival of Music." *Musical Quarterly* 2:365–74, 1916.

Gronow, Pekka. "Ethnic Recordings, an Introduction." In *Ethnic Recordings in America: A Neglected Heritage,* 1–50. Washington, D.C.: Library of Congress, American Folklore Center, 1982.

Günther, Robert, ed. *Musikkulturen Asiens, Afrikas und Ozeaniens im 19. Jahrhundert.* Regensburg: G. Bosse, 1973.

Hamm, Charles, Bruno Nettl, and Ronald Byrnside. *Contemporary Music and Music Cultures.* Englewood Cliffs, N.J.: Prentice Hall, 1975.

Harrison, Frank. *Time, Place, and Music.* Amsterdam: Knuf, 1973.

Herndon, Marcia, and Norma McLeod. *Music as Culture.* Darby, Pa.: Norwood, 1980.

Herskovits, Melville J. *Acculturation: The Study of Culture Contact.* New York: J. J. Augustine, 1938.

Hood, Mantle. "The Challenge of Bi-Musicality." *EM* 4:55–59, 1960.

———. *The Ethnomusicologist.* New York: McGraw-Hill, 1971.

————. "The Reliability of Oral Tradition." *Journal of the American Musicological Society* 12:201–9, 1959.

Hopkins, Pandora. "Individual Choice and the Control of Musical Change." *Journal of American Folklore* 89:449–62, 1976.

Karpeles, Maud. "Concerning Authenticity." *JIFMC* 3:10–14, 1951.

————. "The Distinction Between Folk Music and Popular Music." *JIFMC* 20:9–12, 1968.

Kartomi, Margaret J. "The Processes and Results of Musical Culture Contact: A Discussion of Terminology and Concepts." *EM* 25:227–50, 1981.

Katz, Ruth. "Mannerism and Cultural Change: An Ethnomusicological Example." *Current Anthropology* 11(4–5):465–75, 1970.

Khan, A. H. "Carnival Concerts—Comments on the Subject." *Journal of the Indian Musicological Society* 5(2):37–46, 1974.

Kolinski, Mieczyslaw. "Consonance and Dissonance." *EM* 6:66–74, 1962.

————. "The Structure of Music: Diversification Versus Constraint." *EM* 22:229–44, 1978.

Kuckertz, Josef, ed. *Musica Indigena: Musikethnologisches Symposium, Rom, 1975.* Rome: Consociato Internationalis Musicae Sacrae, 1975.

Laade, Wolfgang. *Gegenwartsfragen der Musik in Afrika und Asien; eine grundlegende Bibliographie.* Heidelberg: W. Laade, 1971.

————. *Neue Musik in Afrika, Asien und Ozeanien; Diskographie und stilistisch–historischer Überblick.* Heidelberg: W. Laade, 1971.

————. *Die Situation von Musikleben und Musikforschung in den Ländern Afrikas und Asiens und die neuen Aufgaben der Musikethnologie.* Tutzing: Hans Schneider, 1969.

Lomax, Alan. *Folk Song Style and Culture.* Washington, D.C.: American Association for the Advancement of Science, 1968.

————. "Folksong Style." *American Anthropologist* 61:927–54, 1959.

Marett, Allan. "Interrelationships Between Musical and Social Change in Japanese and Australian Aboriginal Culture." In *International Symposium on the Conservation and Restoration of Cultural Property,* 63–71. Tokyo: National Research Institute of Cultural Properties, 1981.

McAllester, David P. "The Complexity of the Cultural Process." In *International Symposium on the Conservation and Restoration of Cultural Property,* 1–18. Tokyo: National Research Institute of Cultural Properties, 1981.

McCredie, Andrew D. "Transplanted and Emergent Indigenous Liturgical Musics in East Asia, Australia and Oceania." In *Musica Indigena,* edited by Josef Kuckertz, 117–40. Rome: CIMS, 1975.

Merriam, Alan P. *The Anthropology of Music.* Evanston, Ill.: Northwestern University Press, 1964.

————. "The Use of Music in the Study of a Problem of Acculturation." *American Anthropologist* 57:28–34, 1955.

Metraux, G. S., ed. *Music in a Changing World* [special issue]. *Cultures* 1(3), 1974.

Meyer, Leonard B. *Music, the Arts, and Ideas.* Chicago: University of Chicago Press, 1967.

Nettl, Bruno. "Change in Folk and Primitive Music: A Survey of Problems and Methods." *Journal of the American Musicological Society* 8:101–9, 1955.

————. "Historical Aspects of Ethnomusicology." *American Anthropologist* 60:518–32, 1958.

————. "Some Aspects of the History of World Music in the Twentieth Century: Questions, Problems, Concepts." *EM* 22:123–36, 1978.

————, ed. *Eight Urban Musical Cultures: Tradition and Change.* Urbana: University of Illinois Press, 1978.

Ratanjankar, S. N. "Über die traditionellen Methoden der musikalischen Ausbildung und die Modernen Musikklassen." *Beiträge zur Musikwissenschaft* 8(2):145–48, 1966.

Reyes Schramm, Adelaida. "Explorations in Urban Ethnomusicology: Hard Lessons from the Spectacularly Ordinary." *YTM* 14:1–14, 1982.

Ringer, Alexander L. "Musical Taste and the Industrial Syndrome: A Socio-Musicological Problem in Historical Analysis." *International Review of the Aesthetics and Sociology of Music* 5:139–53, 1974.

Sachs, Curt. *The Wellsprings of Music.* The Hague: M. Nijhoff, 1962.

Šarana, Gopala. *The Methodology of Anthropological Comparisons: An Analysis of Comparative Methods in Social and Cultural Anthropology.* Viking Fund Publications in Anthropology, no. 53. Tucson: University of Arizona Press, 1975.

Schneider, Marius. "Akul'turatsiia v muzyke" [Acculturation in music]. In *Muzyka narodov Azii i Afrika* [Folk Music of Asia and Africa], edited by Victor S. Vinogradov, 285–309. Moscow: Sovetskii Kompozitori, 1969.

Seeger, Charles. "Oral Tradition in Music." In *Funk and Wagnalls Standard Dictionary of Folklore, Mythology and Legend,* edited by M. Leach, vol. 2, 825–29. New York, 1950.

———. "Semantic, Logical, and Political Considerations Bearing upon Research into Ethnomusicology." *EM* 5:77–80, 1961.

———. *Studies in Musicology 1935–1975.* Berkeley: University of California Press, 1977.

Shiloah, Amnon, and Erik Cohen. "The Dynamics of Change in Jewish Oriental Ethnic Music in Israel." *EM* 27:227–52, 1983.

Signell, Karl L. "The Modernization Process in Two Oriental Music Cultures: Turkish and Japanese." *Asian Music* 7(2):72–102, 1976.

Simon, Artur. "Probleme, Methoden und Ziele der Ethnomusikologie," *Jahrbuch für musikalische Volks- und Völkerkunde* 9:8–52, 1978.

Simosko, V. "Cross Cultures." *Coda* 12(5):2–5, 1975.

Stockmann, Erich. "Interethnische Kommunikationsprozesse und die Verbreitung von Musikinstrumenten." *Beiträge zur Musikwissenschaft* 21:189–200, 1979.

Vega, Carlos. "Mesomusic: An Essay on the Music of the Masses." *EM* 10:1–17, 1966.

Wachsmann, Klaus. "Criteria for Acculturation." In *International Musicological Society: Report of the 8th Congress, New York,* 139–49. Kassel: Baerenreiter, 1961.

Wiora, Walter. *Ergebnisse und Aufgaben vergleichender Musikforschung.* Darmstadt: Wissenschaftliche Buchgesellschaft, 1975.

———. *The Four Ages of Music.* New York: Norton, 1965.

# AFRICA (SUB-SAHARAN)

Akpabot, Samuel. "The Conflict Between Foreign and Traditional Culture in Nigeria." In *Reflections on Afro-American Music,* edited by D. R. de Lerma, 124–30. Kent, Ohio: Kent State University Press, 1973.

Ames, David W. "A Sociocultural View of Hausa Musical Activity." In *The Traditional Artist in African Societies,* edited by Warren L. d'Azevedo, 128–61. Bloomington: Indiana University Press, 1973.

———. "Urban Hausa Music." *African Urban Notes* 5(4):19–24, 1970.

Ames, David W., and Anthony V. King. *Glossary of Hausa Music and Its Social Contexts.* Evanston, Ill.: Northwestern University Press, 1971.

Bebey, Francis. "African Musical Tradition in the Face of Foreign Influence." *Cultures* 6(2):134–40, 1979.

———. "Black African Ancestral Music for a New World." *Cultures* 1(3):221–25, 1974.

Berliner, Paul F. *The Soul of Mbira*. Berkeley: University of California Press, 1978.

Blacking, John. "The Role of Music in the Culture of the Venda of the Northern Transvaal." *Studies in Ethnomusicology* (New York) 2:20–53, 1965.

Collins, E. J. "Post-War Popular Band Music in West Africa." *African Arts* 10:53–60, 1977.

Coplan, David. "Go to My Town, Cape Coast! The Social History of Ghanaian Highlife." *Eight Urban Musical Cultures: Tradition and Change*, edited by Bruno Nettl, 96–114. Urbana: University of Illinois Press, 1978.

Coplan, David, with David Rycroft. "Marabi: The Emergence of African Working Class Music in Johannesburg." In *Discourse in Ethnomusicology II: A Tribute to Alan P. Merriam*, edited by Caroline Card and others, 43–66. Bloomington: Indiana University, Ethnomusicology Publications Group, 1981.

Darkwa, Asante. "The New Musical Traditions in Ghana." Diss., Wesleyan University, 1974.

Ekwueme, Lazarus Nnanyelu. "African Music in Christian Liturgy: The Igbo Experiment." *African Music* 5(3):12–33, 1973–74.

Erlmann, Veit. "Marginal Men, Strangers and Wayfarers: Professional Musicians and Change Among the Fulani of Diamaré (North Cameroon)." *EM* 27:187–226, 1983.

Etzkorn, K. Peter. "On the Sphere of Social Validity in African Art: Sociological Reflections on Ethnographic Data." In *The Traditional Artist in African Societies*, edited by Warren L. d'Azevedo, 343–78. Bloomington: Indiana University Press, 1973.

Euba, Akin. "New Idioms of Music-Drama Among the Yoruba," *YIFMC* 2:92–107, 1971.

————. "Traditional Elements as the Basis of New African Art Music." *African Urban Notes* 5(4):52–56, 1970.

Hanna, Judith Lynne. "African Dance: The Continuity of Change." *YIFMC* 5:165–74, 1973.

Hooker, Naomi Ware. "Popular Musicians in Freetown." *African Urban Notes* 5(4):11–18, 1970.

Hornbostel, Erich M. von. "African Negro Music." *Africa* 1:30–62, 1928.

Jones, A. M. *African Hymnody in Christian Worship: A Contribution to the History of Its Development*. Mambo Occasional Papers, Missio-Pastoral Series, no. 8. Gwelo, Rhodesia: Mambo Press, 1976.

Kaemmer, John E. "The Dynamics of a Changing Music System in Rural Rhodesia." Diss., Indiana University, 1975.

Kauffman, Robert. "Shona Urban Music and the Problem of Acculturation." *YIFMC* 4:47–56, 1973.

Kazadi, Pierre Cary. "Trends of Nineteenth and Twentieth Century Music in the Congo–Zaïre." In *Musikkulturen Asiens, Afrikas und Ozeaniens im 19. Jahrhundert*, edited by Robert Günther, 267–83. Regensburg: G. Bosse, 1973.

Kebede, Ashenafi. "Zemenawi Muzika: Modern Trends in Traditional Secular Music of Ethiopia." *The Black Perspective in Music* 4:289–302, 1976.

Keil, Charles. *Tiv Song*. Chicago: University of Chicago Press, 1979.

Kennedy, J. Scott. "The Use of Music in African Theatre." *African Urban Notes* 5(4):57–62, 1970.

Kinney, Esi Sylvia. "Urban West African Music and Dance." *African Urban Notes* 5(4):3–10, 1970.

————, ed. *African Urban Notes* 5(4), 1970 [special issue on ethnomusicology].

Kirby, Percival R. "The Effect of Western Civilization upon Bantu Music." In *Western Civilisation and the Natives of South Africa*, edited by I. Schapera. 1934. Reprint. New York: Humanities Press, 1967.

————. "The Use of European Music Techniques by the Non-European Peoples of Southern Africa." *JIFMC* 11:37–40, 1959.

Koetting, James T. "The Effects of Urbanization: The Music of the Kasena People of Ghana." *World of Music* 17(4):23–31, 1975.

**Martin, Stephen H.** "African Acculturated Music: A Preliminary Study of the Major Genres." M.A. thesis, University of Washington, 1974.

**Mbabi-Katana, S.** "Similarities of Musical Phenomena over a Large Part of the African Continent as Evidenced by the Irambi and Empango Side-Blown Trumpet Styles and Drum Rhythms." *African Urban Notes* 5(4):25–41, 1970.

**Mbunga, Stefan.** "Afrikanische Musik in Gottesdienst." In *Musica Indigena*, edited by Josef Kukertz, 51–71. Rome: CIMS, 1975.

**Mensah, Attah Annan.** "The Impact of Western Music on the Musical Traditions of Ghana." *Composer* 19:19–22, 1966.

————. "Music of Nineteenth-Century Zambia." In *Musikkulturen Asiens, Afrikas und Ozeaniens im 19. Jahrhundert*, edited by Robert Günther, 285–307. Regensburg: G. Bosse, 1973.

————. "Ndebele-Soli Bi-musicality in Zambia." *YIFMC* 2:108–20, 1971.

————. "Song Texts as Reflectors of External Influence." *African Urban Notes* 5(4):42–51, 1970.

**Merriam, Alan P.** "The Bala Musician," In *The Traditional Artist in African Societies*, edited by Warren L. d'Azevedo, 250–81. Bloomington: Indiana University Press, 1973.

————. "Change in Religion and the Arts in a Zairian Village." *African Studies Review* 17:345–59, 1974.

————. "Music Change in a Basongye Village (Zaire)." *Anthropos* 72:806–46, 1977.

**Nketia, J. H. Kwabena.** "Changing Traditions of Folk Music in Ghana." *JIFMC* 11:31–36, 1959.

————. "The Gramophone and Contemporary Music in the Gold Coast." In *Proceedings of the Fourth Annual Conference of the West African Institute of Social and Economic Research*, 189–200. Ibadan: University College, 1955.

————. "Modern Trends in Ghana Music." *African Music* 1(4):13–17, 1957. Reprinted in *Readings in Ethnomusicology*, edited by D. P. McAllester, 330–35. New York: Johnson Reprint Company, 1971.

————. *The Music of Africa.* New York: W. W. Norton, 1974.

————. "The Musician in Akan Society." In *The Traditional Artist in African Societies*, edited by Warren L. d'Azevedo, 79–100. Bloomington: Indiana University Press, 1973.

————. "The Performing Musicians in a Changing Society." *World of Music* 21(2):65–74, 1979.

————. "Tradition and Innovation in African Music." *Jamaica Journal* 11(3–4):2–9, 1978.

**Ouedraogo, Robert.** "La musique sacrée dans les missions du pays Mossi." In *Musica Indigena*, edited by Josef Kuckertz, 72–86. Rome: CIMS, 1975.

**Roberts, John Storm.** "Popular Music in Kenya," *African Music* 4(2):53–55, 1968.

**Rycroft, David K.** "African Music in Johannesburg: African and Non-African Features." *JIFMC* 11:25–30, 1959.

————. "Evidence of Stylistic Continuity in Zulu 'Town' Music." In *Essays for a Humanist, an Offering to Klaus Wachsmann*, 216–60. New York: Town House Press, 1977.

**Smith, Edna M.** "Popular Music in West Africa." *African Music* 3(1):11–17, 1962.

**Tracey, Hugh.** *Chopi Musicians: Their Music, Poetry, and Instruments.* London: Oxford University Press, 1948.

**Twerefoo, Gustav Oware.** "Overcoming Directional Singing in Ghanaian Schools." *Bulletin of the Council for Research in Music Education* 50:67–71, 1977.

**Wachsmann, Klaus.** "A Century of Change in the Folk Music of an African Tribe." *JIFMC* 10:52–56, 1958.

————, ed. *Essays on Music and History in Africa.* Evanston, Ill.: Northwestern University Press, 1971.

**Ware, Naomi.** "Popular Music and African Identity in Freetown, Sierra Leone." In *Eight Urban*

*Musical Cultures: Tradition and Change,* edited by Bruno Nettl, 296–320. Urbana: University of Illinois Press, 1978.

Waterman, Richard A. "On Flogging a Dead Horse: Lessons Learned from the Africanisms Controversy." *EM* 7:83–87, 1963.


# AMERICAN INDIAN (NORTH AMERICA)


Cavanagh, Beverly Anne. "Music of the Netsilik Eskimo: A Study of Stability and Change." Diss., University of Toronto, 1979.

Densmore, Frances. "The Songs of Indian Soldiers During the World War." *Musical Quarterly* 20:419–25, 1934.

Ecklund, Judith Louise. "Marriage, Seaworms, and Song: Ritualized Responses to Cultural Change in Sasak Life." Diss., Cornell University, 1977.

Frisbie, Charlotte J. "The Music of American Indians." In *Music in American Society 1776–1976,* edited by G. McCue, 95–105. New Brunswick, N.J.: Transaction Books, 1977.

Gaus, Dorothy Shipley. "Change in Social Dance Song Style at Allegany Reservation, 1962–1973: The Rabbit Dance." Diss., Catholic University of America, 1976.

Hauser, Michael. "Inuit Songs from Southwest Baffin Island in Cross-Cultural Context." *Etudes Inuit Studies* 2(1):55–83 and (2):71–105, 1978.

Herzog, George. "Plains Ghost Dance and Great Basin Music." *American Anthropologist* 37:403–19, 1935.

Howard, James H. "Pan-Indianism in Native American Music and Dance." *EM* 27:71–82, 1983.

Lutz, Maija M. *The Effects of Acculturation on Eskimo Music of Cumberland Peninsula.* Ottawa: National Museums of Canada, 1978.

Merriam, Alan P. *Ethnomusicology of the Flathead Indians.* Chicago: Aldine Press, 1967.

Mitchell, Frank. *Navajo Blessingway Singer.* . . . Edited by Charlotte Frisbie and David P. McAllester. Tucson: University of Arizona Press, 1978.

Mooney, James. *The Ghost-Dance Religion and the Sioux Outbreak of 1890.* Fourteenth Annual Report of the Bureau of American Ethnology, pt. 2. Washington, 1896.

Nettl, Bruno. "Blackfoot Music in Browning, 1965: Functions and Analysis." In *Festschrift Walter Wiora,* 593–598. Kassel: Bärenreiter, 1967.

———. "Some Influences of Western Civilization on North American Indian Music." In *New Voices in American Studies,* edited by Ray B. Brown and others, 129–37. Lafayette, Ind.: Purdue University Press, 1966.

———. "Studies in Blackfoot Indian Musical Culture." I and II, *EM* 11:141–60, 293–309, 1967; III and IV, *EM* 12:11–48, 192–207, 1968.

Olsen, Poul Rovsing. "Acculturation in the Eskimo Songs of the Greenlanders." *YIFMC* 4:32–37, 1973.

Palmer, A. Dean. "Tsianina Blackstone: A Chapter in the History of the American Indian in Opera." *Liberal Arts Review* 70:40–64, 1979.

Parthun, Paul. "Plains War Dance Songs: A Metamorphosis." *Anthropological Journal of Canada* 16(4):22–26, 1978.

Pelinski, Ramon. "Polyphonie Inuit et Polysémie Occidentale." In *La Musique des Inuit du Caribou: Cinq perspectives méthodologiques* 49–73. Montréal, Quebec: Les Presses de l'Université de Montréal, 1981.

Powers, William K. "Contemporary Oglala Music and Dance: Pan-Indianism versus Pan-Tetonism." *EM* 12:352–72, 1968.

**Rhodes, Willard.** "Acculturation in North American Indian Music." In *Acculturation in the Americas,* edited by Sol Tax, 127–32. Proceedings of the 29th International Congress of Americanists, vol. 2. Chicago, 1952.

————. "North American Indian Music in Transition: A Study of Songs with English Words as an Index of Acculturation." *JIFMC* 15:9–14, 1963.

————. "A Study of Musical Diffusion Based on the Wandering of the Opening Peyote Song." *JIFMC* 10:42–49, 1958.

**Slotkin, J. S.** *Menomini Peyotism.* Transaction of the American Philosophical Society, new series, vol. 42, pt. 4. Philadelphia, 1952.

**Stevens, Bill.** "Indian Fiddling of the North." *Sound Post,* December 1976–January 1977, 6–8.

**Ware, Naomi.** "Survival and Change in Pima Indian Music." *EM* 14:100–13, 1970.

**Witmer, Robert.** "Recent Change in the Musical Culture of the Blood Indians." *Yearbook for Inter-American Musical Research* 9:64–94, 1973.

# FAR EAST

**Blake, C. Fred.** "Love Songs and the Great Leap: The Role of a Youth Culture in the Revolutionary Phase of China's Economic Development." *American Ethnologist* 6:41–54, 1979.

**Bose, Fritz.** "Japanische Musik im 19. Jahrhundert." In *Musikkulturen Asiens, Afrikas und Ozeaniens im 19. Jahrhundert,* edited by Robert Günther, 135–65. Regensburg: G. Bosse, 1973.

————. "Western Influences in Modern Asian Music." *JIFMC* 11:47–50, 1959.

**Chang, Sa-Hun.** "Transmutation of Korean Music." *Korea Journal* (Seoul) 16(12):15–19, December 1976.

————. *Yŏmyŏng ŭi tongsŏ ŭmak* [Western and Traditional Music During the Early 20th Century]. Seoul: Pojin Jai, 1974.

**Chou, Lan.** "A Decade of Revolution in Peking Opera." *Chinese Literature* 4:85–94, 1974.

**Chou, Wen-Chung.** "Asian and Western Music: Influence or Confluence?" *Asian Culture Quarterly* 5:60–66, 1977.

————. "Towards a Re-Merger in Music." In *Contemporary Composers on Contemporary Music,* edited by Elliot Schwartz and Barney Childs, 308–15. New York: Holt, Rinehart and Winston, 1967.

————. "A Visit to Modern China." *World of Music* 20:40–44, 1978.

**Chou Yang** [Chow Yang]. *China's New Literature and Art.* Peking: Foreign Languages Press, 1954.

**Daniélou, Alain.** *Die Musik Asiens zwischen Missachtung und Werschätzung.* Whilhelmshaven: Heinrichshofen, 1973.

**Daniélou, Alain, and Jacques Brunet.** *La musique et sa communication: la situation de la musique et des musiciens dans les pays d'Orient.* Florence: Leo S. Olschki, 1971.

**de Leeuw, Ton.** "Music in Orient and Occident—a social problem." *World of Music* 11(4):6–17, 1969.

————. "Questions, Ideas and Expectations: Premises and Aims of an East–West Encounter." *World of Music* 20(2):19–33, 1978.

**Delza, Sophia.** "Perspectives on the Aesthetics of Change: From the Classical Chinese Theater to the Revolutionary Peking Opera." *Chinoperl Papers* 7:22–48, 1977.

**Fujie, Linda.** "Effects of Urbanization on Matsuri-Bayashi in Tokyo." *YTM* 15:38–44, 1983.

**Garfias, Robert.** "Gradual Modifications of the Gagaku Tradition." *EM* 4:16–19, 1960.

**Gronow, Pekka.** "The Record Industry Comes to the Orient." *EM* 25:251–82, 1981.

**Han, Kuo-Huang.** "The Modern Chinese Orchestra." *Asian Music* 11(1):1–42, 1979.
**Han, Kuo-Huang, and Lindy Li Mark.** "Evolution and Revolution in Chinese Music." In *Musics of Many Cultures,* edited by E. May, 10–31. Berkeley: University of California Press, 1980.
**Harich-Schneider, Eta.** *A History of Japanese Music.* London: Oxford University Press, 1973.
———. "The Present Condition of Japanese Court Music." *Musical Quarterly* 39:49–74, 1953.
**Hughes, David W.** "Japanese Folk Song Preservation Societies: Their History and Nature." In *International Symposium on the Conservation and Restoration of Cultural Property,* 29–46. Tokyo: National Research Institute of Cultural Properties, 1981.
**Jacobs, Kai.** "Deutschsprachige Schriften zur Revolutionären Musik der VR China." *Anschläge* 1:104–11, 1978.
**Kagan, Alan L.** "Music and the Hundred Flowers Movement." *Musical Quarterly* 49:417–30, 1963.
**Kam'bayashi, Sumio.** "Observations on Western Influences upon Japanese Dance." *Journal of the Association of Graduate Dance Ethnologists UCLA* 3:19–25, 1979.
**Kartomi, Margaret J.** "Some Changes in China's Performing Arts." *Eastern Horizon* 16:31–42, 1977.
**Kishibe, Shigeo.** "Japanese Music—Conflict or Synthesis?" *World of Music* 9(2):11–21, 1967.
**Kitahara, Michio.** "Kayokyoku: An Example of Syncretism Involving Scale and Mode." *EM* 10:271–84, 1966.
**Koizumi, Fumio, and others,** eds. *Asian Musics in an Asian Perspective.* Tokyo: The Japan Foundation, 1977.
**Lee, Hye-Ku.** "Impact of Western Music on Asian Music." *Asian and Pacific Quarterly of Cultural and Social Affairs* (Seoul) 8(1):16–18, 1976.
**Lee, Kang-Sook.** "Korean Music Culture: Genuine and Quasi-Korean Music." *Korea Journal* 17(8):70–77, 1977.
**Liu, Marjory Bong-Ray.** "From K'unch'u to Revolutionary Opera: A Study of Continuity and Change in Chinese Society." In *Symposium on the Place of Music in Asian Studies,* 17–30. Arizona State University Occasional Papers, no. 7. Tempe, Arizona: Center for Asian Studies, 1975.
———. "Tradition and Change in Kunqu Opera." Diss., UCLA, 1976.
**Ma Hiao-ts'iun.** *La musique chinoise de style européen.* Paris: Jouve, 1941.
**MacKerras, Colin.** *The Chinese Theater in Modern Times: From 1840 to the Present Day.* Amherst: University of Massachusetts Press, 1975.
**Malm, William P.** *Japanese Music and Musical Instruments.* Tokyo and Rutland, Vermont: C. E. Tuttle, 1959.
**May, Elizabeth.** "Japanese Children's Songs Before and After Contact with the West." *JIFMC* 11:59–65, 1959.
**Mao Tse-tung.** *Five Documents on Literature and Art.* Peking: Foreign Language Press, 1967.
———. *Talks at the Yenan Forum on Literature and Art.* 4th ed. Peking: Foreign Language Press, 1965.
**Neuman, Daniel.** "Towards an Ethnomusicology of Culture Change in Asia." *Asian Music* 7(2):1–5, 1976.
**Nitobe, Inazo.** "Music in Japan." In *Western Influences in Modern Japan,* edited by Inazo Nitobe, 469–523. Chicago: University of Chicago Press, 1931.
**Olsen, Dale A.** "The Social Determinants of Japanese Musical Life in Peru and Brazil." *EM* 27:49–70, 1983.
**Pischner, Hans.** *Musik in China.* Berlin: Henschelverlag, 1955.
**Rockwell, Coralie J.** "Trends and Developments in Korean Traditional Music Today." *Korea Journal* 14(3):15–20, 1974.
**Scott, Adolphe Clarence.** *Literature and the Arts in 20th Century China.* New York: Anchor Books, 1962.

**Sheng, David Shuan-en.** "A Study of the Indigenous Elements in Chinese Christian Hymnody." D.M.A. thesis, University of Southern California, 1964.

**Song, Bang-Song.** *The Korean–Canadian Folk Song: An Ethnomusicological Study.* Ottawa: Nationa Museums of Canada, 1974.

**Sook, Kyung Auh.** "The Education of Musicians in the Republic of Korea." *ISME Yearbook* 2:21–28, 1974.

**Suppan, Wolfgang, and Hachiro Sakanashi.** "Musikforschung in und für Japan." *Acta Musicologica* 54:84–123, 1982.

**Tanabe, Hideo.** "Some Remarks on the Present State of Japanese Traditional Music." In *Proceedings of the Second Asian Pacific Music Conference, 1976,* 23–24.

———. "Western Influences on Japanese Music." *Asian and Pacific Quarterly of Cultural and Social Affairs* 8:17–22, 1976.

**Teng, Chang-Kuo.** "Music Education and Music Activities in the Republic of China." In *Proceedings of the First Asian Pacific Music Conference, 1975,* 31–34.

———. "The Problems of Application of Traditional Chinese Music to Contemporary Music." In *Proceedings of the Second Asian Pacific Music Conference, 1976,* 55–58.

**Trân Van Khê.** "Akulturacija u muzičkum tradicijama Azij [Acculturation in the Musical Traditions of Asia]." *Zvuk* (Sarajevo) 2:143–48, 1974. (English summary.)

**Wu Teh-li.** "The Maoist Struggle in the Musical Arena." *Issues and Studies* 10(8):30–40, 1974.

**Yin, Cheng-chung.** "How the Piano Concerto 'Yellow River' Was Composed." *Chinese Literature* 11:97–102, 1974.

**Yoshida, Hidekazu.** "Housing Japan's Avantgarde." *World of Music* 11(3):6–16, 1969.

**Yun, Isang.** "The Contemporary Composer and Traditional Music." *World of Music* 20(2):57–60, 1978.

# INDIAN SUBCONTINENT

**Albuquerque, Walter.** "Indian Music in Divine Service." In *Musica Indigena,* edited by Josef Kuckertz, 97–116. Rome: CIMS, 1975.

**Ashton, Roger,** ed. *Music East and West: Conference on the Music of East and West, New Delhi, 1964.* Bombay: Indian Council for Cultural Relations, 1966.

**Baké, Arnold.** "The Impact of Western Music on the Indian Musical System." *JIFMC* 5:57–60, 1953.

**Craig, Dale A.** "Fusions of Indian and Western Music." *Eastern Horizon* 17:38–40, 1978.

**Deva, B. C.** *Indian Music.* Delhi: Indian Council for Cultural Relations, 1974.

———. "Tradition and Non-Conformity in Indian Music." *Journal of the Indian Musicological Society* 6(6):27–30, 1975.

**Durga, S. A. K.** *The Opera in South India.* Delhi: B. R. Publishing Corp., 1979.

**Haque, Abu Saeed Zahurul.** "The Use of Folklore in Nationalist Movements and Liberation Struggles: A Case Study of Bangladesh." *Journal of the Folklore Institute* (Bloomington) 12(2–3):211–40, 1975.

**Higgins, Jon B.** "From Prince to Populace: Patronage as a Determinant of Change in South Indian (Karnatak) Music." *Asian Music* 7(2):20–26, 1976.

**Jairazbhoy, Nazir.** "Music in Western Rajasthan: Continuity and Change." *YIFMC* 9:50–66, 1978.

**Jairazbhoy, Nazir, and Stone, A. W.** "Intonation in Present-Day Indian Music." *Journal of the Indian Musicological Society* 7(1):22–39, 1976.

Jha, Akhileshwar. "Indian and Western Music: The Cultural Factor." *Quest* (Bombay) 97:63–65, 1975.

Joshy, D. T. "Das indische Nationalorchester," *Beiträge zur Musikwissenschaft* 8(2):152–53, 1966.

Karnani, Chetan. "Indian and Western Music." *Quest* 94:45–51, 1975.

Kuckertz, Josef. "Die Kunstmusik Südindiens im 19. Jahrhundert." In *Musikkulturen Asiens, Afrikas und Ozeaniens im 19. Jahrhundert*, edited by Robert Günther, 97–130. Regensburg: G. Bosse, 1973.

———. "Reception of Classical Indian Music in Western Countries," *Journal of the Indian Musicological Society* 7(4):5–14, 1976.

L'Armand, Kathleen, and L'Armand, Adrian. "Music in Madras: The Urbanization of a Cultural Tradition." In *Eight Urban Musical Cultures: Tradition and Change*, edited by Bruno Nettl, 115–45. Urbana, Ill.: University of Illinois Press, 1978.

———. "One Hundred Years of Music in Madras: A Case Study in Secondary Urbanization." *EM* 27:411–38, 1983.

Meer, W. van der. "The Influence of Social Change on Indian Music." *World of Music* 20(2):133–35, 1978.

Menon, Narayana. "Music and Culture Change in India." *Cultures* 1(3):59–73, 1974.

———. "The Music Public in India." *World of Music* 5(1–2):17–19, 1963.

Mueller, P. F. "Dhrupad, ein von Untergang bedrohter Gesangstil?" *Neue Zeitschrift für Musik* 6:585–89, 1979.

Myers, Helen. "The Process of Change in Trinidad East Indian Music." *Journal of the Indian Musicological Society* 9(3):11–16, 1978.

Nag, D. "New Trends in Hindustani Rag Sangeet." *Journal of the Indian Musicological Society* 4(1):30–32, 1973.

Neuman, Daniel M. "Gharanas: The Rise of Musical 'Houses' in Delhi and Neighboring Cities." In *Eight Urban Musical Cultures: Tradition and Change*, edited by Bruno Nettl, 186–222. Urbana, Ill.: University of Illinois Press, 1978.

———. *The Life of Music in North India*. London: Faber & Faber, 1980.

Powers, Harold S. "Classical Music, Culture Roots, and Colonial Rule: An Indic Musicologist Looks at the Muslim World." *Asian Music* 12(1):5–39, 1979.

———. "Indian Music and the English Language: A Review Essay." *EM* 9:1–12, 1965.

Rangoonwalla, Firoze. *Indian Filmography: Silent and Hindi Films (1897–1969)*. Bombay: Udeshi, 1970; and complementary volume, *Indian Films Index (1912–1967)*.

Ratanjankar, S. N. "Harmonium and Indian music." *Journal of the Sangeet Natak Akademi* 20:11–14, 1971.

———. "Indian Music and Orchestra." *Journal of the Indian Musicological Society* 3(1):11–13, 1972.

Ross, Israel J. "Cross-Cultural Dynamics in Musical Traditions: The Music of the Jews of Cochin." *Musica Judaica* 2(1):50–72, 1977–78.

Rudolph, Lloyd I., and Susanne H. Rudolph. *The Modernity of Tradition: Political Development in India*. Chicago: University of Chicago Press, 1967.

Sambamoorthy, P. *South Indian Music*. Book 6. Madras: Indian Music Publishing House, 1969.

Shankar, L. "The Art of Violin Accompaniment in South Indian Classical Music." Dissertation, Wesleyan University, 1974.

Shankar, Ravi. *My Music, My Life*. New York: Simon & Schuster, 1968.

Shirali, Vishnudass. "The Problem of Orchestration in Indian Music." *Journal of the Music Academy Madras* 45:68–76, 1974.

Silver, Brian. "On Becoming an Ustad: Six Life Sketches in the Evolution of a Gharana." *Asian Music* 7(2):27–50, 1976.

Singer, Milton. *When a Great Tradition Modernizes*. New York: Praeger, 1972.

Stewart, Rebecca Marie. *The Tabla in Perspective*. Diss., UCLA, 1974.

Tagore, Rabindranath. *Chansons de Rabindranath Tagore . . . précédés d'une préface de Arnold A. Baké.* Paris: Geuthner, 1935.

Wade, Bonnie, and Ann Pescatello. "Music 'Patronage' in Indic Culture: The Jajmani Model." In *Essays for a Humanist, an Offering to Klaus Wachsmann,* 277–336. New York: Town House Press, 1977.


# LATIN AMERICA AND THE CARIBBEAN


Aretz, Isabel. "Music in Latin America: The Perpetuation of Tradition." *Cultures* 1(3):117–31, 1974.

Becerra-Schmidt, Gustavo. "Modern Music South of the Rio Grande." *World of Music* 14(1):3–29, 1972.

Belzner, William. "Music, Modernization, and Westernization Among the Macuma Shuar." In *Cultural Transformations and Ethnicity in Ecuador,* edited by Norman Whitten, 731–48. Urbana, Ill.: University of Illinois Press, 1981.

Borde, Percival. "The Sounds of Trinidad: The Development of the Steel-Drum Bands." *The Black Perspective in Music* 1(1):45–49, 1973.

Epstein, Dena J. "African Music in British and French America." *Musical Quarterly* 59:61–91, 1973.

Herskovits, Melville J. "Drums and Drummers in Afro-Brazilian Cult Life." *Musical Quarterly* 30:477–92, 1944.

Hill, Errol. "The Trinidad Carnival: Cultural Change and Synthesis." *Cultures* 3(1):54–86, 1975.

Hopkin, John Barton. "Music in the Jamaican Pentecostal Churches." *Jamaica Journal* 42:22–40, 1978.

Kolinski, Mieczyslaw. "Suriname Folk Music." In *Suriname Folklore,* edited by M. Herskovits, New York: American Folklore Society, 1936.

List, George. "A Comparison of Certain Aspects of Colombian and Spanish Folksong." *YIFMC* 5:72–84, 1974.

Midgett, Douglas K. "Performance Roles and Musical Change in a Caribbean Society." *EM* 21:55–73, 1977.

Roberts, Helen H. "Possible Survivals of African Song in Jamaica." *Musical Quarterly* 12:56–71, 1926.

Schechter, John. "Corona y Baile: Music in the Child's Wake of Ecuador and Hispanic South America, Past and Present." *Latin American Music Review* 4:1–80, 1983.

Stark, Richard B. *Music of the 'Bailes' in New Mexico.* Santa Fe: International Folk Art Foundation, 1978.

Stigberg, David K. "Jarocho, Tropical, and 'Pop': Aspects of Musical Life in Veracruz, 1971–72." In *Eight Urban Musical Cultures: Tradition and Change,* edited by Bruno Nettl, 260–295. Urbana, Ill.: University of Illinois Press, 1978.


# MIDDLE EAST AND BALKANS


al-Faruqi, Lois Ibsen. "The Status of Music in Muslim Nations: Evidence from the Arab World." *Asian Music* 12(1):56–85, 1979.

Baily, John. "Recent Changes in the Dutar of Herat." *Asian Music* 8(1):29–64, 1976.

Beeman, William O. "You Can Take the Music Out of the Country, But . . . : The Dynamics of Change in Iranian Musical Tradition." *Asian Music* 7(2):6–19, 1976.

Blum, Stephen. "Changing Roles of Performers in Meshhed and Bonjnurd, Iran." In *Eight Urban Musical Cultures: Tradition and Change,* edited by Bruno Nettl, 19–95. Urbana, Ill.: University of Illinois Press, 1978.

Cachia, Pierre. "A 19th Century Arab's Observations on European Music." *EM* 17:41–51, 1973.

Chabrier, Jean-Claude. "Music in the Fertile Crescent: Lebanon, Syria, Iraq." *Cultures* 1(3):35–58, 1974.

———. "New Developments in Arabian Instrumental Music." *World of Music* 20:94–109, 1978.

Cohen, Dalia. "The Meaning of the Modal Framework in the Singing of Religious Hymns by Christian Arabs in Israel." *Yuval* 2:23–57, 1971.

El-Shawan, Salwa. "The Role Of Mediators in the Transmission of al-Musika al-Arabiyyah in Twentieth Century Cairo." *YTM* 14:55–74, 1982.

———. "The Socio-Political Context of Al-Musika Al-Arabiyya in Egypt: Policies, Patronage, Institutions, and Musical Change." *Asian Music* 12(1): 86–128, 1979.

Hickmann, Hans. "Die Musik des arabische-islamischen Bereichs." In *Handbuch der Orientalistik,* 1–134. 1. Abt., Ergänzungsband IV. Leiden: Brill, 1970.

Katz, Ruth. "The Singing of Baqqashôt by Aleppo Jews." *Acta Musicologica* 40:65–85, 1968.

Klitz, Brian, and Norman Cherlin. "Musical Acculturation in Iran." *Iranian Studies* 4:157–66, 1971.

Krishnaswami, S. "Musical Changes in Uzbekhistan." *Journal of the Indian Musicological Society* 5(2):13–17, 1974.

Levin, Theodore C. "Music in Modern Uzbekistan: The Convergence of Marxist Aesthetics and Central Asian Tradition." *Asian Music* 12(1):149–63, 1979.

Loeb, Laurence D. "The Jewish Musician and the Music of Fars." *Asian Music* 4(1):3–14, 1972.

Massoudieh, Mohammad Taghi. "Die Musikforschung in Iran." *Acta Musicologica* 48:12–20, 1976.

———. "Tradition und Wandel in der persischen Musik des 19. Jahrhunderts." In *Musikkulturen Asiens, Afrikas und Ozeaniens im 19. Jahrhundert,* edited by Robert Günther, 73–94. Regensburg: G. Bosse, 1973.

Nettl, Bruno. "Nour-Ali Boroumand, a Twentieth Century Master of Persian Music." *Studia Instrumentorum Musicae Popularis* 3:167–71, 1974.

———. "Persian Classical Music in Tehran: The Processes of Change." In *Eight Urban Musical Cultures: Tradition and Change,* 146–85. Urbana, Ill.: University of Illinois Press, 1978.

———. "Persian Popular Music in 1969." *EM* 16:218–39, 1972.

Petrović, Radmila. "The Concept of Yugoslav Folk Music in the Twentieth Century." *JIFMC* 20:22–25, 1968.

———. "Folk Music of Eastern Yugoslavia: A Process of Acculturation." *International Review of the Aesthetics and Sociology of Music* 5(1):217–25, 1974.

Racy, Ali Jihad. "Arabian Music and the Effects of Commercial Recording." *World of Music* 20:47–58, 1978.

———. "The Impact of Commercial Recording on the Musical Life of Egypt, 1904–1932." *Essays in Arts and Sciences* 6(1):58–94, 1977.

———. "Music in Contemporary Cairo: A Comparative Overview." *Asian Music* 13(1):4–26, 1981.

———. "Music in Nineteenth-Century Egypt: An Historical Sketch." *Selected Reports in Ethnomusicology* 4:157–80, 1983.

———. "Record Industry and Egyptian Traditional Music: 1904–1932." *EM* 20:23–48, 1976.

**Reinhard, Kurt.** "Die Türkei im 19. Jahrhundert." In *Musikkulturen Asiens, Afrikas und Ozeaniens im 19. Jahrhundert,* edited by Robert Günther, 21–48. Regensburg: G. Bosse, 1973.

**Rihtman-Auguštin, Dunja.** "Transformacija radicijske Kulture u Jugoslaviji [Transformation of the Traditional Culture in Yugoslavia]." *Muzika* 21(3–4): 75–86, 1976; English summary, 114–15.

**Shiloah, Amnon.** "The Status of Traditional Art Music in Muslim Nations." *Asian Music* 12(1):40–55, 1979.

**Simic, Andrei.** "Country 'n' Western Yugoslav Style: Contemporary Folk Music as a Mirror of Social Sentiment." *Journal of Popular Culture* 10:156–66, 1976.

**Spector, Johanna.** "Musical Tradition and Innovation." In *Central Asia: A Century of Russian Rule,* edited by Edward Allworth, 434–84. New York: Columbia University Press, 1967.

**Todorov, Todor V.** *Süvremennost i narodna psesn* [Modern Music and the Folksong]. Sofia: Muzika, 1978.

**Touma, Habib Hassan.** *Die Musik der Araber.* Wilhelmshaven: Heinrichshofen, 1975.

———. "Die Musik der Araber im 19. Jahrhundert." In *Musikkulturen Asiens, Afrikas und Ozeaniens im 19. Jahrhundert,* edited by Robert Günther, 49–71. Regensburg: G. Bosse, 1973.

**Zonis, Ella.** *Classical Persian Music, an Introduction.* Cambridge: Harvard University Press, 1973.

———. "Classical Persian Music Today." In *Iran Faces the Seventies,* edited by Ehsan Yar-Shater, 365–79. New York: Praeger, 1971.

# SOUTHEAST ASIA, INDONESIA, AND OCEANIA

**Becker, Judith.** "Kroncong, Indonesian Popular Music." *Asian Music* 7(1):14–19, 1975.

———. *Traditional Music in Modern Java: Gamelan in a Changing Society.* Honolulu: The University Press of Hawaii, 1980.

———. "Western Influence in Gamelan Music." *Asian Music* 3(1):3–9, 1972.

**Budiardjo, Marshal.** "Wayang for Tomorrow." *Hemisphere* (Woden, Australia) 19(11):24–29, 1975.

**de Leeuw, Ton.** "Westerse confrontatie met gamelan: 'Gending' (1975)." *Mens en Melodie* (Utrecht) 30:332–34, 1975.

**Guignard, Michel.** "Mauritanie, les Maures et leur musique au XIXème siècle." In *Musikkulturen Asiens, Afrikas und Ozeaniens im 19. Jahrhundert,* edited by Robert Günther, 241–65. Regensburg: G. Bosse, 1973.

**Haryadi, Frans.** "Modern Music in Java." *World of Music* 20:100–102, 1978.

**Hatch, Martin.** "The Song Is Ended: Changes in the Use of Macapat in Central Java." *Asian Music* 7(2):59–71, 1976.

**Heins, Ernst.** "Kroncong and Tanjidor—Two Cases of Urban Folk Music in Jakarta." *Asian Music* 7(1):20–32, 1975.

**Kaeppler, Adrienne L.** "Music in Hawaii in the Nineteenth Century." In *Musikkulturen Asiens, Afrikas und Ozeaniens im 19. Jahrhundert,* edited by Robert Günther, 311–38. Regensburg: G. Bosse, 1973.

**Kornhauser, Bronia.** "In Defence of Kroncong." In *Studies in Indonesian Music,* edited by Margaret J. Kartomi, 104–83. Monash Papers on Southeast Asia, no. 7, 1978.

**Maceda, José.** "Music in Southeast Asia: Tradition, Nationalism, Innovation." *Cultures* 1(3):75–94, 1974.

———. "Music in the Philippines in the Nineteenth Century." In *Musikkulturen Asiens, Afrikas und Ozeaniens im 19. Jahrhundert,* edited by Robert Günther, 215–32. Regensburg: G. Bosse, 1973.

———. "A Search for an Old and a New Music in Southeast Asia." *Acta Musicologica* 51:160–68, 1979.

McLean, Mervyn. "Innovations in Waiata Style," *YIFMC* 9:27–37, 1977.

———. "Song Loss and Social Context Among the New Zealand Maori." *EM* 9:296–304, 1965.

Morton, David. "Music in Thailand, the Traditional System and Foreign Influences." In *Musikkulturen Asiens, Afrikas und Ozeaniens im 19. Jahrhundert,* edited by Robert Günther, 185–213. Regensburg: G. Bosse, 1973.

Trân Van Khê. "La musique Vietnamienne au XIXème siècle." In *Musikkulturen Asiens, Afrikas und Ozeaniens im 19. Jahrhundert,* edited by Robert Günther, 167–77. Regensburg: G. Bosse, 1973.

Williams, Vernon W. "Folk Ballads of Samoa and Culture Change." *Cultures* 1(3):95–116, 1974.

# UNITED STATES (EXCEPT AMERICAN INDIAN CULTURES)

Baron, Robert. "Syncretism and Ideology: Latin New York Salsa Musicians." *Western Folklore* 36:209–25, 1977.

Erdely, Stephen. "Ethnic Music in America: An Overview." *YIFMC* 11:114–37, 1979.

———. "Traditional and Individual Traits in the Songs of Three Hungarian-Americans." *Selected Reports in Ethnomusicology* 3(1):98–151, 1978.

Forry, Mark. "Bećar Music in the Serbian Community of Los Angeles: Evolution and Transformation." *Selected Reports in Ethnomusicology* 3(1):174–209, 1978.

Herskovits, Melville J. "Problem, Method, and Theory in Afroamerican Studies." *Afroamerica* 1:5–24, 1945.

Hood, Mantle. "Musical Ornamentation as History: The Hawaiian Steel Guitar." *YTM* 15:141–48, 1983.

Hornbostel, Erich M. von. "[Review essay:] American Negro Songs." *International Review of Missions* 15:748–53, 1926.

Jackson, George Pullen. "The Strange Music of the Old Order Amish." *Musical Quarterly* 31:275–88, 1945.

———. *White and Negro Spirituals.* Locust Valley, New York: J. J. Augustin, 1943.

Kirby, Percival R. "A Study of Negro Harmony." *Musical Quarterly* 16:404–14, 1930.

Koskoff, Ellen. "Contemporary Nigun Composition in an American Hasidic Community." *Selected Reports in Ethnomusicology* 3(1):153–73, 1978.

Nettl, Bruno. "Aspects of Folk Music in North American Cities." In *Music in the Americas,* edited by George List, 134–47. The Hague: Mouton, 1967.

Niles, Christina. "The Revival of the Latvian Kokle in America." *Selected Reports in Ethnomusicology* 3(1):211–39, 1978.

Porter, James. "The Traditional Music of Europeans in America." *Selected Reports in Ethnomusicology* 3(1):1–23, 1978.

Riddle, Ronald. *Flying Dragons, Flowing Streams: Music in the Life of San Francisco's Chinese.* Westport, Conn.: Greenwood Press, 1983.

———. "Music Clubs and Ensembles in San Francisco's Chinese Community." In *Eight Urban Musical Cultures: Tradition and Change,* edited by Bruno Nettl, 223–59. Urbana, Ill.: University of Illinois Press, 1978.

Roberts, John Storm. *Black Music in Two Worlds*. New York: Praeger, 1972.

Smith, Barbara Barnard. "Chinese Music in Hawaii." *Asian Music* 6(1–2):255–330, 1975.

Szwed, John F. "Afro-American Musical Adaptations." In *Afro-American Anthropology: Contemporary Perspectives*, edited by Norman J. Whitten, Jr. and John F. Szwed, 219–27. New York: The Free Press, 1970.

Waterman, Richard A. "African Influence on American Negro Music." In *Acculturation in the Americas*, edited by Sol Tax, 207–18. Chicago: University of Chicago Press, 1952.

———. "'Hot' Rhythm in Negro Music." *Journal of the American Musicological Society* 1:24–37, 1948.

Westcott, William. "Ideas of Afro-American Musical Acculturation in the U.S.A.: 1900 to the Present." *Journal of the Steward Anthropological Society* 8:107–36, 1977.

# Index

# Index